HOBOS GOING SOBO IN THEIR OBOZ
and we never looked back ...

Our In-Tents Journey on the Appalachian Trail

FROG & Faith

Copyright © 2022 FROG & Faith.

All rights reserved. No part of this book may be used or reproduced by any means, graphic, electronic, or mechanical, including photocopying, recording, taping or by any information storage retrieval system without the written permission of the author except in the case of brief quotations embodied in critical articles and reviews.

WestBow Press books may be ordered through booksellers or by contacting:

WestBow Press
A Division of Thomas Nelson & Zondervan
1663 Liberty Drive
Bloomington, IN 47403
www.westbowpress.com
844-714-3454

Because of the dynamic nature of the Internet, any web addresses or links contained in this book may have changed since publication and may no longer be valid. The views expressed in this work are solely those of the author and do not necessarily reflect the views of the publisher, and the publisher hereby disclaims any responsibility for them.

Any people depicted in stock imagery provided by Getty Images are models, and such images are being used for illustrative purposes only. Certain stock imagery © Getty Images.

Scripture quotations taken from The Holy Bible, New International Version® NIV® Copyright © 1973 1978 1984 2011 by Biblica, Inc. TM. Used by permission. All rights reserved worldwide.

ISBN: 978-1-6642-7165-4 (sc)
ISBN: 978-1-6642-7166-1 (hc)
ISBN: 978-1-6642-7164-7 (e)

Library of Congress Control Number: 2022912362

Print information available on the last page.

WestBow Press rev. date: 07/27/2022

Dedicated to and written for our grandchildren:
Bryce, Ryan Jr., McKenze, and Lauryn

Our prayer is that you will read this story of our adventure on the Appalachian Trail and go beyond your own limits to accomplish great things for GOD.

> Twenty years from now you will be more disappointed by the things you didn't do than by the ones you did, so throw off the bowlines, sail away from safe harbor, catch the trade winds in your sails. Explore, dream, discover.
> —Mark Twain

CONTENTS

Background ix
Introduction xiii
Our Journey to the Trailhead xvii

1. Groseclose, Virginia, to Damascus, Virginia 1
2. Damascus, Virginia, to Hampton, Tennessee 43
3. Hampton, Tennessee, to Roan Mountains, Tennessee 68
4. A Match Made in Heaven 88
5. Roan Mountain, North Carolina, to Erwin, Tennessee 93
6. Erwin, Tennessee, to Hot Springs, North Carolina 121
7. Lori's Glory Story 148
8. Hot Springs, North Carolina, to Hartford, Tennessee 157
9. Gatlinburg, Tennessee: Newfound Gap to Clingman's Dome 182
10. My Journey to GOD / Brad's Life Song 192
11. Great Smoky Mountains: Clingman's Dome, Tennessee, to Fontana Dam, North Carolina 203
12. Fontana Dam, North Carolina, to Franklin, North Carolina 219
13. We Will Never Look Back 245
14. Franklin, North Carolina, to Helen, Georgia 252
15. The Finish: Helen, Georgia, to Springer Mountain / Amicalola Falls State Park, Georgia 276
16. What We Have Learned 302

Epilogue 309
Months Later 313
Appendix A: Glossary of Words and Terms 315
Appendix B: Setting up Camp, Filtering Water, Our Meals, and Equipment 321
Acknowledgments 327
About the Authors 331

Background

Brad, since the day I met him, wanted to backpack the Appalachian Trail (AT)—all 2,190 miles of it. It had been his dream for at least forty years. I have always enjoyed going on day hikes but really wasn't that interested in overnight or extended backpacking trips.

In 2019, we met Brad's cousins, Sheila and Randy, in Gatlinburg and took a day trip to Newfound Gap in the Great Smoky Mountains National Park, Tennessee. The AT runs through there, so I told Brad to walk along the trail because this would be the only opportunity that he was going to have to walk the AT. Who knew that five months later I would agree to join him in his dream; GOD must have got a good chuckle out of that one. I know we have!

I'm not sure the exact time I agreed to join him, but it was sometime during a three-week trip to Jackson Hole / Grand Teton National Park, Wyoming, in the fall of 2019. We went hiking every day in the mountains (only day hikes), but I loved it and thought, *Well maybe I should give this backpacking adventure at least a try to see if I would like it.*

We didn't officially start planning our trip until 2020 and knew it would take at least a year or more for us to plan a trip of this size. Our original plan was to thru-hike the whole 2,190 miles, traveling north through fourteen states, from Springer Mountain, Georgia, to Mt. Katahdin, Maine, and to do it within six months.

In the fall of 2020, we decided to see if we were capable of a long-distance hike. Throughout the year, we did research and gradually bought and collected our supplies and equipment. We took sixteen days to backpack the 132-mile Northville-Placid Trail (NPT) in the Adirondacks in New York. It was a hard and difficult trail (and many mistakes were made with weight and gear), but we learned so much. It was a great experience, and we found that we really had fun and enjoyed doing it together. I caught the backpacking bug. I was hooked!

> Once the travel bug bites there is no known antidote, and I know that I will be happily infected for the rest of my life!
> —Michael Palin

Our biggest discovery while on the NPT was that we *both* knew a six-month trek might just be too much for us at this time. We knew that there was no way we would be able to complete it within the six months to reach Mt. Katahdin before they closed the mountain by October 15 (which gives us tremendous respect for the thru-hiker).

At first, we felt discouraged and embarrassed that we had told so many people we were going to do a thru-hike, and now we had to tell them otherwise. At the time, we were thinking it was an all or nothing; if we weren't doing the whole thing, it was a bust. After much discussion, we realized we could still have this dream but on a smaller scale; we could become section hikers. Our excitement grew once again!

We went over a lot of different scenarios of sections we could do and finally came up with the section from Groseclose, Virginia, to Springer Mountain, Georgia (545 miles, through four states, within three months.) Our decision to travel southbound (SOBO) instead of going northbound (NOBO) was mainly due to the fact that we didn't want to hit the Smoky Mountains during snow season.

So, on April 7, 2021, we took our first steps on the AT in Groseclose, Virginia, (Route 11) and headed south. This is our journey … full of adventure—the good, the bad, and the ugly. You get it all!

May this instill a desire within you to try something out of your comfort zone.

> Life begins at the end of your comfort zone. So if you're feeling uncomfortable right now, know that the change taking place within your life is a beginning not an end.
> —Neale Donald Walsch

Our Support Team:

May the road rise up to meet you, the wind be ever at your back, and until we meet again, may the good Lord hold you in the palm of his hand! Slainte! Happy hiking! Rob M.

So excited for you!! Looking forward to reading and seeing all the pictures and stories! Praying for a safe trip! Love you guys. Tracy M.

Have an amazing time!!! Sam L.

Oh the places you'll go, the people you'll meet, Godspeed and have fun!! Peg P.

Hugs & prayers for you guys. Diana T.

Make sure you take dehydrated spinach. Just add water and fried eggs and you are good to go. Doesn't weigh much and won't go bad. Claude M.

How exciting! Godspeed my friends! Mary K.

Don't eat all the candy bars the first day! Sandy L.

LOVE YOU GUYS!!!! STAY SAFE!!! (Yes, I am yelling!!) Suzanne M.

Looking forward to hiking vicariously through you both! Have a wonderful journey and enjoy each step. Safe adventures! Maryann V.

Excited for you and your journey! We'll be praying! Have so much fun together!!! Margie W.

Be blessed with every step! Hugs and prayers accompany you wherever you go! Denise L.

I'm looking forward to traveling the road with you via your blog! Here's to your safe adventures! Pat T.

Prayers of protection around you both!! Looking forward to hearing about all the wonders and adventures you encounter! Coleen B.

So excited for both of you! An amazing adventure! I pray God envelopes you in strength, safety, good weather, awesome sights and an abundance of tales and memories! Take care and enjoy every step! Michelle E.

Have a great adventure! Can't wait to live vicariously through you two. Enjoy and safe travels! Bonnie B.

Looking forward to hearing of your adventures!!! Denise A.

Today's your day to go! No turning back! Bethie T.

Wishing you well and safe travels as you begin your next adventure! We love you both! Christine K.

Walking with you in prayer and spirit! Living vicariously on this wonderful adventure with you and Brad! Don't forget to dance along the way and tell Brad to eat his spinach! We love you both! Bev G.

Hugs & prayers continue! Darlene M.

Wishing you many gentle adventures. I look forward to the stories. Penny C.

> The greatest adventure is what lies ahead.
> —J. R. R. Tolkien

Introduction

Every person walking the AT has a trail name. If you don't come up with one, you will be given a name. To save ourselves from getting a name that could potentially be embarrassing, we've chosen our own trail names. Let me officially introduce you to Team Hobos: FROG and Faith. FROG is the acronym for Fully Relying on GOD, and to do that, we know we need *faith*. You can't have one without the other; they go hand in hand, together. I don't know anyone I would rather share this journey hand in hand with than my best friend.

> A *good* friend listens to your adventures; your *best* friend makes them with you.
> —**Unknown**

Our Support Team:

God be the steps in front of you and the stars to light your night and the way to HIS adventures for you ... Faith and Frog. Joyce P.

Beautiful name! Safe journeys. Elaine F.

Love the names, it says so much about you! Bless you in the days ahead. Nancy K.

So excited for you two! Perfect names. Love you both!! Tracy M.

Then you truly are my namesake ... Faith is my middle name! Enjoy both the journey and your partner, my friend! Pat T.

This map is not to scale.
The numbers represent miles.

- Wytheville, VA Bus stop
- Groseclose, VA 545
- Marion, VA 534
- Grayson Highlands 502
- Damascus, VA 470
- The Rabbit Hole 449
- Boots Off Hostel & Campground 428
- Black Bear Resort 420
- Mountain Harbour B&B 395
- Roan Mountains
- Greasy Creek Friendly 368
- Overmountain Shelter 386
- Erwin, TN 344
- Nature's Inn Hostel 320
- Hot Springs, NC 275
- Max Patch 255
- Standing Bear Farm Hiker Hostel 241
- Gatlinburg, TN 208
- Great Smoky Mountains Newfound Gap 208
- Fontana Dam 164
- Nantahala Outdoor Center 137
- Franklin, NC 109
- Albert Mountain 100
- Around The Bend Hostel 69
- Helen, GA 53
- Neels Gap / Misty Mountain Lodge 31
- Blood Mountain 29
- Above The Clouds Hostel 21
- Springer Mountain, GA 0
- Amicalola Falls State Park

Our journey begins at mile marker 545.7 in Groseclose, Virginia, across from the Village Truck Stop on Route 11.

Our journey ends on the AT at mile marker 0 at Springer Mountain.

Finish Line: 8.8 miles on the Approach Trail in Amicalola Falls State Park, Georgia.

> The mountains are calling and I must go.
> —John Muir

Our Support Team:

Wow! Very exciting! We will be praying for good weather and safety as you journey. Coleen B.

Brad and Lori as I drive through all those states to get my 1300 mile journey done from Fla to NY and I start to complain I will think of your feet and how at least I'm not walking it over rocks and creeks etc. You go with God's blessings and it will be the memory you will share for a lifetime. Joyce P.

I'm so excited for you! Cannot wait to see pictures and hear stories of your adventure! Love you guys! Diana T.

Prayers that you and Brad stay healthy and enjoy these miraculous adventures you are undertaking! Pat T.

That's gonna be a great adventure! I'll look forward to seeing updates. Rob M.

Praying wonderful blessings as you trek! Denise L.

Rock on my friends!! Make sure to be near a good supply of spinach along the way!! Claude M.

What a wonderful blog! Wishing the two of you a safe and happy adventure! Shelby S.

Praying for safety and God's blessings as you travel! Look forward to hearing of your adventures! Nancy K.

Have a wonderful and blessed time. I'm sure it will be a fantastic time. You will see some beautiful scenery. Enjoy! Milt K.

> Of all the paths you take in life, make sure a few of them are dirt.
> — John Muir

Please Note:

For a full description on hiking words and terms, see appendix A.

For a full description on setting up camp, filtering water, our meals, and equipment, see appendix B.

For more photographs of the beautiful natural landscape of the AT, see our website: HOBOSOBOBOZ.com.

> We travel not to escape life ... but for life not to escape us.
> —Unknown

Our Journey to the Trailhead

Today, Monday, April 5, starts the adventure we've been planning for over a year. We are excited and so ready to start our journey on the AT. We are not sure what lies ahead, but what we do know with certainty is that we are safely in GOD's hands as He guides and leads us on this journey.

FROG is starting out at 180 pounds and will turn sixty-nine on the trail, I am starting out at—nice try! A woman never shares her age and weight! We are both in fairly good condition (at least we think!). Backpacks are packed and weighed—I will be carrying twenty-five pounds, and FROG, thirty-five pounds. I will probably regret my decision to take as many clothes as I have packed, but a woman just can't go every day with the same outfit on now, can she?

We're all set and ready to go. Nothing can go wrong, right? We will soon find out.

Now let the adventure begin ...

Anticipation and trepidation build as we load up our gear and double-check (more like triple-check) to make sure we have everything packed that we will need. We are as ready as we're going to be at this point. Let's do it!

We are fortunate that we have cousins who live a couple hours away from where we will finish in Amicalola Falls State Park, Georgia. Sheila and Randy have graciously opened up their home for us to stay with them this Easter weekend (even going as far as giving up their comfortable bed, knowing we wouldn't have that luxury for a while) and have offered to take us to the bus depot today to meet our 8:20 p.m. bus to Wytheville, Virginia. We will forever be indebted to them for all they did in helping us.

We are early people and want to make sure we arrive in plenty of time before our departure, so we head out forty-five minutes early. Fifteen minutes later, we are sitting in front of what looks like an abandoned building, with a Closed sign in the window. There is no one around. "Are you sure this is it?" FROG asks. Randy is pretty sure this is it, so we pull in and sit for a minute, still not totally convinced. I see a bathroom available to use, and since my nerves have kicked in, I'm ready to get out. As I am preoccupied, they have noticed the Southeastern Stages, Inc. Bus Station sign off to the side of the parking lot, so it is indeed a bus station. I had made arrangements with Greyhound, so seeing another name on the sign still makes me wonder if this is it. They are still pretty sure this is it; there isn't another bus station here in town.

They sit and wait in chairs in front of the building, while FROG and I pace back and forth. Not so much due to anxiety over this being the right place or not, more about the journey ahead. So many questions: *What in the world are we doing? Can we really do this? Are we ready for this? Are we sure we really want to do this? Will we be calling them soon to come and get us? What lies beyond this?*

Our departure time of 8:20 p.m. comes and goes—still no bus, still no other people around. What's the worst that can happen? If no bus arrives, we go back with Sheila and Randy to their nice, comfy house and stay in their nice, comfy bed. That sounds perfectly fine to me. I will bet Sheila is praying otherwise, because soon after that, we see our bus approaching.

And we're off!

There are mixed emotions as we say our goodbyes and give last-minute hugs. I am sure I hold on longer than I need to because of fear of letting go and doing something that is so out of my comfort zone.

I take one painstaking step at a time toward the bus, not out of fear; it's because my backpack is way too heavy! I don't bother strapping it on properly but instead just drape a strap over one shoulder and try to carry it all on one side. My trekking poles that are attached to the outside with Velcro have come loose and have slipped down; they are now going in different directions and are tripping me up. I know I am fumbling and trying desperately to act as if I can carry this heavy thing with no problems, but I'm sure those on the bus and our cousins can tell otherwise! This is not at all how I envisioned it would go! Can we just go back home now? Oh, that's right—we sold our home so we could do this; hence why we are the wandering nomads, the Hobos. No turning back now.

It doesn't get any better when we board the bus. There are no seats together as we walk all the way to the back, hoping we find some. Nothing. Not even two seats close to each other. One person notices our dilemma and stands up and tries to get people to switch their seats so that we can sit together, to no avail. No one is budging. One girl did volunteer her seat that is close by another vacant seat, so at least we are an arm's length from each other. We are thankful for her kindness and willingness to make the ride a little better for us if we can't be together.

Observing the people all around me and looking up front, I notice no one our age takes the bus. It is filled with young people in their twenties or thirties. My twenty-something bus mate doesn't necessarily respect my personal space. He's fast asleep, sitting spread-eagle and definitely on my seat, and he's a big dude! I'm glad I was able to at least sit comfortably with one cheek on the seat.

When did kids their age come up with their own dialect? We have no idea what most of them are saying! It is English, but certainly they aren't putting words together that I can decipher.

There is a lot of aggressive behavior at times between the passengers in the back. I have no idea why they are so riled up and yelling at each other. This whole time, I am thinking my bus mate is fast asleep when all of a sudden he jumps up and starts yelling at another person three rows up on the other side. He immediately sits back down, rants in unintelligible words, and falls back to sleep. What in the world is happening around me? It's a circus of craziness! (I never got one bit of sleep on that leg of the bus ride. Didn't dare.)

After a while, it quiets down again, and the young man who tried to help us find two seats together comes back to the bathroom and says something to me about "dropping my smile." What in the world does that mean? How could he tell anything about my smile since I am wearing a mask? I'm trying to figure out if he is hitting on me and this is his pickup line or what. Maybe someone can enlighten me on this new language and let me know.

What a relief when we hear the bus driver say we are nearing our transfer station. Please, GOD, don't let the second bus ride be like the first! Remember all those questions I had before the bus arrived in Monroe? Yep! I'm asking myself those all over again!

A new bus means we have to get our heavy backpacks out of the bottom of the bus, and they're not in an easy spot to just reach in and get. Our bags have been moved and are now in the center with suitcases all around them. There is no way unless we crawl in there to get them. After a hair-raising bus ride, we are both frazzled and becoming short with each other. Finally, after not knowing what else we are supposed to do and not getting any help from the bus driver, we start taking suitcases off the bus so that we can climb in to reach our packs. It takes some maneuvering and finagling, but we finally get those heavy things out and lay them down by the bus to go and ask the bus driver where we need to go to catch our next bus.

We even find that the bus drivers are not the friendliest either. Maybe it is because they deal with these kids' behaviors every night. I am not sure. We ask the bus driver where we are to go, and I guess because we didn't immediately go the right way, he starts yelling at us, "I told you it's that way!" We hold our composure and *nicely* reply that we need to get our backpacks that we laid down by the bus first.

> *Never mess with a hiker; we know places where nobody will find you.* 🐸

We find our second bus, put our packs down in the baggage compartment, and hope that they are easy enough to get out once we reach Wytheville. I guess we got here before a lot of others because we find two seats together in the front of the bus. Already starting out positively! I am happy to report that this bus ride is a complete 180 from the first. We are both able to get some shut-eye but we still arrive at our destination pretty whipped. We are so glad that part of the journey is over!

Don't always assume the bus station is located directly in a town surrounded by hotels. There are those that stop in no-man's-land, and you'll need to figure out how to get yourself to civilization. For a planner, this is hard to just be winging it, but I'm determined I am going to learn to just go with the flow and trust GOD (and FROG) to figure it out for me.

There is a convenience store here, but since it's only six o'clock in the morning, it is still closed. Well, I'd say that is not very convenient. So, what are we to do? We look around; it's just us and another gal who got off the bus here. She is not headed in our direction and has another ride that is coming. On a nearby window of the Laundromat, we see a sign for taxi drivers. FROG gives them a call. Success! There will be one coming to pick us up within half an hour. It is a cool morning, but we keep moving to stay warm so it's not so bad. (Plus, at this point, we still have a lot of available clothes to put on to stay warm. More on that later.)

As we are waiting, a guy pulls up in his car and parks it right where we are and jumps out; full of energy this one is! I'm hoping he is just full of life and not full of something else. I will give him the benefit of the doubt. He is friendly and is willing to take us into town if we want. No, we have a taxi coming, so we're okay. This other gal who is waiting, her ride has not shown up yet, and he offers her a ride too, going in the other direction. We are hesitant for this exchange and tell her she can take the taxi with us into Wytheville until she can connect with her ride. She is a young girl in her twenties, and we are concerned for her safety. I'm assuming he is harmless, but still, if this was our daughter, we would want someone looking out for her safety. She decides to go with him. Hmmm ... you can't force someone to make other choices. We left before she did. We just pray that everything went okay for her.

We get taxied into town and decide to stay at the Days Inn right next to Shoney's. We will be able to have a nice place to stay and be able to get a good meal for dinner tonight, our *last supper*.

> Wilderness is not a luxury but a necessity of the human spirit, and as vital to our lives as water and good bread.
> — Edward Abbey

Our Support Team:

Brad's dream about to come true—shows all over his face! Bethie T.

Sounds like an interesting first day. It will be better when you hit the woods, I hope. Mary K.

You got hit on! The younger ones are drawn to you!! Probably your hair again!! Suzanne M.

Have wonderful adventures!! Can't wait to hear about them! And if your pack gets too heavy put some clothes in Brad's while he's not looking. Love you guys!! Casey M.

Looking happy and ready!!! Joyce P.

… and they're off!!! Tracy M.

> On a hike, the days pass with the wind, the sun, the stars; movement is powered by a belly full of food and water, not a noxious tankful of fossil fuels. On a hike, you are less a job title, and more a human being. A periodic hike not only stretches the limbs but also reminds us: Wow, there is a great big world out there.
> **—Ken Ilgunas**

Groseclose, Virginia, to Damascus, Virginia

> He who dwells in the shelter of the Most High
> will rest in the shadow of the Almighty.
> —Psalm 91:1

Wow! It is finally here! Months and months of planning and buying supplies; months of anticipation building and excitement growing—to now. The day has finally arrived!

We spend the night in Wytheville, Virginia, which is about thirty minutes away from our planned start on the AT. Last night, we made arrangements for a driver to pick us up at our hotel lobby around eight in the morning, Wednesday, April 7, 2021.

Our driver, Rambunny (her trail name), arrives early at our hotel, full of excitement for us and with great tips to share about life on the AT since she has hiked the whole trail, from Georgia to Maine, herself. Conversation is fun and comfortable, so we don't hesitate to ask about her leg since we notice she is in a leg brace. She mentions that she has recently fallen from a step ladder and is also battling cancer and going through chemo treatments, which explains the knit cap she is wearing on her head. Most people would be down and out about their circumstances, but not Ms. Rambunny; she is so positive with a bright outlook on her life, despite the circumstances that she is going through. She freely shares her love of GOD and knows that He is going to heal her completely of her cancer. May we learn from her as we journey forward to have a faith so strong to know that no matter what circumstance we will face, GOD is in the midst and will get us through it. (And believe me, circumstances did we have!)

When we arrive at the gas station, we both look around in wonderment and ask, "Are we here? Is this it?"

She points to the other side of the road to a worn path with tall weeds next to it. "Right there is where you will start your southbound journey." Our expectations of what the trailhead would look like once we arrived in no way matched what it actually looked like. Excitement mixed with some fear set in. *Are we really ready for this? What lies beyond the start of the trail?* There are those questions again.

After praying with Rambunny, which was a great honor and privilege, I put on my *Faith over Fear* cap, and we both step out of her truck in faith, knowing we can do this. We are, after all, FROG and Faith. GOD will be with us every step we take as we fully rely on GOD in faith.

Here we go!

> Fear has two meanings: "Forget everything and run" or "Face everything and rise." The choice is yours.
> —**Zig Ziglar**

HOBOS GOING SOBO IN THEIR OBOZ and we never looked back ...

Day 1 (Wednesday, April 7)—Today Is Our Day!

After a sorry attempt at taking a good selfie at the trailhead, we both take our first step together. The first 2.7 miles through meadows, over an active railroad track, crossing dirt roads, and walking across a footbridge seem easy and effortless, maybe because it is mostly flat or maybe it is because of the adrenaline and excitement of finally hiking the AT. We are not sure.

We Begin!

From a distance, we see the Lindamood School coming up, a one-room schoolhouse built in 1894 and active through 1937. Rambunny had told us to make sure we made a stop there to look around and go inside the schoolhouse, which they keep open for hikers to go in. (We later found out that they allow hikers to spend the night in there as well, which would have been so cool to do!) As we make our way to the school, we drop our packs out front and walk in. If you've ever seen other one-room schoolhouses before, it was as expected: potbelly stove in the middle, chalkboard in the front behind the teacher's desk, and student desks (that could hold up to three students) lined up front to back on both sides of the stove.

Lindamood School

We take a seat at one of the desks and imagine what it might have been like to have attended school this way. Being a former teacher, FROG remarks on the challenges it must have brought to teach different grade levels throughout the day and the additional duties of the teacher to keep the building warm in the cooler days. It would have been his responsibility, as their teacher, to bring a bucket of water and a scuttle of coal each day.

How appropriate it is that our first stop on the AT is a schoolhouse. FROG taught in the Owego-Apalachin School District for twenty years. His first year was in Owego Elementary, and the remainder in Apalachin Elementary. He never graduated from the fourth grade. Since I am writing this, I can brag on my husband. He was made to teach. He loved his students, and they loved him, and he did an awesome job! I can visualize him standing here in this one-room schoolhouse at the front, with his students all around him, looking at rocks and minerals or doing science experiments. I know he is thinking about this as well and missing his former students.

Outside, behind the school, are two outhouses labeled *Boys* and *Girls*. Off to the other side is the Settler's Museum, which we had hoped to go into, but unfortunately, it is still closed for the winter season. Next to that is a bathroom, also closed, and a huge pavilion beyond that, with electrical outlets and a spigot with running water. If we were ready to camp for the night, what a great place it would be to set up here, but our adventure has only just begun, and it is time to move on.

A little over two miles, we come to what is our very first shelter on the AT, Chatfield Shelter (many more to come in our future!) with a privy up behind it. A privy is another name for an outhouse; this particular one is fully enclosed, which, as you can guess, stinks! We wear a neck wrap that has three benefits: you can soak it with water to keep cool, you can use it for warmth around your neck if cold out, and lastly, for a face mask! The latter comes in handy for such a time as this!

Most people will start their journey from the south and walk north, NOBOs. We decided to be different (hmmm … no comments needed!) and go the opposite direction; we start north and are heading south, SOBOs. At this point, we haven't really run into anyone going in either direction.

When we arrive at the shelter, there are already two guys taking a lunch break, and after we take off our packs and settle in to eat our lunch, a few more people show up. I am an introvert, so to walk in on people and to have more show up instantly makes me uncomfortable and quiet. FROG easily makes conversation and feels at ease, but for me, I know it is going to take time to get used to this new way of living on the trail and to be able to open up and just be me.

Everyone we talk to is friendly and excited to be on the trail, some for the second time. A new term we hear from a couple groups we run into is that they are COBOs (COVID-bound hikers.) A new term for those who started their hike in 2020 but had to get off the trail due to COVID restrictions and shutdowns. They are back on the trail, starting where they left off the previous year.

As we venture farther and farther into the woods, it doesn't take long to discover our pack weight is way too heavy and that we will have to do something about it soon. After what would be an eight-mile day our first day, we stop at an unofficial campsite for the night, a flat spot just off the trail not designated as a camping spot (we're rule breakers!). We are just so tired and ready to set up camp, eat dinner, and conk out for the night.

As we are planning out our next day's adventure, we know there is just no way we can walk all the way to Georgia with such heavy packs. We have heard from some hikers that the next town we are coming to has shuttle service that would take us into town, so we decide to make a pit stop at the visitor center and catch the bus into Marion, Virginia, to their post office to send some items back.

As we lay down for the night, we can feel our legs and feet pulsing and twitching from our day's hike. They don't cramp up; they just seem to be responding to an event that is foreign to them (this was to happen for the next week or so until our bodies got used to fact that we were walking and this was our new way of living!).

It is a warm evening, so we have the window flap open on our door to the tent to allow a breeze to flow through, and off on the horizon, a great ending to our first day, is a beautiful sunset. Thank You, Lord, for blessing the end of our day with Your magnificent masterpiece!

Day 2 (Thursday, April 8)—Travel Light

We had a wonderful night's sleep. We are so refreshed and ready to get up (our legs and feet not feeling tired anymore). We break down camp and decide to eat breakfast on the trail. We are so ready to get moving and see what lies ahead for us today.

As our journey begins, we come upon "Kitchen Sink." We don't get an explanation for why he is called that (we will continue to run into a lot of people with very interesting trail names), but I'm pretty sure it wasn't because he was carrying everything but the kitchen sink (since the goal is to travel light). We think his name may refer to the fact that he is recording good water sources along the trail through the Guthook app.

He tells us about the next upcoming shelter, Partnership Shelter, that is well-known and the only place (at least on the long section we are doing) where you can get pizza delivered to you. (Because the shelter is so close to Virginia Route 16, pizza delivery is common to this shelter.) He had walked thirty-one miles the previous day just to get that luxury the night before. Food is a huge motivator!

After 3.2 miles of trudging along with our heavy backpacks, we finally come to Virginia 16, and there sits the W. Pat Jennings Sr. Visitor Center, the Mt. Rogers National Recreation Area Headquarters. What a sight for sore eyes (or rather, sore backs!). We can't tell you how excited we are to know that finally we are going to get some relief from our heavy load. (We think we can safely say that it is a number one problem with most hiking the AT for the first time: you overpack and will most likely be unloading either at a post office or a hiker box soon after you start your journey.)

The visitor center is closed, but we learn from Kitchen Sink that if we walk out back, there is a phone on the building that we can use to call for shuttle pickup, the same one he used for pizza delivery. There is also a water spring back there that is nice and cold and doesn't need filtering. Oh yeah! What a day this is turning out to be!

The shuttle driver picks us up out front at the gate of the visitor center and drops us off at the post office in Marion, Virginia. He gives us tips on a place to eat and where to get supplies and then gives us a time and place for our pickup to return to the trailhead. We try to give him money, but he won't take it. We find a place to sit down out behind the post office and empty everything out of our packs. We sit there analyzing each item and whether it is needed or not. Okay, so our first bit of advice:

> Don't send items home on a warm, dry day!
> **—FROG and Faith**

Our logic in that is that we are of course walking south, so it is only going to get warmer, so we won't need our heavy long johns, blanket liner, gloves, rain pants, waterproof gloves, and warm hats. (We would later find out what a big mistake that decision was!) Another bit of advice:

> Carry as little as possible, but choose that little with care.
> —**Earl Shaffer**

We have set aside our down vests to put in our box to send back as well, but in the end, they don't fit. (We would later realize that was a gift from GOD that they hadn't fit in the box; we sure needed them!) Other items we ship back include our small bear canister (we had two, a large and small one); a lot of food that we don't think we would need before our next resupply in Damascus, Virginia; one of our power chargers; some clothes (there goes more of my outfits!); and several other miscellaneous items we think we can live without. By the time we are done, we ship back two boxes of things, and our packs are about five pounds lighter for each of us. What a relief!

We take time to eat at the Sisters Café and Gifts. We can't say enough about how nice they are and how they go out of their way to make these hikers feel comfortable. Their hospitality and friendliness are top-notch, not to mention how delicious their food is. We aren't able to finish our sandwiches, so they wrap them up for us so that we can finish them later after we get to camp. I decide I will carry them and put them in the very top part of my backpack so that we can easily get to them later.

FROG is designated (by me!) to be the one to go into the army/navy store in town to get a replacement gas canister since we remember that our second one is in our bounce box, and we might need a new one before we reach Damascus. My job would be to sit outside the store and watch the backpacks and make sure nothing happens to them. My only job, y'all ...

HOBOS GOING SOBO IN THEIR OBOZ and we never looked back ...

We set our backpacks upright on the bench outside the store, with me planted between them. I am pretty sure I did not hit my pack at all (maybe because it's lost weight, just not sure), but within seconds, it has toppled off the bench and has landed top-side down. Yep! Right on our sandwiches! I don't dare look inside at the damage, afraid to see that tonight's dinner might just be smooshed sandwiches. Well, even if they are, they will still taste better than the trail food we would have had.

We spend about three and a half hours in town, then catch the shuttle back up to the visitor center (shuttle driver still would not take any payment) and continue our journey southbound. Just past the visitor center is the infamous Partnership Shelter, the Taj Mahal of shelters. It has two floors, can hold up to sixteen people, has a water spigot and a shower (not available to use this season), a privy off to the side, and a nice sitting area near a campfire ring. We aren't ready to stop for the night, but of course we had to stop and check it out since we've heard so much about it. No one is here at the time we are, but we hear that it is always full nightly—understandably so, since many look forward to a night of pigging out on pizza and washing it down with a lot of soda! (Beer/alcohol is forbidden, but we wonder how often that rule is broken.)

We hike another 4.1 miles, which brings us to Pugh Mountain Road, and decide to stop for the night, this time at an official designated campsite just south of the road. We only hiked about 7.3 miles today because of stopping in town, but no regrets; we have lighter packs and, yep, very smooshed sandwiches to eat! Life is good!

Day 3 (Friday, April 9)—Plans Change

Our plan today is to walk to a designated campsite about nine miles ahead. It's okay to make plans, but you need to hold on to them loosely, as we would soon find out in just a few hours. It is another beautiful, warm day. We just finished our cold-soaked oatmeal (which is really pretty good and worth the try if you've never tried it) and head out on the trail. After about five miles of walking through woods, crossing roads and footbridges, we come to a meadow that is (supposedly!) fenced in to keep cows in. We use the gate and make sure we close the gate, as the sign indicates, only to see off to the side a wide-open gate. Well, that totally seemed pointless. Looking around the meadow, we see no cows. We wonder, *Are there really cows, or did they escape out of the open gate?* Doesn't matter. That is not the point of this day's story.

Something is really wrong with FROG. His energy level is so low, his heart is racing, he has shortness of breath, and he can't walk more than a few feet before having to sit down. We decide to just stop and rest in the open meadow, eat our lunch, and wait it out to see how he feels after getting some much-needed protein and lots of water in his body.

At this point, I am so worried. I'm not sure what we'll do if medical attention is needed. We are out here in Timbuktu land, with no one around. How will we get the help we may need? I just can't figure out how serious this situation really is.

After a good hour of sitting under a tree in the shade, we get strapped up again with our packs, only to get about a quarter of a mile uphill when I see FROG throw his trekking poles in frustration; he is still not feeling well, and we need to stop again. At this point, I am feeling I better do some research to see if I am able to figure out exactly where we are to alert 911 of our location. FROG doesn't want me to call for help—just give him some more time to rest.

After sitting another half hour, we decide to give it another go. We go exceptionally slow and make plans to stop at the next shelter, Trimpi Shelter, which is 0.6 miles away. Six-tenths doesn't sound far, but believe me, when you're in this situation, it seems like an eternity!

Walking SOBO allows us to come across people who are walking NOBO who will give us tips on places to stay, how the terrain will be coming up, water sources, and so on. This particular group of NOBOs lets us know that if we are going to the Trimpi Shelter, to beware: there is a snake that frequents the shelter. Lovely! Another scare on top of the scare I am already facing!

Finally! We see the sign for the shelter and make the descent. After hearing that we may encounter a snake, I have mixed feelings about being here but know that we must stop to give FROG time to lie down. He goes into the shelter to lie upon the raised bunk that is inside, which is totally stressing me out, just thinking about the snake. After all, snakes love to swallow frogs! I convince him to at least come out and lie on the picnic table, and I will run down to the stream to get water to refill our water bottles and get a wet rag to put on his forehead to cool off.

As FROG is relaxing, I take the time to filter water and check out the area. If we need to, it really is a good spot to set up camp for the night. Well, no, I don't mean in the shelter but in one of the tent sites they have around the area. It would only make for a six-mile hiking day today, but we would soon learn that GOD needed us to stop at this particular shelter so divine intervention could happen.

After a short time, FROG is feeling so much better, but we make the decision to stay the night anyway and so start setting up camp for the night at one of the tent sites just below the hill from the shelter. We get everything set up and put all our gear inside the tent. (Take note of that point.)

FROG does better if we are able to sit at a table instead of sitting on a log to eat dinner, so we head back up to the shelter to fix our dinner, eat, and play a game of cards (which would be our entertainment nightly here on out).

By this time, other hikers have shown up and plan to camp: one who decides to stay in the shelter (trail name Godfather, who I did warn about the snake); a group of four walking a short section of the trail going SOBO (yay for the SOBOs!); and three others going NOBO. So, in all that night are ten people, me being the only woman. And I must add, a loud group of men, were they! And you talk about women! Hah! Who can tell the biggest (and loudest) story seems to be the theme tonight.

As we are playing cards, the wind picks up substantially. It gets to the point that we can't successfully play cards anymore without them blowing around, but before we have a chance to pick up, we just happen to look down at our tent. Lo and behold, our tent has come up off the ground and flipped over on its side. Now tell me. How is that possible with all our heavy packs inside holding things down?

We abandon everything at the picnic table to rush to our tent and grab it before it decides to take flight again. We get it upright and this time stake it down, all the while laughing at ourselves for not staking it down in the first place. Not taking any more chances, I decide to climb inside and call it a night. FROG returns to the picnic table to gather up our things that the guys have so graciously made sure didn't fly away, and he decides to hang out with the group of guys for a while as they set up their tents and hammocks for the night. Must be FROG has a bigger and better story to share.

We never did see the snake, but we sure weren't without excitement or drama that night!

Day 4 (Saturday, April 10)—Hike Your Own Hike

FROG had a good night. He is all rested, not feeling as he did yesterday, and thinks he will be able to walk 9.2 miles today to Hurricane Shelter. There are a few tent sites there, and we hope at least one will be available when we arrive to set up. Weather is looking pretty iffy today—much cooler and is calling for some rain.

Camp is still jovial as we all break camp this morning. Everyone is excited to hit the trail and venture forward. One of the campers (Johnny) had set up his hammock just above our tent site on the hill. After he rolls his sleeping bag up and bags it, it rolls down the hill into our camp. He scurries down the hill to retrieve it and apologizes. It's no problem at all. Back up he goes to roll up his hammock, and when he sets it down, down rolls his hammock into our camp. He's so apologetic, but we think it's pretty funny. FROG asks him if he has a trail name, and he says that he does not. So, FROG gives him the trail name of "Rollin'." Very appropriate!

Breakfast at the shelter before heading out is fun, as we take extra time to get to know the group of four guys going SOBO: Barry, Craig, Butch, and Johnny (Rollin'). They are doing a short weekend section hike and will be ending their hike tomorrow. They are going to celebrate their hike by getting beer and steak dinners! The thought of eating real food makes our eyes light up with anticipation of the day we will be able to do that. Unfortunately, it is still four days away! We are happy and jealous at the same time for them.

FROG is keeping a daily journal and is writing in it when one of the guys asks if he can write in his journal. What a great idea! (From that day forward, FROG had several people sign his journal.)

> **April 10, Trimpi Shelter we headed there southbound from Partnership Shelter, 10.5 miles. My limit is 8 miles so I was spent. But feel a lot better today. Great to meet you guys, hope your journey is fantastic. Keep on truckin'. Butch**
>
> **Happy Trails! Johnny**
>
> **Keep doin' it! Craig**

They are planning to walk farther than we are today, so we wish them well and say that we'll probably see them on the trail again when they pass us. We know we are slow; we have adopted the motto "slow and steady wins the race; we will go at our own pace." Another saying you will hear often on the trail is "hike your own hike." It really doesn't matter what anyone else is doing. Do *you*.

About three miles after we leave Trimpi Shelter, we run into a detour at Comers Creek Falls. The bridge over Comers Creek has been removed due to structural damage. They have rerouted us, which means we have to take the Dickey Gap Trail and Comer Creek Road for a couple of miles, which is so much harder on the legs and feet than the trail is; no soft landings on a paved road. We don't want to take any chances and not be able to cross at the falls, so we take the detour. Hikers who are purists try to avoid any detours away from the original white blazes on the trail. Purists we are not! Realists we are!

Needing to give our legs and feet a rest from the hard surface, we stop at Hurricane Campground to rest and have lunch before heading back on the marked trail in the woods. Weather is starting to get even cooler, and there is a light mist in the air. Being on the safe side, we put our duck covers on our packs as precaution against the wetness in the air. No one wants to sleep in a damp sleeping bag!

We are finally following the official white blazes again as we make a gradual incline through the deep woods. We still haven't seen our group of four men that we stayed with last night in the shelter, so we figure we must have missed them when we stopped at the campground for lunch or they didn't take the detour and took a chance at the falls.

We are passing a lot of NOBOs, not only those hiking but also people who are running the trail with lighter packs. Unbelievable! We can't even walk the trail without stumbling; we can't even imagine trying to run it! The trail is quite rocky in many places, so now we can understand why many have to leave the trail due to injuries. Nope! Not us. We will continue to walk our turtle pace, thank you very much!

As we continue our ascent, we realize we are again rule breakers. Going uphill allows you the right of way when hikers are coming down the hill. We always pull over when trekking uphill to allow others to go by, not so much out of kindness as it is to catch our breath!

> **PRO TIP: Carry binoculars when hiking so when making frequent stops, it looks like you're appreciating nature not fighting for air!**
> –The Pilgrim Life

About a mile away from our stopping point for the night, Hurricane Mountain Shelter, the rains start to pick up some. At this point, if you remember, we only have our duck covers on, so we need to stop to put on our ponchos (Frogg Toggs), which will completely cover our backpacks for additional protection to keep all our contents dry. Before we can go through the complete process of stopping, getting into our packs for our ponchos, and getting them on (which is not a quick process), the skies open up, and we are in the worst rainfall we have experienced thus far. You've never seen two older people move as quickly as we did to get our ponchos on and over our gear. Talk about dancing and moving, we are rockin' it! I love to dance, and we are moving fast, but I will tell you, this is one dance I am not having fun at! I instantly become upset and miserable. We have another mile to go, and to top it off, we know it is a steep climb up. Ugh! I storm (no pun intended) off and don't even wait for FROG to catch up. Let him hop around and jump in the puddles. I'm outta here! I can honestly say this was one time I was not proud of how I treated my best friend. After all, it wasn't his fault that the weather had turned bad. I guess human nature wants to blame someone, and he was the one who got it. Still, no excuse, and once we got to the shelter, I did apologize. (But not until we were in the shelter. I needed to stew in my own juices for a while until we got there.)

It is a long haul to the shelter. Visibility is poor due to the rain, and having to have the poncho up over my head blocks my eyes so I can't see much of the time. We are still not very conditioned from hiking the trail yet, so our endurance level isn't very good. We are struggling. Once we round the corner, we think we are at the top of the hill where the shelter is; to our dismay, it is a false summit, and there is no shelter. The trail continues uphill, and I wonder if I have the energy to endure anymore of this. I turn around to wait up for FROG, who is quite a ways back; I guess being mad gives you the extra drive to push yourself up the hill faster. The look on his face is exactly what I am feeling ... utter defeat! This is kicking our butts!

It is a total miracle that we make it up that hill and into the shelter. I shake my head and believe it must be the Lord who gives us the extra push we need, because we just don't physically have it in us; we are spent.

Our original plan of spending the night at a tent site below the shelter is not going to happen tonight for two reasons: the tent sites are already taken by the time we arrive, and it is much too wet to go farther to see if there are any more sites close by, so the shelter is our only option. So hopefully it is available and not already full. It is off-trail about 0.01 mile, uphill. As we turn in, we are both silently praying that it won't be full and we can set up our sleeping bags in the shelter. In addition to the pouring rain, the wind and cold are picking up, and we are chilled to the bone. Remember all those wonderful warm things we sent back home?

Rounding the corner of the shelter, we look in and see just one other person in there; we are so full of relief and joy that there is room in the inn—or rather shelter—for us tonight! Thank You, GOD! We don't hesitate and quickly get our air mattresses blown up and sleeping bags out to claim two spots off to the very right side.

Even though we had our ponchos on, the clothes that we were wearing got really wet, so we change into any remaining clothes we have tucked away in our packs. We are so cold and chilled we snuggle down into our sleeping bags (which miraculously stayed dry), just trying to stop shaking and to warm up. (This is where we start beating ourselves up for sending home our waterproof rain pants and gloves, as well as our blanket liners that would give us additional warmth now as we lay in our bags.) Oh, to live and learn the hard way!

> There is no such thing as bad weather,
> only inappropriate clothing.
> — **Sir Rannalph Fiennes**

Soon after we settle into our sleeping bags, who should show up at the shelter looking for a place to stay? Rollin'! And our new friends from the shelter the night before. We hadn't met up with them on the trail, and we thought we had missed them, but no, they got a late start this morning from Trimpi Shelter, and with all the rain, they knew they wouldn't be able to make it to their planned destination, which was supposed to be a tent site near Iron Mountain Trail.

It didn't take long for some NOBOs to show up: another young man, an older gentleman, and "Texas." After Texas got dried off, had his supper, and climbed into his quilted sleeping bag, we didn't hear or see him again for twelve hours. He hiked with his travel companion, Squirrel, and they average about fifteen miles a day. We weren't the only ones spent after a long day's hike!

Texas

By night's end, we have ten of us (Gangster, Trebek, Squirrel, Texas, Rollin', Craig, Barry, Butch, FROG, and Faith) all planning to stay in the shelter. It is tight, but thankfully, with so many huddled bodies close together, we feel much more comfortable and not so cold. Never mind that we are going through a pandemic; we all just want to stay warm and not die from hypothermia.

Sidenote from FROG: Oh yeah, speaking of hypothermia. In 1982, my buddy Rick and I were backpacking in the Teton Mountains in Jackson, Wyoming. We had been out about two weeks. On the last day, we discovered we were on the wrong side of the river and needed to cross. It is June, and the water is snow melt from the mountains so is frigid. So halfway across the river, I slip and start floating downstream. I finally find the shore and, on all fours, climb up onto dry land. I have never been so cold in my life. Luckily, Rick got a dry shirt and sweater on me, and we continued our hike. I got some idea of what hypothermia was like.

It was really cold at the shelter, but at least we were dry. A wet cold is the worst!

Since the floor is so packed, seven lined up one way, two going the opposite way at our feet, Barry decides to strap his hammock up over us. With so many of us in here, there is hardly any moving space, so I am not able to get pictures, but it is definitely a sight to see.

Despite conditions surrounding us and the day we all experienced, we make the most of it, and it turns out to be a fun night! Who knew sleeping with eight guys and a dog in a shelter would lead to a whole lot of fun and laughs and, well, a chorus of noises at night, if you know what I mean!

At the time of our hike, we have been married thirty-six years. We learn that night that two of the other guys in the shelter are also in the thirty-year club and are happily married. Barry makes my FROG look pretty bad, I must say, with all his romancing stories of flowers and secret rendezvous he does for his wife that he shares with us that night. There are several times I smack FROG for not doing this for his wife. His response is to say, "But you get a nice backpacking trip that she doesn't get." Hmmpf! Smack!

> **Hey guys! Great spending time on the trail with y'all! Hope you liked the romance stories/tips HAHA! Stay safe and enjoy the remainder of your time in the woods. Happy Trails. Barry**
>
> **Northbound to Pearisburg, Virginia. Squirrel and Texas**

Day 5 (Sunday, April 11)—Be Bold, Start Cold

What a rough night's sleep. We feel like we didn't get much sleep at all with the storm happening around us and all the noises happening throughout the night in our shelter. It seemed to take me forever to finally get to sleep, and come to find out ... I snore. I never knew I did but was startled awake a few times as a snort was escaping. And to think for years I have been waking FROG up to tell him to roll over because he was snoring; I wonder now if it was really *me*!

At least the weather has cleared up, and it's supposed to be a sunny day today. A lot of the clothes we hung up to dry last night did not successfully dry, understandably so with the wet and damp conditions we had throughout the night. Hopefully they will dry out throughout the day as we're hiking.

We pray mornings and read a daily psalm (depending on what day we are on, we read that psalm, i.e., Psalm 5 today) before we leave camp. Today we decide to stand off to the side of the shelter to pray, to be out of everyone's way as they are packing up. Our good friend Rollin' notices we are praying and calls out, "Come pray with us too. We need it." We gladly walk back and pray with the remaining five guys (and Texas) who are left at camp. As we're leaving camp and rounding the corner of the shelter, FROG gets emotional, and with tears in his eyes, he turns to me and simply says, "Wow!" I know exactly how he is feeling. I feel it too. What a great blessing to have developed such a strong bond of friendship within two nights of being together and to have shared that moment together before our Lord.

We then knew without any doubt this is why we had to have a day where FROG was low on energy and we needed to stop early; we never would have met our new friends, formed a bond, and had that special moment together. Our biggest lesson so far: don't always get upset with how things turn out. There may be a divine reason why it happens the way it does. Trust GOD to lead.

We are getting low and in need of water, so we plan that our next stop will be at State Route 603, Fox Creek, where we hear there is a nice stream with easy access for getting water to filter. Turns out to be a beautiful area with a great water source! We decide as we're refilling our water bottles to take an extended break by the water, to rest up and eat a snack. FROG decides to hang his long-sleeved, sun-screening, breathable, brand-new blue Columbia shirt up on a bush to dry out since it is one of the items that didn't thoroughly dry the night before.

Breaks are always nice, but sometimes it's hard to get moving again after such a long time, so we don't try to get too comfy and stay a long period of time, and at this point, I am in desperate need of finding a bathroom. Since this is an area with many picnic tables and a parking lot full of cars, we assume there must be a bathroom around here somewhere, and hopefully it is unlocked. In some places we have encountered so far, due to COVID, the bathrooms have been closed. So my only options have been the privies if I find one on the trail or, worst-case scenario, the great outdoors. As a woman, you can imagine it's not my favorite place to go. I spend my whole time worrying that someone might see me, but the real kicker is I ask myself, *"Why in the world didn't I study up on what poison ivy looks like and what to do if a rattlesnake bites?"* I don't even want to think about what would have happened if I had been bit or developed a rash in such a sensitive area. TMI, but just sayin'! Am I the only one who thinks like this?

After looking around for a while, we finally spot some porta-potties down the road (okay, that will work!) from the parking lot, so off I go. FROG decides to stay and wait in the parking lot since the trail picks up at that spot, greeting the hikers as they come off the trail. I guess he's in practice for his next job as a Walmart greeter.

I say all this to emphasize that after leaving our spot by the water, we didn't just head back out on the trail. We have plenty of time to think about anything we may have left behind. No, it wasn't until two miles *up* the trail that FROG stops suddenly. I crash into him with the bill of my cap (wasn't the first and won't be the last time that happens). "Oh no! I think I forgot to get my shirt off the bush before we left," says FROG in a panic. He is frantically digging through his pack, and yep! He forgot it. To all those hikers out there, you know if you have a big day planned of hiking and still have plenty more miles to go, you do not make the decision to add more miles to your day, especially over a shirt, and go back to get it. It was a sad moment to have to say goodbye to his favorite shirt (and his only warm long-sleeve shirt, I might add.)

Our journey onward and upward brought us to the next shelter for lunch, Old Orchard Shelter. We are there only a short amount of time when three young adults in their twenties show up, two guys and a gal. They are part of a larger group, but what we find out from them is since they all have their own pace when hiking, they hike separately and meet up at night and camp at the same place. Sounds like a neat arrangement for them. During our conversation with them, FROG mentions that he left his shirt on a bush down by the stream, that if any of the guys are interested, "It's brand-new. Just smells pretty bad, but you're welcome to take it if it's still there." You didn't have to tell the guys twice about it. They took off soon after to go find it. FROG always had dreams to hike all the way to Maine. Maybe his shirt will make it there to Mt. Katahdin since he won't be able to.

The gal, going by the trail name Dance Party, gives us a bit of advice, "Be bold. Start cold." Referring to the start of your hike, instead of piling on a bunch of clothes (not really a problem for us since we sent most of them home anyway!) and then in five minutes having to stop to remove the layers, start cold with no layers. It is good advice for those who don't mind starting cold, but I never could do it! I like to be warm!

Our planned destination tonight is Wise Shelter just outside the Grayson Highlands State Park. We are getting so close to seeing the wild ponies that every person we meet going NOBO talks about. We are just so excited and can't wait for our opportunity to see them as well. We've been told that we'll most definitely see a bunch of them (if not before) hanging out at the Thomas Knob Shelter. If you're wearing shorts, they will lick your legs for the salt, which after a while becomes annoying some say. Weather has still been cold, so I am sure we won't have shorts on when we pass there tomorrow.

We approach The Scales, a large horse corral in an open meadow that is fenced in. We are 4,634 feet in elevation, and it is so windy and cold. There are many campsites within the fenced-in area, and we wonder how anyone could successfully keep their tent upright with such high winds. We do spot two horses just outside the fence and wonder if those could be the infamous ponies, but we are just not sure if they are someone's horses and are supposed to be in the fenced-in area. (Now that we are professional pony watchers, we believe they were ponies and not just someone's horses, which we originally thought! Man, we would have gotten much more excited if we had only known.)

We head out of the fenced-in corral and head up Stone Mountain, a grassy ridge with great views. We don't stay too long to admire; it is just too windy. Best to just keep moving. With such high winds, our pace isn't fast, but eventually we get some relief when we reach Little Wilson Creek Wilderness, where we are out of the open and in the woods once again. We notice a couple girls who have come to a complete stop and are looking out into the woods. This of course makes us curious, so we stop and ask what they see. There, in the distance, behind trees is the back end of a pony! Yep, we see it! We tried but didn't get a good picture of it (it seemed to know we wanted a picture and was camera shy), but at the time, we think this is our first pony, so we're pretty excited! The back end is better than no end!

We have gone 10.7 miles for the day and decide to stop just 0.01 mile before Wise Shelter. Off to the right side is a beautiful spot right next to Big Wilson Creek. It has our name all over it. The evening is cool, and sleeping right next to the running water will have such a calming and relaxing effect. We are ecstatic to have gotten such a spot for the night!

Less than thirty miles to our first zero day (and a shower!) in Damascus, Virginia.

TMI sidenote: I have not mastered the farmer blow. My nose has never dripped so much my entire life as it does now. My attempt at blowing leaves more on me than on the ground. Sorry … I know, TMI!

Day 6 (Monday, April 12)—Listen to Your Partner

Sleeping next to a creek does have a calming effect, but it also triggers the bladder into thinking it needs to go a little more often than normal. We have made an agreement—if I have to get up in the middle of the night, I wake FROG, and he goes with me. I'm not going out there in the dark by myself; one never knows what may be lurking out there.

It's a beautiful, cool morning, and today is the day we are headed to Grayson Highlands and will be seeing wild ponies! It isn't hard to get motivated to move this morning, knowing it is going to be the day we finally get to experience all the hype everyone has been talking about for the last six days. Bring on the day. We're psyched!

After crossing the bridge over Big Wilson Creek and walking only 0.01 mile, we come to Wise Shelter, our planned stop for last night. It's nice up here, but we think we made a great decision by staying down by the creek.

Did you know that rhododendrons grow wild in Virginia? We sure didn't; they are everywhere! (Not only are they in Virginia: they are in Tennessee and North Carolina as well). There are so many of them that those volunteering for the ATC (Appalachian Trail Conservatory) had to make the trail go through them so you're walking through tunnels of them. They are spectacular! What would make it even better is if they were in full bloom (depending on the area, we hear it doesn't happen until mid-May through June).

Someday my Prince will come ... it has become the norm that each time we enter a tunnel, FROG will turn to kiss his princess. Not sure why it was started, just one of those silly things you do to bring fun into your day. I can't even tell you how many kisses I ended up getting by the time we hit northern Georgia, when we ran out of wild rhododendron tunnels. It was a lot! By the last kiss he most definitely turned from a frog into my prince charming!

Rhododendron Tunnel

As we're almost to Grayson Highlands State Park, we see a sign indicating the Appalachian Spur Trail off to the right. Just seeing the words *spur trail* conjures up all sorts of bad memories for us. We learned our lesson when we hiked the Northville-Placid Trail (NPT) in 2020 to never take another spur trail. We thought to take one would mean cutting miles and the trail would be a lot easier. The NPT Spur Trail in Long Lake, New York, was anything but that! We were so tired, so we thought, *Hey, this trail will be good to take.* Don't do it. It's a trap! There were so many ups, downs, and zigzagging this way and that; it seemed to go on for an eternity before we finally came to civilization. Lesson learned ... taking shortcuts in life aren't always easy or the best choices to make.

We quickly boogied away from the spur trail and didn't fall for that twice!

> A lot of people want a shortcut. I find the best shortcut is the long way, which is basically two words: WORK HARD.
> —**Randy Pausch**

HOBOS GOING SOBO IN THEIR OBOZ and we never looked back ...

It's a cold and windy trek up into Grayson Highlands; we have on our light jacket and down vest and are shivering uncontrollably. It is truly unbearable and so hard to walk against the winds. We are passing a lot of NOBOs. It seems as though we have hit a bubble. We don't stop to talk; much too cold. We just need to keep moving.

Once we enter into the park, there are a lot of people around who have come from the Massie Gap parking lot, which is the major access point for those visiting Grayson Highlands State Park and is often very crowded. After being in the woods, almost always just the two of us, to see a lot of people seems good and overwhelming at the same time.

As we are wandering through the park, still not seeing any ponies at this point, we get a tip that there are four coming up very soon. Forget the wind. We hightail it up those stairs as fast as we're able, and as we round the corner ... there they are! They are just as we've been told, beautiful and magnificent! We know they are wild, and the desire to just reach out and touch one takes all the restraint we have. We stay back and admire them, as they are intent on eating the grass before them. We are so enamored with them that as we head off to continue the trail, we don't see the sign (the ponies are in front of it) that indicates we are to hike to the right, and instead we head straight on another trail, unaware that it is not the correct trail.

On the AT, you follow the trail, looking for white blazes that they have painted throughout on trees located near the trail. Any side trails are usually indicated with a blue blaze. There were very few trees in this park, so blazes were painted on the rocks.

As we head onward and upward, we see our first blaze—but wait! It's blue. I immediately freeze and ask FROG if we are going the right way. He assures me and says we are on the right path. There is a white blaze under the blue blaze, so it must mean the two trails intersect. I'm not seeing the white under the blue as he sees it, but okay, we continue. Hmmm ... something is just not right. We see no one with backpacks on, and everyone walking this trail is without a pack. An argument pursues, where I am saying this is not right, and FROG is adamant that we are going the right way. I ask FROG to *please* look at the Guthook app and see if they indicate we are still on the trail.

(One of the great features on that app is it has a GPS and will tell us where we are—if we are on or veered off the AT.)

Yep! I was right! We are off trail according to Guthook! Turns out someone needs to listen to their partner better! We backtrack, and sure enough, we took the wrong trail (Wilburn Ridge Trail). We head in the direction we are supposed to go and start to once again run into a whole bunch of NOBOs coming down the hill. Ahh, now I am at ease, knowing we are headed in the right direction toward Thomas Knob Shelter. (In FROG's defense, we did find out later that the trail we were on would have eventually connected to the AT, but we would have missed a good portion of the trail had we taken it.)

> It feels good to be lost in the right direction.
> **—Unknown**

It is a tough climb up and through Fatman's Squeeze (the AT passes through a tight squeeze between a cliff and a boulder). They do make it so you can go around it if your pack doesn't fit through, but we want the full experience of going through, so we make it fit; it is tight, but we do it!

Fatman's Squeeze

Weather continues to be so cold and windy! It's taken us four and a half hours to go only five miles, which totally saps our energy.

Winds are so strong at one point I start to go sideways and FROG reaches over to pull me back. If FROG was not here with me or I didn't have my backpack for the added weight, I really think I could have been blown away. (Grayson Highlands was our first of many more areas where we will experience cold, high winds, and pouring rain.)

"Could you please take my picture?" says a man attempting to do a selfie in front of a huge rock. We say sure, although we aren't sure why he would be wanting a picture of himself with this particular rock. As we walk around the rock, we notice 500 painted on the front, and realization hits that it's been five hundred miles that this gentleman has walked from Springer Mt., Georgia. Congratulations to him! That definitely is picture worthy! We also ask if he will take our picture because that means that we've walked forty-five miles, and to us, that is picture worthy as well! Only five hundred more miles to go!

500 mile marker

We are so close to Thomas Knob Shelter now, one of the most talked about shelters on the trail. We heard so many stories about ponies hanging out here. We wonder if we will be fortunate enough to see more. We needn't have wondered; even before we reach the shelter, we spot one! Then when we finally arrive at the shelter, there are four just waiting for us. Aw! They aren't afraid of us and have no problem coming right up to us, I'm sure looking for a handout. We want to, but we do not feed them. They don't even get the pleasure of licking our legs for salt; much too cold for us to have shorts on! We stay and visit with them for quite a while, and when we are ready to leave, two follow us for about a quarter mile. What a memory that we will cherish for as long as we're able to remember!

The Wild Ponies

Our journey out of Grayson Highlands State Park and through Lewis Fork Wilderness leads us to a beautiful hilltop meadow where we can see views in all directions. Looking back to where we just came from, we can still spot the ponies that have followed us down the trail, just grazing and enjoying life in the wild. Oh, to have no cares in the world and to live as carefree as they are.

After our descent into an open meadow and pasture, we end our 9.4-mile day at Elk Garden, a parking lot on VA600. There are some campsites just into the woods off from the parking area, where we find a campsite next to a gentleman wearing all purple. We soon strike up conversation with JPG (Jolly Purple Giant) and find out he is a NOBO and plans to walk all the way to Mt. Katahdin.

Rations are getting low, and we want to save our dehydrated meals for our last two nights on the trail before Damascus, so it's oatmeal tonight. Blah! We really like oatmeal but not after a long day's hike when you want substantially more than just that. At least we have a couple Snickers bars that we're looking forward to! Tonight, we dream of soon being able to eat some juicy hamburgers!

Day 7 (Tuesday, April 13)—Oh, the People You Meet

> We got to share a lovely sunrise this morning, April 13, at a campsite at Elk Garden. It's a bit cold, but I have a feeling it's going to be a lovely day. Good luck making it to Damascus (and later Springer). You are going to love it there! If you make it by the Dancing Bear Inn, please tell Pat and Elizabeth JPG says hello.
>
> FROG, you gave me great words of wisdom yesterday evening; compromise and listen. I admire your relationship and look forward to putting your advice to practice.
>
> I'll leave you with some wisdom passed on to me by a former thru hiker doing trail magic at Stecoah Gap: you can quit tomorrow but you can't quit today.
>
> JPG (Jolly Purple Giant)

As we say our goodbyes, he is all dressed in purple. We wish him the very best, to enjoy the ponies coming up and to have a safe journey as he heads to Mt. Katahdin. We have no doubt that he successfully made it there!

In what has been a short hike so far, we have met a lot of great people. We all seem to have a common interest and goal. But as we head out on our hike this morning, we run into a guy who is definitely disoriented, drugged, and headed in the wrong direction. The hike and scenery alone are a high; there is no need for drugs. We truly feel sorry for this young man. (We would discover throughout our journey that there were, unfortunately, others who had the same goals and ambitions as this young man. Some upcoming hostels that we would stop at were a den for drugs and drinking parties. So sad and disappointing!)

We are in need of water after using most of what we had at the campsite for last night's dinner. JPG reassures us we will run into a few smaller water sources as we head up to Whitetop Mountain (Virginia's second highest mountain at 5520 feet) but to look out for a natural piped spring coming up within three miles, soon after crossing Whitetop Road.

What we aren't prepared for is the amazing views once when we get to the top of the mountain! Spectacular! As we're enjoying our surroundings, we come to a sign hidden behind some bushes. Just twenty-five feet off-trail, and there it is! The piped spring! A sight to behold! What an incredible water source, and the best part, no filtering needed. Ahh ... the water is so cold and refreshing! What a great place to camel up, eat a snack, and enjoy the view! After refilling our water bottles, we are off to our next stop, where we'll be eating our lunch.

Relief for us going SOBO as we head downhill into the open, grassy ridge, heading to a secondary summit of Whitetop called Buzzard Rock (5080 feet elevation). We see the rock in the distance, so we know we're close, but it's the views in every direction that are knocking our socks off! Wow! Sometimes you just don't have words other than a simple *wow*.

It's a small ascent to the rock as we wait our turn to get pictures, since there has been a small group that has gathered there. The wind is just cool enough that we don't linger long. We head downhill a few feet and hide behind a boulder that is blocking the wind to eat our lunch. This is the spot I begin to notice the wildflowers all around me. The fields are full of them. I think prior to this, spring had not sprung yet, or maybe I just hadn't noticed. Either way, I see them now and am in awe of how beautiful they look as the sun shines down upon them and they stand regally reaching up to receive the sun. I start to feel overwhelmed by the beauty around me but at the same time so full of joy to be here, right now, with my love, taking this all in.

Buzzard Rock

We make the hard decision to continue onward from our nice warm spot behind the boulder, surrounded by such beauty, and head to our destination for the day, Lost Mountain Shelter. It will be an 8.2-mile day, which really isn't too bad. We don't put in a lot of miles, but the miles we do put in are full of adventure.

> It does not matter how slowly you go
> as long as you do not stop.
> **—Confucius**

It is mostly downhill (1800-foot drop in elevation), which is really hard on our knees, but we'd say better than going uphill, which we have to do the last mile to reach the shelter. It's midafternoon when we arrive, so there is only one other person there with their tent up. FROG wants to wait it out to see if we should put our tent up or just grab a spot in the shelter. He knows there is threat of rain so would much rather set up in the shelter. Ugh! The shelters are my least favorite place to stay. It's not so much that we're sleeping with others (well, okay, there is that, I like my privacy!) as it is that the floor is so hard that our air mattresses make an awful, loud crinkle sound when we move around throughout the night, and then there are the mice and snakes. I never feel like I am getting much sleep, worrying and stressing that we are bothering others with our noises, especially now that I know I snore! (Sleeping in the shelters ends up being the biggest disagreements we have between the two of us.)

Not setting up our tent right away gives us time to explore the area around us and just relax before we have to get our nightly chores done. First things first. Off come the hiking boots and on with our Crocs. Ahh, relief for our weary feet!

We are in need of refills on our water bottles, so I volunteer to head down to the water source. After a long day's walk, any extra walking seems a long way to have to go. "No problem. You rest. I've got this." As I follow the blue blazes that indicate a side trail to water, I finally spot the stream. Oh, this will be interesting! The pipe that disperses the water is clear on the other side of the stream. I have to maneuver my way from rock to rock to get to the pipe. My Crocs are not the best support, but at least if I do fall in and they get wet, it's no big deal. Why does my mind even go there? Once you start thinking about falling in, what do you think is going to happen? I get all the way over to the pipe, so proud of myself for not falling, bend down to get water from the pipe, and lose my balance. Down I go, on my knees as water is rushing around me, soaking up my pant legs. I laugh at myself as I'm trying to get up, praying to GOD that no one just witnessed that tumble. I finally get up and look around. Phew! The coast is clear. I fill the bags of water that we will need to filter. Now to get back to the other side with full bags of water without another mishap. I proceed to step from one rock to another as though I am a professional rock hopper. Oh yeah, rock on, baby. I definitely have this! I am almost to dry ground; I can feel a victory moment coming on soon, and then ... splat! I miss the last rock, and my right foot goes down into the water. So close! It still warrants the victory dance I give myself once I am on dry ground.

As we are filtering our water, two of the three young adults who will be our shelter mates (FROG decided we would stay in the shelter, although it never did rain that night, grrr!) have arrived. We immediately love them! They are so much fun! Racehorse and Man Alive have cheated and walked the Virginia Creeper Trail, which runs parallel to the AT. It is flatter and a beautiful walk alongside Laurel Creek. (Lux, part of their *tramily*, is a purist and wasn't going to take the easier route so walked alone and stayed on the AT.) They had taken a zero day the day before and stayed in a cabin in Damascus. Knowing we are headed there, they have all sorts of tips on places to eat, great outfitters, and where to resupply.

The moment Racehorse and Man Alive sit down at the picnic table, they start pulling out all the food they have in their bags. I wonder how they were able to walk the fifteen miles with so much food. It had to have been so heavy! They are definitely experiencing what you would call hiker hunger. I think they didn't stop eating until it was time for bed. At this point, they have almost hiked five hundred miles from Amicalola Falls; we wonder if we'll be eating like that after walking that many miles. Right now, we aren't really hungry but eat because we know we need the nourishment. We pull out our Chili Mac dehydrated meal and have that for dinner and feel completely satisfied, especially after adding the spices that Man Alive shares with us from his stash. He generously gives us a small bag of the spices to use for future meals. (It lasted up to our final day. Thank you, Man Alive!)

Lux has arrived and is (playfully) upset with them for cheating and not walking the AT. Watching them banter back and forth and eat is certainly a highlight of our evening. They even include us in their bantering and just make it such an enjoyable time.

They are the ones to notice that inside the privy (which they say was one of the nicest they've seen as far as privies go), someone has written out the whole story of the Lorax by Dr. Seuss. Why would someone stay in a privy that long to write that much? It smells horrible in there, nice privy or not.

> **We have been *so* lucky to meet you guys up here after our cheat day on the Creeper Trail! We hope Damascus is filled with hamburgers and milkshakes. We wish you the best of luck on your journey to Amicalola, enjoy it! Racehorse, Lux, & Man Alive**

Days 8–10 (Wednesday, April 14–Friday, April 16)–Happy Birthday, FROG!

Backpacking the AT was always FROG's dream, never mine. For many years, I told him he'd have to find someone else to hike the trail with because I was never going to do it. I like showers, a soft bed, and a home-cooked meal too much to do that. Well, never say never, as the saying goes. He must have been praying that GOD would change my heart, because here we are today as we celebrate his sixty-ninth birthday on the trail. I am so excited to be able to give him his dream for his birthday! Happy birthday, FROG!

Our plan today was to hike to Saunders Shelter, which is approximately seven miles away, and then tomorrow we'd get up and walk nine miles into Damascus, since we know a sixteen-mile day is definitely not doable for us. But after speaking with Racehorse and Man Alive, they encourage us (since we're not purists!) to bypass the AT and walk the Virginia Creeper Trail (VCT) when we come to it. It is flat and an easy fifteen-mile walk into Damascus. They assure us that there are many campsites along that trail if we decide we need to stop before arriving in town, since it is a long walk and we aren't sure we will be able to make it.

We couldn't have picked a better day for FROG's birthday; it was so warm and sunny. Just perfect! The VCT is all they said it was: a flat trail walking next to Laurel Creek, crossing a whole lot of bridges. Such a beautiful walk and a welcome change from all the ups and downs from the AT.

We have heard that we will walk through a small town on our way to Damascus, and with it being a warmer day, we keep thinking how nice it will be to have a cold soda. Might not have been one of our wisest choices today. We see a gentleman (humph!) standing outside and ask him if there is a restaurant close by to get a soda. He points out one just ahead on the left. We proceed to walk there. Of course we're all excited for the possibility of getting a cold drink and maybe something to eat, only to find out he failed to mention it is a closed restaurant! (Now we know why another guy started laughing after he told us about the restaurant.) We look around the building to see if they have a soda machine, but they don't, so we sit down at one of their picnic tables and eat a protein bar and drink our water. After about fifteen minutes, we head back on the trail. Soon after we start walking, we look back, and we're being followed by a cop car with two policemen in it. As they approach us, they stop to ask where we're from and where we're headed. How do you explain we're just a bunch of Hobos traveling on the AT when in fact we are not even on the AT? Well, we manage to say all the right things because they let us continue on. We're positive someone called us in for stopping at the restaurant. (Could it have been the sweet, dear gentleman who led us astray? Hah!) All we can say is what a great neighborhood watch they have!

Another couple miles down on the VCT, as we stop to have another water break, here comes security riding along on his bike. Really? We look that much like a threat? He must have gotten the "they're okay" report because he just stops where we are, says hello, and turns around and heads back. Glad we didn't have to call our kids to bail us out of jail! They might not have!

On the road to Damascus, I share a dream I had last night with FROG, a Jesus encounter that I will share with you in a later chapter. Hang in there. It's a good one! I'm just not ready to share it with you yet.

Food! Bed! Bath! It's amazing what you start to think about after you've been on the trail eight days straight! After only averaging about seven to nine miles a day, we decide we're going to push through and walk the whole fifteen miles. We want to celebrate FROG's birthday in style and have ourselves a nice juicy hamburger!

Damascus, Virginia, is our first stop after traveling seventy-five miles. The AT goes directly through town, and it is a trail town for sure! So many amenities to suit the backpacker. By the time we arrive in the late afternoon, we are totally exhausted. Our first stop is at Subway to get that huge, cold soda we've been dying to have for several miles now.

We haven't made any plans for where we will stay the night, so we feel like we are aimlessly walking through town, looking this way and that to see where to go. We really are hoping to just FROG—fully rely on GOD—to find us a place since we are just plain pooped! As we walk by, Larry (owner of Crazy Larry's Hostel) is out front and offers us an ice-cream sandwich. He invites us to look through his hiker box to see if there is anything we might need. We thank him for the ice cream (I've never tasted an ice-cream sandwich as good as this one was) and tell him we will be back another day to check the box; we are headed into town.

We round the corner and head into town. We pass the Appalachian Trail Town Inn, which says Open but looks deserted, so we move on. We cross the bridge, and off to our right is Dancing Bear Inn (where JPG said he stayed). The place looks nice. We are just getting ready to cross the road when we hear, "Are you guys looking for a place to stay?" from behind us. We turn around, feeling so relieved that someone has noticed how tired and lost we feel and wants to help. "Yes!" we both answer. "I've got rooms available at the Appalachian Trail Town Inn. Someone else is waiting to register, but if you head back there, I can give you a room too," the gentleman answers. "We actually need a room for two nights, and possibly three," we tell him. "No problem. I'm pretty sure we can do that for you," our good Samaritan responds. Timing was perfect! Thank You, Lord, for taking care of us and providing a room at the inn. (We ended up taking three zero days—a much-needed rest for our feet, legs, and especially our calves, which hurt so much our first week.)

We are so exhausted and tired, but this gives us the burst of energy that we need to backtrack to the inn. We laugh on our way back there and comment on how it is a miracle for sure, but it doesn't escape us that he never offered to give us a lift back to the inn. Not that it is very far to walk, but we are just so tired. Do you think it may have something to do with us not having had a shower in eight days?

We wait on the porch as Scott (the owner) checks in another hiker/biker (Tom), and then it is our turn. As it turns out, because we are planning to stay longer than Tom, we have first dibs on which room we want. We take the room that has access to a bathtub. The thought of soaking our tired, aching muscles helps in making our decision. We have the whole upstairs to ourselves for the first two nights. It is wonderful!

Note to self: take a shower before you soak in the bathtub after *just* getting off the trail. Talk about ring around the tub! It is horribly disgusting! Not sure why I felt you needed to know that, but I guess because I promised you the good, the bad, the ugly!

After taking a nice, hot, relaxing bath, we head to the Damascus Diner! It isn't that we are famished; it is that for eight days we've been eating nothing but trail food, and it is time to have that hamburger that we've been dreaming about to celebrate FROG's birthday. Damascus is not a big town, but do you think we could find the diner? We are expecting it to be located right on main street, but instead it is located on a side street, so we have to stop, ask directions, and backtrack to find it. What would have helped is if they had had white blazes to follow to get there (or maybe not! We still can get lost *thinking* we are following the white blazes, right, FROG?)

Once we find it, we aren't disappointed! The food is phenomenal! (We recommended it to everyone we saw on the trail after we left Damascus.) It is here that FROG learns what "regular tea" means to southerners. Up north, regular tea is unsweetened tea, so he asks for regular tea. After he tastes it, he asks the waitress about it, and in her sweet southern accent, she says, "Honey, regular tea *is* sweet tea down here in these parts." After a good laugh, we learn that being SOBO would also mean that we need to ask for unsweetened tea as we venture farther on our journey south.

The Appalachian Trail Inn has a really nice common kitchen area that is available for guests to use, so we do eat most of our breakfasts and lunches here, but for dinners, we eat out and enjoy the luxury of being pampered and catered to. Our recommendation if you're ever in the area is, of course, the Damascus Diner. Then there is Wicked Chicken, and we really enjoyed Mojo's Café and Coffee Shop for their orange creamsicle smoothie—very delicious!

So, what do you do when *all* your clothes are dirty and you need to get your clothes washed? You find a Dollar General and buy some cheap clothes to wear while they are getting washed at Crazy Larry's Hostel. That's what you do! When we put our bounce box together before the trip, we hadn't given this situation much thought. Now we know it's pretty important to have something to put on while everything is getting washed. (How forgetful we are with this important point, as you'll find out in a much later chapter!) So, after we have our clothes washed, we add our newly bought clothes to the bounce box and have it shipped to our next big stop, Black Bear Resort in Hampton, Tennessee, fifty miles away, so that we'll have them again when we arrive and have to do laundry again.

We remember that Racehorse mentioned to us to check out Mt. Rogers Outfitters when we got to town. We have not been able to find the store, so FROG heads across the street to the bike shop to ask them if they know where it is. Not long after, I see FROG and a store employee head outside, and she points to the store right next door. Well, that is embarrassing! How many times have we walked past there and not even recognized it was there? We couldn't find the diner, now this. (It's really quite astonishing that we were even able to hike this trail without getting lost!)

Last year for Christmas, we thought it'd be fun to include our grandkids on our journey on the AT, so one of their presents was an AT map so they could follow us daily, and we also included with that a priority mailing box for them to send us goodies while on the trail. I guess that was more a dual present, as we would benefit from it as well. I mention this to say my son's family had the first resupply box sent to us in Damascus. It is like having another Christmas as we open up the box to see what kinds of goodies they thought to send us: raisins, fruit roll-ups, Nutrigrain bars, gummi worms, peanut butter sandwich crackers, granola bars, and a warning to watch out for bears! A very thoughtful gift to us, for sure! We enjoyed it all! (To our amazement, we enjoyed the fruit roll-ups and the gummies the best. Who knew that having something to savor in your mouth that tasted fruity would taste so good to us old folks! Good choice, family!)

Day three in Damascus brings Purple Streak and Paisley to the Appalachian Trail Town Inn. FROG has been sitting outside enjoying the sun when they stop by and inquire of him if there is room in the inn. Thanks to FROG (I'm thinking he should have been given a referral fee for that one), they become our floor mates and will share our bathroom with us for our last night here. Ahh man, now we have to share the tub! Thank goodness we cleaned the dirty ring around the tub!

To finish up the errands we need to do before heading back out on the trail tomorrow, we head across the street to Mt. Rogers Outfitters to see about buying a new long-sleeve shirt for FROG (remember, he left his on the bush?) and new hiking boots for me since I have blown out my current hiking shoe and am in desperate need of new boots. They didn't have the particular trail runner shoe I was looking for, but I settled on a woman's Oboz, and FROG found a really cool AT long-sleeve blue shirt to replace his long-lost shirt on its way to Mt. Katahdin. (This new shirt we can proudly say made it the whole way south to Amicalola Falls in Georgia, a total miracle!) I highly recommend this outfitter store; they were so knowledgeable and nice to us, and on top of that, they gave us a 10 percent discount, so we left happy campers, or rather, happy hikers.

Now anyone knows that if you aren't used to a certain shoe and you're wearing it for the first time, you are very susceptible to blisters and hot spots on your feet. We made sure we bought moleskin to go along with the Hike Goo I was putting on my feet as safety precaution from blisters and sore feet that were bound to occur. (I shake my head in disbelief as I write this. I didn't need to use the moleskin; I never got a blister or hot spot on my feet from my new shoes. And on warm days, I was not even wearing socks. Another miracle!)

Great sharing stories with you in Damascus. Tom

FROG used his connections to get us into an inclusive inn. Much appreciation! Paisley and Purple Streak

> We don't stop hiking because we grow old.
> We grow old because we stop hiking.
> —Finis Mitchell

HOBOS GOING SOBO IN THEIR OBOZ and we never looked back ...

Our Support Team:

Thank you for posting & sharing. :) 15 miles for burgers?!?!! Bethie T.

You're an inspiration!! Can't wait to hear about your Jesus encounter. Blessings! Cheryl K.

I admire you so much for your fortitude! Stay safe! Pat T.

Great pictures! Thanks for taking us along!! Enjoy those hot showers!!! Denise A.

Thanks so much for sharing your experience with all of us. We look forward to your posts. You both look like you are holding up well so far. What a wonderful adventure. Mary K.

These are fantastic! I am enjoying your journey, albeit from the comfort of my dining room!! Thank you for sharing your trek, and am looking for more of your pics and commentary!!! Linda H

Sounds exciting! Keep up the good attitude ... love the pictures ! Nancy K.

God is blessing you! Beauty, new "friends," blessing others. Keep going in grace, safety, joy, and wonder. Thank you for sharing! Denise L.

Thanks for the update and photos! Prayers for your continued journey! Coleen B.

Loving your updates and your pictures! I'm so glad you figured out how to take us along with you. Diana T.

Glad you guys are finding your groove and having a great time while you do! Stay safe! Meg F.

Those ponies are worth the trip! Doing good… that's a lot of miles in a day … kick back and pat yourselves on the back. We haven't gotten off the couch!! Joyce P.

Thank you for sharing your adventures! Can't wait to read the book! Did you leave a geocache travel bug with the shirt!? Thanks for sharing the pics and the humor! Cathy L.

Love your blog and pictures! Stay warm! Shelby S.

Awesome! Rob M.

You guys are amazing! Renee M.

Great stuff!! Clarissa F.

You are awesome and I am amazed and proud of you. Casey M.

Might have been worth it to stay there just for the pizza!! (Partnership Shelter) Lol Tracy M.

We are thinking of you two today, wondering if your feet are hurting? Sandy L.

> Only those who will risk going too far can possibly find out how far one can go.
> **—T. S. Eliot**

Damascus, Virginia, to Hampton, Tennessee

I will say of the LORD, "He is my refuge and
my fortress, my GOD, in whom I trust."
—Psalm 91:2

Day 11 (Saturday, April 17)—Leaving Virginia

Our first frost! We are thankful we weren't in our tent last night but have started shivering just thinking about having to walk in the cold this morning. So much for thinking we wouldn't be encountering any cold because we were heading south. Okay, so again, not one of our most brilliant thoughts.

Grabbing our hot tea and sitting down to do our daily devotions, we notice Paisley and Purple Streak are also preparing and planning for their hike out; they are going NOBO. We mention that we read a psalm every morning; would they like to join us? What a blessing to share that special time with them as FROG reads our daily psalm. We pray that this made an impact in their lives.

We say our goodbyes and well wishes, bundle up in all the warmest clothes we have available, and make our way out into the chilly morning. There is no way we are going to be bold, start cold; just isn't happening today! The backpack feels heavy since we haven't had it on our backs for a few days, but today we look past all that just to have an extra layer of warmth on our backs.

We thoroughly enjoyed our zero days in Damascus, so saying goodbye is bittersweet as we first start out. Walking through town, following those white blazes again, gives us a pep in our step that, unless you've hiked this trail, you may not understand. We are ready and excited! We have a big day ahead; four miles up and out of Damascus, we will hit the Virginia/Tennessee state line.

It is an uphill climb out of town (as we would discover, all of the hikes out of towns are uphill!), and turning around allows us to get our last glimpse of Damascus. As we're looking at the view, we meet three guys walking down the trail, excited that they are almost to town. We immediately tell them to stop at the diner in town; they won't be disappointed. Food is always the topic of conversation with hikers, who are hungry and thinking of food all the time. So, of course, it wasn't a surprise that they continue the topic and highly recommend Mountain Harbour B&B to us and tell us we must plan to stay; their breakfast is to die for! It is thirteen dollars per person, but the food is out of this world and done by a professional chef. They go into detail on the different entrees and choices they had, and it doesn't take long for our stomachs to start growling in anticipation! They also mention that if you do stay overnight, they have a food truck there that also serves gourmet hamburgers and french fries. We are sold! It is definitely going to be a stop we plan to make, even though it's not on the schedule. Learning to be flexible and not sticking with a plan is turning out to be pretty sweet! They also mention there is another option farther up the road to stay, the Station at 19E, but that would be more of a party place for the younger crowd, and I guess after looking us over, they thought we'd feel more comfortable hanging with the older crowd. They are right in that assumption, but we still like to think we're young, hip, and cool just like the young crowd and that we could still fit in. Probably *not*!

We make it to the state line! One foot in Virginia and the other in Tennessee, we take pictures to document the completion of our first state and seventy-nine miles behind us. What an accomplishment!

Virginia/Tennessee State Line

We meet a lot of people on their way to Damascus. I think we hit another bubble of hikers on this stretch. One gentleman we stop to talk to, trail name "Camel," is section hiking. His wife dropped him off fifteen miles back and is going to pick him up in Damascus. (We would come to learn that a lot of people walked the AT in sections and would try to complete the whole 2,190 miles a section at a time.) He is planning to do more sections within the next couple weeks, so we might just run into him again. "When you get to Damascus, go to the diner," we tell him.

We continue hiking and walk past a side trail and the ruins of an old stone cabin foundation and come to Abingdon Gap Shelter, six and a half miles after leaving Damascus. We decide not to stay here since they don't have a privy, and so we move on. (We find out later that Tennessee does not have privies to use. The only thing available to use is the great outdoors. Oh joy!) About one mile farther, we run into McQueen Gap Road, but it just seems to be a pull-off for cars and not really a place to camp. At this point, we are starting to feel tired and could easily call it a night if we could find something.

In the distance, we see what looks like a shelter coming up and start to feel some relief that we might just have a place to stay for the night. Even though I prefer not to stay in a shelter, I am so tired and will agree to anything right now. As we get closer, we see that it is a tiny shelter, only able to hold two people, and there are two people already in it. Disappointment at seeing them fades as we hear the gal on the phone upset with whomever she is talking to. We find out that they are trying to find a place to set up their tent while in Damascus and are being told that no tents are allowed within the city limits, that they have to set up on the Virginia Creeper Trail (outside the city), and they're not wanting to do that because of the distance. In conversation, we find that they are not planning to stay in the shelter; they're just taking a rest there to make calls. The young man is very nice, but the young gal is still reeling from her conversation on the phone and tells us we are not able to spend the night at the shelter; it is McQueens Knob Shelter and is only for emergency situations, so we'll have to find another place. He's trying to tell her he thinks it's okay if we stay, and she is adamant that we can't. Oh! My! Get me out of here! I am starting to feel uncomfortable and just want to get away — we don't know if she's right or not; at this point, we're just ready to move on, so that they can figure out their own dilemma, and we can figure out ours.

Just under four miles later, each step filled with pure exhaustion and not believing we can go one step farther, we finally find a flat area (unofficial campsite) near a swamp where we're able to put up our tent for the night. We are low on water, but even though we're near a swamp, we decide it is not suitable to drink, even if we filtered it. To conserve the water that we do have and energy that we don't have, we don't bother to fix a hot dinner; it is just tortilla shells with mayo, cheese, and salami tonight. Thirteen miles of hiking, and we're calling it a night at only 6:30 p.m.! Good night, y'all!

Day 12 (Sunday, April 18)–Trail Magic!

After a good night's sleep, we awaken to sunshine but cool temperatures. Mornings like this are perfect for either a hot tea or hot cider. For me, on cooler mornings, I tend to take longer getting around, whereas FROG is already up and whistling along with the birds, making our hot drinks, enjoying the early-morning stirrings of nature. I don't get how someone can be so cheerful in the morning! A short time later, I hear him talking to those passing on the trail, which convinces me to get myself in motion; the day seems to be starting without me. Morning routine quickly sets in: pack up, drink our hot cider, read our psalm, and pray for the Lord to lead us through this day. And we're off.

Well, lookie there! Less than a quarter mile up the trail and off to the right, we see an official campsite that would have been a perfect spot for us to have camped last night. So close yet so far away. We never would have made it up the hill to that spot, not with the amount of energy we had left.

Three miles later, we come to Low Gap and cross the road, and there we see a welcome sight: a stone picnic table to sit at and a good water supply flowing next to it! We are in desperate need after using water this morning for our hot cider and drinking most of what we had left on our walk here. After filling our water bottles, we sit at the stone picnic table to relax, camel up, and eat our lunch. As we're sitting there, a man and woman show up who are dressed and ready to go out and do trail maintenance. The trails thus far have been in immaculate shape, so it is nice to meet those we could thank for their service in keeping the trails in such good shape.

Hah! Not only were the trails in good shape, but the people maintaining them were in good shape as well. We watch them *effortlessly* walk up the steep hill with their chainsaws, toolbelts, and work gear in hand.

As we finish our lunch, another vehicle arrives and parks in the lot next to the picnic table. I think nothing of it, just assuming it is another maintenance worker showing up to help out. The driver gets out and calls out to us, "Do you guys need anything?" I am still not sure what exactly he is referring to, but before I answer, FROG replies, "Good looks and talent." "Well, I can't help you with either of those, but I do have food here if you'd like some." *Wait, what?!* Could this be our first trail magic? We heard about the generosity extended to hikers by trail angels, but we hadn't encountered it yet, so we just weren't sure. He opens up his trunk, and lo and behold, there's food everywhere! Yes! It's our first trail magic! He's got candy bars, fruit, granola bars, chips, and soda, and he mentions that they will be setting up the grill and doing hamburgers and hot dogs soon. We really wish we hadn't just had our lunch and had waited just a bit more, but how could we have known? Nonetheless, we have to pass on the burgers and dogs but do take apples, tangerines, Little Debbie Swiss Rolls, a Gatorade, and a Pepsi to enjoy later. With sincere appreciation, we thank him so much for his generosity and trudge up the hill with our newfound treasure. Of course, everyone we meet up with on the trail going NOBO, we just have to tell them what is coming up. We come upon a single hiker off to the side, sitting on a log, eating some snacks, but once we mention what is ahead, she immediately throws her food in her pack and hurries off. You don't have to tell hungry hikers more than once; their faces light up, and their steps are hurried in anticipation.

    It doesn't take us long to realize that the fruit, Pepsi, and Gatorade have become heavy to carry (you notice I didn't mention the Little Debbie Swiss Rolls; they were gone soon after we received them) and that maybe our gluttonous decision to take so much wasn't such a good idea. That is probably why most hikers sit and eat their food before heading back out on the trail; next time, hopefully, we will do it right and not load up. Although, is there really any difference if we eat the same amount or carry it? Won't we still feel the heaviness? Hmmm.

    Hearing the trail maintenance crew in the distance, clearing our path with their chainsaws, is a sound that brings a mixture of emotions to FROG. Before we sold our home, we strictly heated our home with wood, which meant that every summer, he would prepare for the winter by going out with his chainsaw, cutting wood, and then hauling it back to the house with his beloved rotted-out wheelbarrow. He'd stack it up in our lopsided but functional woodshed for the winter months. It was a chore he loved to do. Now being homeless means he is no longer going to be doing that; it brings both joy and sadness as he recounts his past. We have no doubts that we made the right decision to sell our home; it's just that change can be so hard sometimes, especially since it's been his norm for forty-three years now. He will have to create a new norm.

Our goal is to go 6.5 more miles until we reach TN91 trailhead parking lot and call for pickup to stay at The Rabbit Hole in Shady Valley. Our friends at Lost Mountain Shelter (day 7, Racehorse, Lux, and Man Alive) gave a great review on this hostel and told us if we're able to stay here, it's a must! They raved about the accommodations, the showers, the breakfast, and the *milkshakes*! Another place that we hadn't planned to stay, but who in their right mind can pass up on a milkshake? Not us! We love our sweets!

We are so focused on getting to our destination that we pass Double Springs Shelter without taking a rest and continue onward, which eventually brings us to a fenced-in pasture with a beautiful view of the countryside atop Cross Mountain. We know we must be close to the trailhead parking lot as we start to see more people out on the trail. We stop and have an interesting conversation with an elderly man in his eighties who frequently walks this particular section and is now on his way back to his car. We try to insist that he go ahead of us so he doesn't show us up and pass us. That would be much too humiliating! But being the gentleman he is, he insists we go first. Oh boy, step it up, FROG! As it turns out, he stops at the top of the mountain and enjoys the view so we can easily put distance between us. He probably did that on purpose because he knew he could take us! Such a gentleman and a scholar!

Approaching the other end of the fenced-in gate, we struggle somewhat with the lock, only to find out that it is broken and there are instructions on how to maneuver and shimmy it just right to let yourself out. It takes some doing and some reassuring ourselves that we are smarter than a silly lock and that we *can* do this! After what seems like an eternity, we finally must have shimmied it just right because we are set free! A celebratory high five and a look back to see that our gentleman friend has still not caught up with us—yes! Life is good!

Just a short distance away, we see two women taking pictures of a barn sitting in a field and assume it must be picture worthy for them to be taking pictures with their professional-looking cameras. As we get closer, we see a huge AT symbol on the side of it. Aww ... we need a picture next to that! They are still there by the time we arrive and offer to take our picture next to it. What a momentous moment! We're only twelve days in, and the AT has become our home as we stand proudly next to it with big smiles and huge dreams of completing what we set out to do! (Picture on front cover.)

About one hundred yards from the barn sits an old truck just parked out in the field next to the fence. Not that it is anything special; it's more of an excuse to continue taking breaks, so we take time to look at it. We hear behind us, "Nice shirt!" Seems FROG has a hiking twin who is wearing an identical shirt in brand and color. Fist bump and well wishes as his twin heads to Maine with a shirt identical to his! Another shirt that may make it to Mt. Katahdin but won't be on FROG. (He is at peace with the fact that he won't be hiking all 2,190 miles of the AT and realizes just how much of an accomplishment it truly is to complete such a hike all the way to Maine. We truly hope that his shirt twin made it all the way and stood proudly in his green Arctic Cool shirt next to the sign on top of Mt. Katahdin!)

As we make the short descent down the hill, we see the road (TN91) and the parking lot full of cars. With a welcome shout, we know soon we will be having a *milkshake* and a *shower*! Of course, not at the same time! (Hmmm ... that might not have been such a bad idea!) Oh, the joys of civilization! We can hardly contain our excitement as we pass those on our path on our way down. Being hikers, I know they understand.

It's early, around 2:30 p.m., as I plop myself down with our gear next to the road and FROG goes to the signboard to see if there is any information on calling for pickup for The Rabbit Hole. He is able to locate the number and calls, asking if there is any availability (another place we failed to make reservations ahead of time) to stay for the night. We are hoping to stay in their only private cabin for the night, but he finds out that it is reserved already. There is availability in the bunkhouse. I am disappointed that we won't have privacy, but the thought of getting off the trail for the night wins out.

Soon a car pulls up, and out pops a very casual, no frills, down-to-earth, barefooted guy who greets us and introduces himself as "Rabbit." We instantly like him and feel comfortable as he drives us down a windy road into Shady Valley.

Arriving at the hostel, he helps us unload and takes us into the bunkhouse. I immediately feel the warmth and welcoming scents that await us as we walk in. This place is homey and so inviting! There is a nice comfy couch, a TV, a couple gas fireplaces, a refrigerator, and some hiker boxes full of unwanted food and other miscellaneous items. The inside doors were painted with chalk paint so that everyone who stayed could write their trail names on the door (the door was full, but we found space to add *Faith and FROG 2021 SOBO*). The room has six sets of foamed bunkbeds with towels and washcloths on them, waiting for weary hikers to arrive and shower and bed down for the night. We are the first to arrive, so we're able to pick our bunks first. We choose the last bottom two on the left side and share a nightstand between the beds.

As we're setting up our sleeping bags, Rabbit asks us which flavor milkshake we would like. There are so many different flavors, but I choose peanut butter, and FROG, vanilla. Can I just tell you ... the peanut butter milkshake was the bomb! I can't attest to the vanilla, but wow! I never tasted something as yummy, creamy, and delicious as that milkshake was! It was well worth the four dollars we paid for it! Now I know why our friend Racehorse said she had three of them! We sign up for the shuttle into town later (to the local restaurant) as well as for the five-dollar breakfast they will serve in the morning.

The shower is equally as nice! There are three outside showers available for use with shampoo, conditioner, and soap provided in each. Ahh! My very first time taking a shower outside in the great outdoors—a little awkward at first, but I soon *warmed* up to the idea! Oh, the modern conveniences that we took for granted before starting this hike are now true luxuries out here on the trail!

We have only one other person show up to stay in the bunkhouse tonight, Man Card. He is travelling NOBO and is doing long sections, not entirely sure how far he will be going. His wife, Pit Crew, isn't doing the long hikes but is meeting up with him along the trail to help with resupply, short hikes, and spending time with him when he takes zero days. He is the one to introduce us to the Sutton family. He had met four-year-old Harvey (who turned five on the trail and currently is the youngest person to complete a thru hike on the AT), his mom, Cassie, and his dad, Josh, while they were just finishing up in the Smokies. He finds the video on YouTube to show us the presentation he had made to Harvey (trail name Little Man) by giving him a man card—hence his trail name. We enjoy hearing about Man Card's adventures thus far on the AT while we enjoy dinner together at the restaurant in town. FROG and I each have the hamburger combo meal, and Man Card (who has been on the trail a lot longer than we have) has two meals, the hamburger combo and the chicken dinner. He completes both meals before I finish my single dinner! Again, I wonder if we will be like this after our hiker hunger sets in. After dinner, we are picked up by Rabbit's wife, Cat—also free-spirited, down to earth, long dreadlocks, and barefooted. We really like her as well and enjoy learning more about her and Rabbit's family and life at the hostel. What a great couple! So glad that we included this stay in our journey.

Just keep walking! Man Card and Pit Crew

Day 13 (Monday, April 19)—Hundred-Mile Marker

Breakfast in the morning is plentiful (for us anyway!) and delicious! It is delivered to us in the bunkhouse about 8:30 a.m. on paper plates with tin foil covering the plate. As we open up our plate, we see a generous supply of eggs and potatoes (from their chickens and garden) with a side of toast. The portions are so big neither FROG nor I can finish all that is on our plate. Now Man Card, on the other hand, has woofed down his plateful of food in a hurry. I know I can't eat anymore and turn to Man Card and say, "This may sound weird, but I can't eat anymore, so you're welcome to eat what is left on my plate if you want." He turns to me and says, "That is not weird at all, and *yes*, I would love to finish what's on your plate." We laugh as I hand over my plate. He finishes what's left on my plate, and then FROG offers him what's left on his plate. He eats some but finally has hit a wall; he can't finish it all. At least we feel good that we didn't waste much and that we all are full.

We are taken back to the trail about 9:00 a.m. along with the woman who stayed in the cabin (our first time seeing her.) When we arrive at the trailhead, Man Card is in a panic because he can't find his wallet and thinks he left it at the bunkhouse. He is looking through his backpack and just can't seem to locate it. Cat has driven us and calls Rabbit to see if he can see if it's still in the bunkhouse. All I can think about is, *Does he think we might have taken it since we are the only ones who were in the bunkhouse with him?* The thought of someone thinking ill of us and knowing we didn't have it weighed heavily on me and must have on FROG too because he ends up calling Rabbit later to see if Man Card found it. Thankfully, he did; it was in his backpack, just not in the usual place he put it. Relief for both parties!

It is a cold and windy day as we travel up Iron Mountain. Less than four miles later, we come to the gravesite of Nick Grindstaff, a local hermit who was found dead in his bed one day, guarded by his dog, Ganter. He was laid to rest near his cabin on the highest peak of Iron Mountain right off the Appalachian Trail, where he lived for forty years. On his tombstone reads UNCLE NICK GRINDSTAFF, *Born December 26, 1851, Died July 22, 1923. Lived alone, suffered alone and died alone.* It saddens me to know he died alone (but glad he at least had a dog he loved by his side).

We just hit a milestone! Today we have hiked one hundred miles! Woohoo! Our celebration tonight after dinner will be a Snickers bar and a Payday candy bar! It's usually one or the other, and we share a bar, but not tonight. This is a special occasion!

Our plans today are to stop at Iron Mountain Shelter for lunch and then to make it to Vandeventer Shelter for the night, 11.5 miles if our plan pans out.

On our way to the first shelter, we run into a seventy-two-year-old man who goes by the trail name of "506." He is walking 506 miles to honor his military unit—you guessed it, #506. He is one of those guys who is so personable and friendly we wish we had more time to talk with him to hear more of his story. What is interesting to find out is that all three of us have something in common, and it isn't just hiking; we all have a background with National Cash Register (NCR). We have all worked there; actually, this is where FROG and I met, which we will be sharing with you in detail in a later chapter.

As we arrive at Iron Mountain Shelter, there are already two young guys there eating their lunch. As we sit down, a third young guy shows up and seems to know the other two. They have plans to hike all the way to Damascus from there, 26.2 miles away. Our mouths just drop open; we can't even fathom trying to push out that many miles in one day. Not to mention they have put in several miles already to get to this point. They are young, energetic, and very confident. I'm sure they will do it! They were a fun bunch and very encouraging to us old folks to keep keeping on, and they were sure we'd successfully reach our goals as well.

> **Just keep walking! Swamp**
> **Best wishes! May the stars guide you. Arrow**
> **Have a great hike! Floorboard**

Well, hopefully we do meet our overall goal of reaching the finish line in Georgia, but we don't successfully meet our goal for the day. After a day of many ups and downs, we call it quits after ten miles. We just don't feel we can walk the extra 1.5 miles to reach the next shelter. We find an official campsite on the ridge of a cliff, overlooking the beautiful Tennessee countryside. What a view and spot! We make sure we have our door faced away from the cliff so when we have to inevitably get up in the middle of the night, we don't accidentally fall off the cliff. Good thinking, huh?

Day 14 (Tuesday, April 20)–Awkward

Nature does call, but fortunately it is light enough out that I don't wake FROG to have to go out with me this time. As I open the door flap of the tent and peek out (I'm always on the lookout first), I turn to FROG, who is in a deep sleep, and loudly exclaim, "You *have got* to get up and see what I'm seeing!" Not sure what I am so worked up about, FROG immediately gets up (well, as fast as FROG can immediately get up, that is!) and looks out the flap. "Wow!" There before us is a beautiful display in the sky, all lit up with pinks, yellows, and oranges—our first sunrise that we've seen since we started the hike. It is beautiful! That, my friends, is put here by GOD specifically for us to see at this time. I don't believe it is a coincidence. We usually have to use the bathroom way before sunrise and could have easily missed it if we had gotten up earlier. We thought we found this perfect spot; oh no—GOD found this perfect spot for us so to bless us with His creativity! What a glorious way to start our day! Can our day get any better than it is right now?

As we walk to Vandeventer Shelter, we start to see fantastic views of Watauga Lake off in the distance. The shelter sits high on the ridge overlooking the lake, so views out behind the shelter are spectacular! Time to just sit, get a few photos, and eat our breakfast. We are in need of water, and they do mention in Guthook that a water source is close by and that it's 0.3 miles off-trail. Ugh! Too far off-trail to go for water, which will definitely be downhill and straight up on the return. Nope! Next one is over 1.5 miles; we will ration what we've got and try to make it work.

Watauga Lake

We've run into a lot of solo female hikers on the trail, and it surprises us that so many are willing to walk alone with so many unknowns. Not that it's a bad thing, just surprises us is all. A lot of them carry the Garmin InReach as security, some have dogs, and some latch on to others and become a tramily, but there are those who choose to hike purely alone, avoiding much contact. It's not something we would feel comfortable doing by ourselves, but thank goodness there is a wide range of different personalities, which makes life so interesting!

On our descent, we first hear running water, and then we see it!

Our water source! And we don't have to go off-trail to get it! Time to camel up and fill our water bottles. A common thing we notice at most water sources is if they don't use a pipe to help with the water flow, they will use a leaf as a spout in helping to fill your bottles. Very clever idea, as it works quite well. (That is, if you have a water flow. There will be days to come when we come to water sources that have dried up or only have a small trickle coming from them, and it takes a long time to get a full bottle.)

Our views of Watauga Lake are getting closer, and we're starting to run into more people on the trail, which usually indicates that we're close to a trailhead and will soon be approaching the parking lot at Wilbur Dam Road. We've decided we're going to stop at the road and call Boots Off Hostel and Campground and see if they have any availability there for the night and if they offer pick up.

What a relief to drop all our gear and just rest along the road while FROG calls the hostel. The bunkhouse is full, but there are some campsites available to use for the night, and no, there is no pickup. We have to walk the five miles to their place. (We misunderstood the comments on Guthook, thinking they offered pickup, but it is only for those who slackpack, which we would learn about later.)

We gather up our packs and try to convince ourselves that we can handle five miles. It's only five miles for goodness sakes! What you don't take into consideration is nothing is just a straight shot (unless you cheat and take the Virginia Creeper Trail); there are many ups and downs and road walking that make five miles seem to go on forever.

We cross over Watauga Dam, which offers great views of the lake, and proceed walking on the Watauga Lake Lookout Road, passing a Boy Scout troop with about eight boys and just one leader. We can't imagine trying to keep that many boys in line, especially with the excitement they express as we pass by.

Just before we reach Shook Branch Rec Area (a large lakeside park), we hear, "Faith, FROG!" Not quite sure who it is, we get closer and see that it is Camel, who we ran into on day 11 as we were leaving Damascus. He had mentioned to us that we might run into him again, and here he is. His wife has dropped him off again, and he is walking another section of the AT and will be picked up at Wilbur Dam Road. I'm tired at this point and start wondering why in the world I am not more like his wife and just have FROG walk sections on his own. I'm sure I would be a good dropper offer and picker upper. We've run into several solo men out hiking on their own who have mentioned that their wives would never be out here doing this. Hmmm ... there was that time I said *never* too, so maybe there is hope with those wives. Hang in there!

Crossing road US 321 is *scary*! We are not sure if there have been a lot of fatalities with crossing this road or not; but it is insane! I can guarantee you those are not hikers who are passing by at high speeds without any care at all for those who are trying to cross the road to connect to the AT on the other side. They need to come up with some alternative; this road is too busy and fast. I am in a panic to cross this road.

It gives me flashbacks to the time I was a young child trying to cross a busy road to reach my parents' car on the other side. I was with my brother and didn't notice when he started running to the other side; when I looked up, I panicked and started running too, not looking to see that a car was close enough to hit me. It was close. I wasn't hit, but that was traumatic enough to put fear into me when crossing busy roads. When my son was young, while we were vacationing in the Catskills in New York state and staying at a hotel that had a pool on the other side of the road, he wanted to make sure he was the first one to cross the road to the other side, so he started running full speed, not knowing a car was coming right at him. I screamed for him to stop; he stopped but inches from being hit. I am positive there was an angel between him and that car that prevented him from being hit that day. Busy roads just scare the bejeebers out of me! By the grace of GOD (again), we safely cross the road, but I don't think it will shock you to know I have a *tight* grip on FROG's arm as we cross.

We're not sure where Boots Off Hostel and Campground is exactly. It's supposedly on this road somewhere. We're just hoping it's not that much farther; we are really whipped! It's been a 10.8-mile trip today, with so many ups and downs; we're just ready to lay down! Ah, there's a sign at the end of the road. Maybe that is it. As we get closer to the sign, we see that it is indeed the place we are looking for. Relief turns into complete discouragement as we look to our right and see that there is a huge hill for us to climb up to get to the campground. It's embarrassing to admit: these two senior adults had a complete meltdown at the bottom of that hill. You have to be kidding me, right? With tears in our eyes, we start to take slow deliberate steps, one slow step at a time, up that long walk to the top. I am secretly hoping that someone, anyone, will be driving up this hill and will give us a lift. Doesn't happen. (Had we known what lay ahead, we never would have made that awful climb up! We would have just plopped down and camped right on the side of the road!)

Finally! After what seems like forever, we reach the top and break out into complete busyness—there are people everywhere! We are relieved to finally be here, but now where do we go? There are no signs to direct us where to go, and no one greets us as we continue to shuffle along, one slow step at a time. A quick survey of the people around us reveals they are very young adults, early twenties. Oh boy, we're already feeling out of place.

We finally decide to enter the side door of the first building we come to, and hopefully once inside there, there will be some indicator as to where we need to check in. Nope. Still no indicators, only a lot of young adults inside all over the place, yelling, socializing, partying. We figure out that this must be the common area that is used to prepare meals: there are microwaves to use, food items scattered all over the place, a big table off to the side, a crowded room with people everywhere. Feeling like all eyes are on the old people, FROG finally asks someone where we are supposed to go to check in. Talk about awkward! If we had had the energy, we should have hightailed it out then! Finally, someone points to another side door to indicate the office. Well, good. Now we're getting someplace.

Inside that door is the camp store and indeed the office for check-in. This may not be everyone's view of their experience at this hostel, but for us, from the moment we step up to the desk, we are treated as though we are imbeciles. Okay, granted, we are extremely tired and might not be thinking straight, but there is no reason to treat us this way. Everything we say or ask about is followed by disrespect and annoyance. FROG is usually pretty good about coming up with something to lighten the mood, but he isn't able to change this guy's demeanor. Okay, fine, just tell us where to go to put up our tent, and we'll get out of your hair. No, that would have been too easy. Instead, we are told he *thinks* there are a couple spots left, and we'll need to go and find a spot on our own. What? You don't even know if you have a spot available, and we have to go and hunt for a vacant spot? We, of course, are not saying this out loud, but we're both angrily thinking it inside.

If we hadn't been so tired already, maybe we would have welcomed this better than we did. With no clear direction, we grab our things and try to figure out where we might need to go to find the tent sites. There is a huge firepit to our right with seats around it, and to the left of that are individual cabins. We hear a dog barking below the cabins and turn to see where it is coming from and notice there are tents set up down there. Ah! Success! We walk past the cabins and around the bend and see the long line of tents set up. FROG has reached his limit and is telling me he can't walk another step; I know how he feels, but we can't stop now. We need to find a site. We can do this! Each step we take is met with disappointment; we are just not finding a site that is available to use. FROG is just ready to set up in someone else's spot that looks big enough to hold our tent too, but I lumber on, not agreeing with his rash decision. We finally spot a place, tent site #12! If we had had the energy, we would certainly have done a victory dance in celebration. (We would soon find out why this spot had been vacant.)

From the distance, it seems to be a nice spot: a tall tree covering for shade (not that we need it, as by now it is getting cold) with a good-sized log to sit on to eat our dinner. But as we get closer, we realize why it hasn't been snatched up yet. The area we need to use to put up our tent is on a slant! Oh! My! Goodness! Too bad! We're going to have to make it work. We are not moving another step farther to see if there is another site available. We maneuver the tent so that our heads are uphill and hope, due to the slant, that we don't slide all the way to the bottom of the tent by morning.

As is our standard, after putting up the tent, we crawl inside and lay down for a while before getting up to have dinner and do our nightly chores. I'm sure we could easily call it a night and just stay right here, but we are pretty excited knowing there are showers available to use, so that is our motivator to get back up and try to get moving again. The thought of taking a long, hot shower is exactly what the doctor ordered on a day like today. After our shower, FROG must feel brave (probably more like thirsty) because he says he is headed into the camp store to buy us some sodas. I have no desire to walk back in there and encounter any more confrontations with our *friendly* camp host. "You're on your own. I'm headed back to our tent."

We don't get to sleep until 8:00 p.m. (our latest so far) because of the partying that is going on around the firepit. (We later learned that it lasted until about ten that night, later than the hiker midnight. There would be some tired hikers the next day.)

We found out that not all hostels are created equal. This was not one of our favorites. Maybe if we had been in our twenties and wanted to party, it may have been, but for us old folks, it wasn't our cup of tea!

Day 15 (Wednesday, April 21)—Blue Hershey's Kiss

It was a cold night; it was supposed to rain during the night but didn't. There's nothing worse than packing up a wet tent and having to carry the extra weight in water. And more good news: we had the best night's sleep! We prepared for the worst and ended with the best. Who would have thought you could sleep so well on slanted ground? Flat ground is overrated!

We find out before we leave that there are those who stay at hostels, especially this one, who work-for-stay. Maybe the guy we met yesterday working check-in was one of those, and he just gave us the wrong impression of this place. Hopefully that's the case and Boots Off Hostel and Campground is really a great place to stay.

We shook our *boots off*, left, and never looked back. The highlights of our stay: showers, cold sodas, and a good night's sleep! That's it. Oh and maybe the fact that now it's all downhill to get out of here.

It will be a shorter day today—only eight miles to Black Bear Resort, and then we plan to stay a couple nights. We previously got a tip from another hiker to make sure we made reservations; if you don't, most likely they will be sold out. Thank goodness we followed through with that, and we have our own private cabin awaiting our arrival when we get in later. We also have three boxes that were shipped directly there, waiting for us, two resupply boxes and our bounce box.

It's such a cold, windy, and rainy day; we are bundled up as much as we can to stay warm and also have our ponchos on over our clothes to keep things as dry as we can. Today, being an exceptionally windier day, caught me by surprise when the wind blew up behind me with a huge gust. FROG got a picture of me in my poncho looking like a giant blue Hershey's Kiss! Good glory be, we're going south, y'all! Isn't it supposed to be warmer in the South? Don't believe it; it's a lie! It's freezing here! Temps have been getting into the thirties.

Blue Hershey's Kiss

HOBOS GOING SOBO IN THEIR OBOZ and we never looked back ...

A note of caution: be wary of tree roots. They have a way of jumping up and tripping you, leaving you flat on the ground with a face full of leaves and no way of getting up, due to a heavy pack on your back. All you can do is lie there and laugh—and hope your sidekick stops laughing enough to help you back up. (He did check that I was okay first, before full-blown laughter.)

The walk along Laurel Creek is beautiful! Directions are a little confusing. As we approach an intersection, one way straight up is the Laurel Fork Shelter, and the other off to the right indicates a trail to Laurel Falls. We think this is an option to go and see the falls and that the trail really goes up past the shelter. (This is where looking at your Guthook app would have been a good thing.) We are just anxious to get to the resort, so we opt to just continue on the trail (what we *thought* was the trail anyway) and bypass the falls. It is a climb up to the shelter, so by the time we reach the top, we are ready for a drink and something to eat. It seems strange that since we've encountered a bubble of NOBOs, we aren't seeing any people, but still not thinking too much about it, we decide to head farther down the trail. Unbeknownst to us, we're walking on another trail within the park, the High-Water Route Trail instead of the AT. Something is just not right; we haven't seen a white blaze in a long time. Maybe we better stop and backtrack to find a blaze before we continue further. FROG heads back to see if he sees any white blazes going the other direction. Nothing. Hmmm ... we head back to the shelter—still nothing, so we decide to go back to the intersection. Maybe we missed something. Yep! At the intersection, the white blazes continue off to the right. It isn't an option; you're supposed to take the trail to the falls. Oh brother! We tried to avoid going out of our way so as not to add additional steps, and by doing so, we end up going a mile out of our way. Jiminy Crickets!

> We chose the road less traveled, and now we don't know where we are.
> **—Unknown**

The falls are spectacular! To think we opted to not see them makes us so glad that it isn't an option! It is so worth our walk to see them. We have pictures, but like most pictures you take, you don't get the full appreciation unless you see them firsthand. What a sight to behold. As we turn to head up and make the climb out, we run into a NOBO coming down the trail. We tell him he'll enjoy the view coming up. He kind of chuckles (instead of showing exasperation, I'm sure) and says this will be his third time walking this half mile, and he has already been down here once. Come to find out it wasn't clear on the NOBO side either, and he thought it was an option to see the falls, so the first time, he left his backpack at the top so as not to carry a heavy load down, only to find out once he got down here, this was indeed the trail you continue to follow. Up he had to go to get his pack, and this is when we meet him, coming back again with his pack. (Ugh! And I'm telling you, that half mile up was treacherous, steep, and rocky. So, I can imagine how frustrated he was having to do it three times, both directions!)

Laurel Fork Falls

He asks us where we are headed, and we tell him Black Bear Resort. He asks if we have reservations because they are always booked. Yes, we called ahead of time. He says we will love it and raves about his stay, since he is just coming from there, and gives us a great tip. Use the bathroom/shower located in the laundry room. No one knows about it, and it's very private. Good tip. We'll check it out!

After seeing cliff views of Laurel Fork Gorge and going through Pond Mountain Wilderness, we come to the south trailhead located on Dennis Cove Road. Black Bear Resort is located a half mile on this road. Not sure which direction we are supposed to go, we consult our Guthook app but to no avail. It says we have arrived, and we know that isn't true; we are standing in a parking lot. One thing we have noticed traveling SOBO, the signs and directions posted on roads cater mostly to the NOBO. (We would find out on our first slackpack day that across the road were directions on which way to head to the resort.)

We see no one for some time and are afraid to start walking the wrong direction, so we just try to wait it out to see if anyone comes along. Finally, a young NOBO hiker shows up, and we ask if she knows where the resort might be. She points the direction we need to go and says she is headed there too. She asks us if we have made reservations, because if we haven't, we would most likely be wasting our time going there, since they are always booked. We laugh and nod the affirmative. Hearing that again is confirmation to us that it is a good idea that we made reservations and didn't just wing it this time. Yes, we're good. We'll just follow you so we know where to go since you know where the resort is.

Hah! We really do try to keep up with her, but she is gone in a flash! This girl is bookin' it! I like to think the cold air motivates her since she is wearing a skirt and her legs look cold, but I'm betting this is a normal pace for her. We can't see her due to her rounding a corner, but we know this is the way, and hopefully it is obvious when we get to it and we don't just walk past it. We needn't have worried; it is obvious when we get to it. A really nice area on the other side of Laurel Creek with a bridge that you cross to reach it—truly a gem in the woods.

> A walk in nature is to witness a thousand miracles.
> —**Mary Davis**

Our Support Team:

Sounds like an uncomfortable week. You just might wish for some of this cool weather in a few weeks when it starts getting too warm hiking the trail. Thanks for the updates. It is great taking an armchair hike with you guys. Stay safe. Mary K.

I finally sat down to see your pictures from my large screen computer—didn't want to do so from just my phone. LOVELY! Love ya! Bethie T.

I've been thinking about you guys. So nice to hear your updates! I am not surprised to hear how freezing you are as one of the first lessons learned lol. Enjoy some rest. Can't wait to see what the next leg of your adventure brings. Diana T.

Thanks for the updates and photos! What an adventure! Makes one appreciate a bathroom and a comfy bed! Prayers for safety as you continue your journey!! Coleen B.

I see a book in the making here! Your stories and pictures take us with you on this adventure ... minus the rain, the cold, the wind, the lack of bathroom facilities and most importantly living this incredible adventure. You two are amazing! Stay well and can hardly wait for the next update. Love you both! Bev G.

Thanks for the updates! What an adventure! Sorry you're cold. I know the cold would really bother me! Take care. Praying you remain upbeat and safe! Nancy K.

HOBOS GOING SOBO IN THEIR OBOZ and we never looked back ...

You two are so brave and open to experiences! We love reading about them and seeing the photos! May God continue to bless and keep you both!! Hugs across the many miles! Denise L.

Sounds like you are having a real learning, thanks for keeping us updated. Milt K.

These updates & the photos are awesome. And you have an excellent sense of humor which just might be the most important gear you can carry on this sort of adventure! Walk on & have fun! Linda M.

I am very proud of you, my friends. And you seem to be doing it without spinach! Claude M.

Your blog is wonderful full of humor and great pictures! You're doing great! Stay healthy and keep living your dream! Shelby S.

Lori we are so impressed. Love your blog! Keep up the great trekking! Bonnie B.

Thank you for the update! And the Humor! You guys are soooo fabulous! Wonderful adventure for sure. God Bless—Stay Safe! Darlene M.

Awesome photos!! Keep it up! Glad you guys got to get some rest along the way!! Love you. Tracy M.

> Live your life, forget your age.
> **—Unknown**

Hampton, Tennessee, to Roan Mountains, Tennessee

> Surely he will save you from the fowler's snare,
> and from the deadly pestilence.
> —Psalm 91:3

We arrive so cold and just ready to settle into our cabin, hoping that it is heated and ready for us. We have to wait in line due to the amount of people checking in, and lookie there, two people ahead of us in line is our little speed walking friend who blew our doors off in getting here. FROG tells her we tried to keep up, but we were just too tired to maintain her pace. Hah! Even if we weren't tired, we never would have kept up to her pace! We are humbled but certainly don't want to admit it out loud in front of everyone.

We immediately love Linda and Travis, really good people, new owners of Black Bear Resort. They are a lot of fun, such personable, down-to-earth Christians and just lovers of people. They are definitely right where GOD needs them to be at such a time as this.

Our cabin, Mountain Mama, is ready for us, and Linda even took the time to go outside to show us where it is located so we wouldn't have to go all over looking for it. What a change from last night's adventure at Boots. It is a cute cabin: a nice porch on the front, a small sitting area with a table just inside with a microwave and small refrigerator, and then another room with two sets of bunk beds. It is cozy but *cold* in there. The heater is on, but it keeps coming on and shutting off, so the room hasn't really heated up much. We don't want to be a pain, but we need to be warm, so FROG heads back to the office to see if we can get another heater or at least see if this one can be fixed. Within minutes, Travis is at our door to inspect the heater. It's working, but he decides to get us another heater so that we can have two going at the same time. It takes us awhile huddled around those heaters to thaw out, but eventually we do.

We noticed when we were in the office for check-in that the camp store had frozen pizzas available to heat up and plenty of sodas, so we head back down to see about that for dinner tonight and to get our three boxes that we had shipped to us. Linda jokes with us about having sent so much. "You know you have to carry all that, right?" We laugh because it does seem ridiculous that we've sent so much to ourselves. One is our bounce box that we will continue to send forward, and the other two are full of food. We'll go through and decide what we want, and what we don't use, we'll include in our bounce box, getting it down to one box, and then send that to our next stop. The fear before you set out to do a backpacking trip like this is that you'll run out of food, so you tend to over plan your food, as is our case. No one wants to go hungry, and you hear that eventually the hiker hunger will hit, and you want to be well prepared for that time. But when will that happen? Hard to plan for it when you're just not sure. It's been two weeks, and it hasn't hit yet.

Day 16 (Thursday, April 22)—We're Going to Hollywood!

Zero day! We wake to frost on the cars. Brrr! What a great day to have deemed a no-hiking day. Our cabin has become comfy and warm, so to leave to go to the bathroom brings out a groan from both of us.

But we put on our big-boy and big-girl pants and head out despite our reservations to do so. With such cool temperatures, even the walk to the bathroom seems longer than it really is. So far, we have been fortunate that no one has discovered the bathroom/shower in the laundry room, and it's been available each time we've gone there. Today is no exception. We feel free to take a long, hot shower and not feel rushed. Oh, the joys of life that are taken for granted!

Today we are headed into town. We need to ship our bounce box ahead to our next stop and send home our big bear canister that has become more of a burden than functional. But what we are looking forward to most is we're headed to McDonald's for some Big Macs! We are so excited! Now in real life, FROG and I do not go to McDonald's other than to get drinks. We never get their food, but after you've walked 125 miles, it just sounds so good!

Travis shuttles us into the town along with Poncho, who is taking a zero day as well. He has already thru-hiked the AT, PCT, CDT (a triple crowner) and a trail in Mongolia and decided he wanted to do the AT again. He is a NOBO, so he's already hiked 420 miles to date, and he's hungry! None of us left disappointed and felt full after our meals and shakes. We shipped our bounce box to the next destination, where we plan to take our next zero day, Natures Inn Hostel and Cabins located near Sam's Gap, in Flag Pond, Tennessee—100.2 miles away. (All the zero days that we preplanned to take we did take off. We'd soon find out that due to weather and health, additional zero days were needed that we didn't plan for. As with life, things happen that you don't or can't possibly plan for ahead of time.)

The buzz around the resort is about the weather expected for Saturday; they are calling for 100 percent chance of rain all day, which makes us rethink our plans. Today is our only planned zero day, but what if we take the next two nights and stay here (in our nice, warm cabin) and leave the day after the storm? With that plan in mind, we head to the office to check with Linda to see if it is possible to add nights to our stay. The resort has been full both days, so we're just praying that it will work out. There is just no way that we can get to our next destination and out of the rain before Saturday.

HOBOS GOING SOBO IN THEIR OBOZ and we never looked back ...

As we're waiting our turn at the desk, we hear others talking about slackpacking. Our first time hearing about this option. I turn to FROG and ask him, "What do you think about checking to see if it's possible to get shuttled tomorrow to a drop-off point, and then we hike back to the resort? Tomorrow is supposed to be a nice day, so why waste a day? Let's try to put in some miles if we can." FROG is all for it, just isn't sure they offer it, but he figures it doesn't hurt to ask.

Our turn. "Two questions," says FROG. "What's up?" asks Linda. "First one, is it possible to stay two more nights?" asks FROG. Linda looks at her computer, "No ... at least not staying in Mountain Mama. It's already reserved for the next two nights. We can move you to Hollywood if that works for you." "Yes, that works!" I chime in quickly. I am so relieved; it doesn't matter to me if we don't have the same place as long as it is warm and I don't have to sleep in the tent on a day that is expected to be miserable. She mentions that she just cleaned Hollywood and that right now there is no one scheduled to go in there tonight, so to make life easier for her, we offer to move over to Hollywood tonight so they can clean ours and have it ready for their guests tomorrow. (Linda not only handles all the duties at the front desk, she also does all the cleaning. She is amazing!)

Since question one is affirmative, "Question two" says FROG. "Do you offer slackpacking options? We would like to get dropped off tomorrow morning and hike back here if it's possible?" If it works out, it will be the first time we will walk as NOBOs but would only be for a day.

"Yes, we do offer it. Let's schedule you in for eight o'clock tomorrow morning to be dropped off at USFS 293, and you can hike back here. We have day packs available for use; you will find them in the laundry room." Sweet! Two for two! Eleven miles and only a small day pack on our backs! We are beyond thrilled and can hardly wait for tomorrow's hike.

We hurry back to our cabin at Mountain Mama to pack everything up to move over to Hollywood for the next three nights. Hollywood is located farther away and sits the highest of all cabins, two flights of steps to enter. The cabin looks like the other one inside, although there is only one set of bunk beds and two doors (one in front and another in back) on this one. Knowing that we like a lot of heat, they even provided us another heater to stay extra toasty with the cold and damp weather expected. Out of the two cabins, I like this one the best, so I feel it was a good trade.

Day 17 (Friday, April 23)—Our First Slackpack Day

Up with the roosters this morning! Last night before bed, we had arranged a day pack with our essentials needed for today's hike. It feels so good to only have water, a water filter (in case we need to filter), snacks, lunch, and toilet paper packed. We should be able to fly today with the lightness of our packs—or rather, pack (singular). I have no excuse since I am pack-less.

The thought of leaving our cozy, warm cabin and heading out in the cold, chilly air today doesn't even faze us as we are filled with so much excitement about doing something new in a something not so new, if that makes any sense to y'all. The woods are calling, and we are ready to see what the day holds!

> And into the forest I go, to lose my mind and find my soul.
> —Unknown

It's buzzing and busy at the office with hikers all around, getting ready to be shuttled or heading out to continue their hike NOBO. We are the only ones who will be shuttled to USFS 293, as they have all completed that section already to have gotten here.

We hadn't noticed before that there are two scales on the front porch, one to weigh our backpacks and one to weigh ourselves. We figure we'll weigh our backpacks tomorrow before we leave, but let's just for fun step on the scale and weigh ourselves. Hah! Was fun for FROG as he lost ten pounds, but I never should have stepped on that horrible thing. How in the world after walking 125 miles does someone *gain* three pounds! And FROG can lose ten pounds? We hiked the same number of miles, for goodness sakes! All you women out there know the frustration this brings! My purpose for hiking was not to lose weight, although I did figure I would just naturally do so. Months before the hike started, I ate as I pleased and gained five pounds *expecting* that I would probably lose weight, so I could justify my indulgences ahead of time. Grrr! That's it! I refuse to step on another scale or even talk about my weight until we reach the finish line in Georgia!

While waiting outside for Travis to shuttle us to the trailhead, we are surrounded by a lot of hikers going about their business of getting ready. We spot two guys, a father/son duo, sitting on the porch, waiting for their ride to pick them up. They have just finished a section of the trail together and are ready to go home to North Carolina. Conversation turns to where we are from, and we always say, "Upstate New York," not to be confused by just saying New York, because it is always automatically assumed we are from New York City. The father mentions that he is from upstate. At this point, we are very interested to find out just where he is from. Our mouths couldn't have dropped any lower when he said, "Owego." FROG taught fourth grade in Apalachin Elementary (Owego-Apalachin School District), and our church is located in Owego. His son couldn't believe the odds of this and just kept shaking his head. They say small world; in this case, it really is.

As we're standing there, FROG mentions out loud that he wished he hadn't sent back his warm gloves because his hands are so cold. He is going to go check the hiker box to see if anyone left some that he can take. Another hiker pipes right up. "I just found these on the trail yesterday." He shows FROG a really nice, thick pair of black gloves. "I already have a pair, but I didn't just want to leave them there. Do you want them?" You would have thought this guy gave FROG the moon the way he is so appreciative of receiving them. What a true gift and blessing this is! Hikers look out for one another, as we found out firsthand.

We arrive at the trailhead about 10:00 a.m. and start our journey NOBO. We keep a good pace, but it doesn't really matter; we are still passed by so many going the same direction we are. I know it's not a race, go your own pace, but we find it somewhat stressful at times to constantly be looking over our shoulders to make sure we get out of the way of those needing to pass. In spite of that, we really do enjoy the hike. The terrain is really good, views are phenomenal, it isn't raining, and we feel lighter—so light that we don't even stop for lunch at Moreland Gap Shelter; we just hustle right on through. Toward the end of our hike, we meet up with a man who is walking SOBO. Since we rarely run into our own kind, we stop to talk with him. He is parked at the parking lot and has walked in to meet his daughter, who has been on the trail for weeks. He can't wait to see her! Aww... I'm sure she was one of the young gals sitting in the shelter that we passed. What a reunion that will be!

About 0.2 miles from the end, we come upon an old rotted-out cabin and stagnant pond. Since our current state is homeless, we kid about the possibility of taking up roots here at this luxurious waterfront property! We've always wanted a tiny cabin to live in. Check out the picture and let us know your thoughts!

Our Future Home?

And there it is! The sign that tells us where Black Bear Resort is that we didn't have on the other side of the road! Yep, catering to the NOBOs they are! SOBOs matter too!

We are feeling great, not tired at all. What a new and wonderful feeling to be experiencing! The last time we walked this direction to Black Bear, we were so tired and trying to keep up with our young speed walking friend. Okay, where is she? We want a rematch! Maybe today we would have a chance to keep up with her or at least not have such a gap between us. Instead of getting that rematch, we hear a truck stop beside us. "Do you two need a ride to Black Bear?" It's a sweet woman who has hiked the trail before and wants to extend a good deed to others, the same as she was given when she hiked. If someone wants to give us a ride, we ain't refusin'! We jump in her truck and enjoy not having to take the half-mile walk by foot; works for us! The whole time, I'm thinking, *Where were you two days ago when we were really tired and needed a ride?* Of course, I'm kidding and would never say anything like that out loud; I am appreciative of what I am given at the moment. It just wasn't supposed to happen two days ago; we needed to be humbled by that twenty-something-year-old, I guess!

Day 18 (Saturday, April 24)—Wet Zero Day

It's raining cats and dogs out there! So thankful for our warm and toasty cabin but not so thankful that it doesn't have indoor plumbing. In the pouring rain, it seems a long walk to the bathroom, and it's so *cold*! We're still fortunate that no one has discovered the laundry room bathroom, because it's free and available for us to use. Of course, there aren't a lot of people out and about anyway; a lot have decided to zero it today too, and they are hunkered down in their cabin or the bunkhouse.

It rained most of the day. It was a smart decision to stay here and not be on the trail during all this. Yeah, we could have walked in it and been completely drenched by the time we arrived at a shelter for the night, but it more than likely would have made us miserable and not so nice to each other had we done it.

A deck of cards is one of our luxury items that we included in our backpack, knowing that there would be times like today that we would need some form of entertainment. So far, it has become our nightly routine to play a game of cards before going to sleep, but today we end up playing a lot of card games of 3-13 and Golf. We also update our journals, read our Bible, organize our pictures, hang out and relax, and talk about our amazing adventures thus far. It is good for us to have a day like today, but we both agree we miss being on the trail and are ready to get out there again.

By late afternoon, the rain has let up to only a drizzle, and we start to see people and activity happening around the resort. Everyone else is feeling as we are, cabin fever! Time to get out and stretch and at least go buy some ice cream. It might be cold outside, but there is always a need for ice cream!

We settle our account with Linda and make plans to get shuttled to USFS 293 again and start hiking SOBO from where we left off. We are on the 8:00 a.m. shuttle along with others who will be going the other direction. We thank her for making our stay with them so enjoyable, and if we're ever in the area again, we'll definitely stop in. What a night-and-day experience between this place and Boots Off. We highly recommend that if you're ever in the area, give them a shout. You won't be disappointed! Well … that is if you're a woman and don't step on that horrible scale, you won't be disappointed. I'm for sure going to need therapy over this, I can tell!

> **ANXIETY/DOUBT/WORRY**
> **It is easy to worry about weather and if you are going to get to a shelter in time. But you must have faith that GOD is going to provide and look after you. FROG**

Day 19 (Sunday, April 25)—Four-Hundred-Mile Marker

> We loved having you for four days at Black Bear Resort. Come back soon! Linda & Travis

It's time to hit the trail once again! We are full of excitement this morning as we gather up our gear and head to the office. Weather is still pretty cold, but at least it is not raining. So many have gathered out front, getting ready to head out, going over last-minute details, and making sure they have everything until they can stop again. We take time to weigh our packs: twenty-six pounds for FROG and twenty-one pounds for mine. Not having had them on our backs for four days, they feel heavy, but compared to what we started out with nineteen days ago, they are not bad at all. We will adjust quickly to the weight once we get moving.

As we're waiting for our shuttle time, a young woman (everyone compared to us seems young!) approaches me about my down vest. She is really liking it a lot and wishes she had one instead of the full down jacket that she has. I appreciate it and thank her for liking it, but when it gets warmer, I won't really need a full coat. (Hindsight would have me trading!)

Travis is ready to shuttle us, but there is a change in plans. There is another hiker who really needs to get to the trailhead at Wilbur Dam Road in the opposite direction that we are going. Would it be okay to drop him off first, and then he will take us to our trailhead at USFS 293? The agreeable couple that we are, we say, "Sure, it's no problem." It really isn't a problem, but I'm sure even if it had been, we would have been agreeable. Neither one of us likes to be disagreeable.

After we drop off the eager hiker, we head back to where we will need to get dropped off. Conversation with Travis is fun and easy flowing; we find out how he met Linda and how they came to buy the Black Bear Resort. FROG mentions that he noticed the fish sticker on the van and also that there was a Bible in the common area. "Are you believers in Jesus Christ?" asks FROG. "Absolutely! We couldn't do what we are doing without Him," replies Travis. Once we reach the trailhead, FROG asks him if it would be okay if we pray for him and Linda. We have the tremendous blessing of praying with him before we head out. What a way to start the day!

We are headed to Mountain Harbour B&B, which is 13.6 miles away, located in Roan Mountain, Tennessee. Remember, this is the place that was highly recommended to us on day 11; we were told we must make plans to stop so that we can partake of their fabulous gourmet breakfast. We have called and made reservations for Monday night for their semiprivate room off the bunkhouse. Our goal for tonight is to get as close as we can so that our day tomorrow will be a short day, a *nero* day.

Today is a big day for us! We will be hitting the four-hundred-mile mark (145 miles for us)! Crossing many footbridges, dirt roads, and seeing many views brings us to the split; if we go 0.01 mile off the trail, we can enjoy our lunch at Mountaineer Falls Shelter. Not that far—let's do it! This shelter is unique in that it has three floors and holds about fourteen people. It really is nice and a great place to stay if we were in need (hah!), but instead, we just enjoy our lunch there. There are already three guys in there when we arrive, and then two more arrive after us. It is interesting to see what others eat for lunch. I am pretty intrigued with the guy next to me as he spreads peanut butter on a tortilla shell (okay so far) and then dots it with pepperoni and cheese (lost me there), rolls it up, and eats it. I know the point is getting a lot of protein, but I just don't think I could mix peanut butter with pepperoni and cheese. Granted I have never tried it, but I guess I'm not desperate enough to try it yet. Tip for the day from those hikers: make sure you stop and see Jones Falls; it is so worth the 0.01 mile off-trail. You won't regret the extra steps.

Not very far from the shelter and right on the trail is Mountaineer Falls, a waterfall on the north side of Big Pine Mountain. Had it been a warmer day, the mist from the falls would have been refreshing, but the day has been cloudy and cool. We just happen to turn back around to take a last-minute look at the falls, which are spectacular, and notice a gnome village set up off to the side. Ahh, an added bonus! There are three tents set up, with a Santa gnome and a mushroom in front. Cute that someone took the time to set that up for us hikers to enjoy. If we hadn't turned around, going SOBO, we might have missed it. All about the NOBOs!

Right before hitting the four hundred mark, we come to the split. If we go left 0.01 mile, we will see Jones Falls; if we go right, we will continue on the AT. We've become accustomed to listening to the advice and tips of other hikers; we haven't been led astray yet in their recommendations.

We drop our backpacks and make the short trek in. What a hidden gem! Jones Falls is absolutely breathtaking! I agree—so worth the extra steps in to see it! Great place to sit and enjoy a snack and the view.

Jones Falls

We know we are in the right vicinity; Guthook says we are here. As it was for the five-hundred-mile marker, we had to look behind us to see it, so probably the four-hundred-mile marker is right around here some place. Keep alert and look around. FROG is the first to spot it. "Look behind you." Right there printed in red with a white background on the tree behind us was a good sized 400. Well, hot diggity dog! There it is! No one is around, but it doesn't matter. I'm sure we still would have danced around and high-fived each other even if there were others there! Wow! We've gone 145 miles!

Four-Hundred-Mile Mark

We are getting to the point that if we could find a good place to set up the tent, we would. Nothing seems to be working yet, so we decide to push through; something will come up. We come to Buck Mountain Road, and there to the left is a Baptist church. We wonder if they would be opposed to our staying on the church grounds for the night. I designate FROG to go and search it out and see if anyone is around to ask. (FROG was designated by me a lot to do the uncomfortable things!) He comes back unsuccessful in his endeavor. He thinks it would be okay to just camp there; I don't want any confrontations if it's not, so we cross the road and continue on the trail.

We have a hard time finding something that will work; no flat spots that aren't by a swamp. Trudging up the hill, we finally get to the top, where there is a huge, open field where we could easily set up camp. There is no tree protection, and it is really windy up here, so we don't take long in setting up our tent and calling it a night. Our view is Isaacs Cemetery just over the way. Hmmm. Well, at least it should be *quiet* here since everyone close by is resting in peace. We fall asleep with a bright full moon illuminating our tent.

Day 20 (Monday, April 26)—Hamburgers And Fries

What in the world is that noise? We both awake in the middle of the night to high-pitched noises outside our tent. Either it's a bird of some kind, or there is a lot of activity going on in that quiet cemetery next door. Not choosing to believe the latter, we wonder what type of bird sounds like it's in such distress. It went on for a long time, so a restful sleep didn't happen for us through the night.

Not only the noise, but we also woke up to a super soggy, soaked tent from the dew that was all around us. Oh boy! FROG is so upset that he hadn't even thought about this possibility and swears to never set up in an open field again. Now he has to carry a drenched tent, which adds so much additional weight to his load. At least it's just a little over three miles to Mountain Harbour B&B, and then we can spread it out to dry.

It is expected to be a warm and sunny day today, so that adds an additional pep to our step this morning as we head out with thoughts of hamburgers, soda, and a gourmet breakfast on our minds!

Passing by the cemetery, we find that there were better tent sites (under cover) if we had just walked a little farther. Oh well, it's just one of those things that you just wouldn't know unless you looked at your Guthook app a little more and read the comments of other hikers. We aren't very tech savvy, so it wasn't on our radar to keep checking the research we had available.

Walking through a meadow, we notice a woman sitting under a tree eating her lunch, so we stop to see how she is doing. We first notice that she is sitting on her bear canister, so we ask her how she likes it. She says she loves hers and is thrilled that it doubles as a chair when she stops. We tell her we had one too, but because it was heavy and couldn't conform in our pack, we decided to send ours back home. Our concern is the Smokies and what is needed there because of the number of bears roaming in the area. We are reassured that although a canister is ideal, they do have bear cables to hang your food up at night. Relief! We kept getting mixed messages on what was needed in that area.

As we continue the conversation, we find out she was a massage therapist before COVID-19 hit, and due to the shutdowns, she had to close her business. She is out on the trail, hoping to find answers to what she is going to do next in her life; 2,190 miles gives you plenty of time to think about that and ask GOD what's next. She mentions she isn't going to give massages anymore, but I'm thinking, *You have a group of hikers all around who would love to have massages and would gladly pay for them (start with me!).* She could have a small business while hiking the trail trying to figure out what to do next, if she wanted. We wish her well and believe GOD will give her the direction she needs.

We walk with a neck wrap or gaiter; FROG has a bright orange one, and I have a blue one. Today it is warm, but instead of putting it in the water to cool our necks (since we are so close to our destination), we take them off and strap them to our packs. We pass a hiker going NOBO and hear her yell back to us, "Did you drop this?" There lying on the ground is FROG's orange neck wrap. We had not seen that it fell. I make this point to say it happened again toward the end of our hike, because we did not come home with it. Maybe that is another thing of FROG's that made it all the way to Maine!

When we come to Bear Branch Road, we know we are close to where we need to go to find our way to Mountain Harbour B&B, but there are no signs indicating which way we are supposed to go. If you go down the road to the right, you can see a main road. If you continue to cross this dirt road, the AT continues. We are very confused! We stand there in bewilderment for a while, hoping maybe someone will pop out of the woods to give us some direction, but no one does. Where is the bubble of hikers when you need them? We finally decide to cross the dirt road and head back into the woods to see where it might lead us. We eventually run into someone on the trail who tells us to keep going; it's a short distance to the main road, and then across the main road is where the AT will continue. Okay, so good, this does eventually come out to the main road that will lead us to Mountain Harbour. (We could have easily saved ourselves quite a few steps if we had gone right and just headed to the main road when we first saw it.)

The hiker is right. It is a short walk to US19E, and there across the road is a parking lot with people. Let's go ask them if they know where this place is. This group is waiting to be picked up to go to the Station at 19E, the other hostel in the opposite direction (the place we were told might not be for us due to the young crowd and partying). They point the direction we need to go and tell us to walk that way; we will surely run into it. A common remark on the trail to others is, "Happy trails," which we bid everyone and move on.

After a quarter mile, we come to a sign to the right that reads "Hikers Trail to Mountain Harbour B&B, Enter at Your Own Risk." Hmmm ... that's a good way to scare people away! We hesitantly take the trail down into the woods (noting exactly where our bear spray is if we need it), round a corner, and pass a small tree house cabin with a creek flowing in front of it (very cute), then continue following the path that eventually opens up to a beautifully landscaped property. Whoa! It took our breath away it was so beautiful!

Up on the hill is the main house, a log cabin home (where breakfast was served and with private rooms available for stays). A porch runs the full length of the house and around the side, with steps down to a bridge. The bridge crosses the creek that is running through the property to a barn (bunkhouse and private rooms, laundry room, bathrooms with showers, common kitchen, camp store). There is a food truck close by (for hamburgers tonight!) and plenty of places to sit outside, with a decorative pond and firepit close by for enjoyment later.

We arrive late morning, and there is no one around that we can see. Hikers have already had their breakfast and are back on the trail by now. We are the first to arrive for the day/night. Taking our time and just wandering around to enjoy all that surrounds us, we eventually see someone up on the porch spraying down the walkways. We decide to head up to see about checking in. Such a friendly guy who lets us know he is part of the staff takes us to the camp store for check-in and to show us around. We love the saying on his shirt: *The Journey Is the Destination.*

He shows us the laundry room first and stresses that it is free.

Hmmm. We can read in between the lines! We stink! Thankfully, they have a loaner clothes box available, so we decide to shower first and put on their clothes, which are anything but stylish and are a mismatch of assorted clothes. (One of the hikers later would be walking around with pajama bottoms on with Cookie Monster all over them as he was waiting for his laundry to finish. We had a good time teasing other hikers on their clothes options!)

Our semiprivate room has a queen-sized bed, a lamp, and a chair. It is tight quarters in there, but it is our home for the night, and it is comfy! There is a bathroom with a shower close by for us to use that will be shared with other hikers tonight. Well, no, we won't share the bathroom *with* them; we will take turns!

The weather is actually on the warm side today, so after hanging our tent over the balcony and putting our boots out to dry, it doesn't take long for them to completely dry out. It seems forever ago that we've had weather nice enough to sit outside and enjoy the heat, so we take full advantage of this, as do the swarms of bees all around us! Maybe now we will be getting the warmth the South is noted for! (Never have such high expectations!)

We finally have great cell service and are able to catch up on emails and messages. We are so thrilled with the amount of people following us and encouraging us along on this journey. Every message has meant the world to us and gives us the drive we need to keep at our goal of finishing in Georgia. We have even gotten quite a few encouraging us to write a book about our adventures. Hah! Not sure about going that far, but we'll see. (Last laugh on us!)

When contacting family to let them know we are doing fine; we find out from my sister that FROG has been summoned for jury duty (she has been collecting our mail for us since we've become homeless). Oh. My. Goodness. Please send me a copy of the notice so we can try to get him dismissed; there is no way we will be finished with our hike and back to New York by the time he is scheduled to appear. He is able to get excused *this time*, but he will be notified again in six months. (They didn't miss a beat; he did receive another summons exactly six months later.)

We aren't sure if the food truck will be providing burgers tonight or not. We found out it's usually based on how many show up to stay (same as the breakfast in the morning). This is one time we are praying for a large group. We're hungry! By the time dinner rolls around, we have enough hikers to stay the night. Yay! The food truck is open! You didn't have to tell us more than once; we were second in line, after Cookie Monster. I can't even tell you without drooling how delicious those gourmet burgers and fries were. They literally knocked our socks off—oh, we didn't have any on, but they sure would have had we had any on!

Following dinner, a whole group of us sat around the firepit, remarking about our adventures and experiences on the trail. What a great way to end a wonderful day! If we had had it planned, taking a zero day tomorrow would have been just fine in my books! But after breakfast tomorrow, it's time to conquer those tough Roan Mountains, so off we go to get a good night's sleep.

Day 21 (Tuesday, April 27)—Gourmet Breakfast

Talk about southern hospitality! The owners, Shannon and David, have put on the most elaborate gourmet breakfast we have ever experienced! Everything is homemade. French toast, fresh baked pastries and muffins, sausage gravy and biscuits, smoked pork sausage, egg souffle, quiche (to name just a few), along with fresh fruit, assorted drinks, coffee, and tea.

As we look around waiting to indulge, there are at least twenty-five to thirty people waiting to eat this scrumptious feast. Okay, well, I don't want to sound selfish, but I start to wonder if I might not get my fill with this many waiting. I scope out the hungry crowd and spot some of the larger partakers and think, *If I can just wiggle my way in front of them, I might have a chance.* What if we act as if we are going to get our juice, and once they call out, "It's ready," we can jump in the front of the line, knocking out those who are in our way? I'm a dreamer. Never happened that way. We were toward the end of the line, but we certainly got our fill; we left satisfied and full. Now we are asking ourselves, "How in the world are we going to make it up the mountain with such a full stomach?"

Sidenote: This is definitely a place we would return to even if we weren't hiking. Highly recommend this bed-and-breakfast to anyone reading this book. It's not just for hikers and offers beautiful rooms inside the house. The thirteen-dollars-per-person rate for the all-you-can-eat breakfast is well worth it!

We slowly take our time to gather up our things, say our last-minute goodbyes and well wishes to our new friends, and then backtrack through the woods to find the main highway, US 19E.

Time for a climb! We start at an elevation of 2,861 feet and are expected to reach our highest today at 5,559 feet, with elevation dips and heights going even higher in the next few days before we completely leave the Roans—which my brother so appropriately renamed for us, the Groans! Perfect name, David! They were so difficult, with a lot of groaning going on between us!

It is just over three miles to reach our next state, North Carolina. That doesn't sound so bad and certainly shouldn't take very long to accomplish. Hah! Maybe if we hadn't had our backpacks, full stomachs, and there wasn't any elevation, it would have been a breeze ... not today. We kept climbing and climbing and climbing until we finally broke out into a large, open area that had space for quite a few tent sites, called Doll Flats. It took us all morning to just get to this point, but since it's way too early to camp, we take a long recovery break before crossing into North Carolina.

> **The road I've travelled hasn't been easy, but I'm still here. The only reason I'm here today is because GOD was walking the road with me, every step of the way. Amen.**

Our Support Team:

Wow! Looking forward to lots of stories in Texas but we love your updates! Hike on!! Denise L.

HOBOS GOING SOBO IN THEIR OBOZ and we never looked back ...

Awesome photos! Safe travels! Chrissi W.

Love your blogs! Glad you are having a good time. Beautiful pictures. The scenery is amazing! Stay safe, love you Tracy M.

Love seeing the pictures and hearing about your travels. Feels like we're walking along with you without the backpacks and putting in all the hard work. Bev G.

Lori, thanks for the laughs. Keep posting. We love hearing all about your adventures! Bonnie B.

Thank you for sharing your journey. Can't wait to hear all about it next winter. Elaine F.

Great pictures as always but I really enjoy hearing your "lessons" as well. Diana T.

You guys are amazing! Keep up the good work. Nancy K.

What beauty! The trail magic is awesome! Cathy L.

Love reading your blog. You make me laugh! Continue having strength to keep on going! Pictures are wonderful! Shelby S.

Amazing photos! What a journey. You are both inspirational. Penny C.

I love reading this trail log, and "slack packing" might be my new fave phrase ... Didn't know it had a name! Thanks for sharing!! How awesome, keep on trekkin'! Ariel S.

> It's time to do it. Whatever it is, find it and do it.
> **—Unknown**

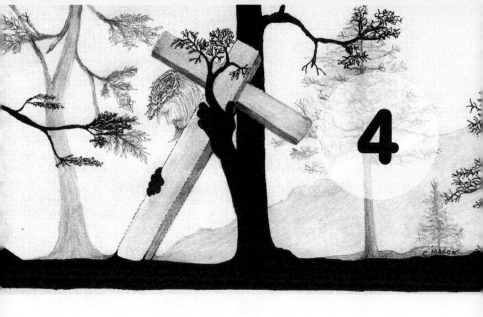

A Match Made in Heaven

> He will cover you with his feathers, and under his wings you will find refuge; his faithfulness will be your shield and rampart.
> —Psalm 91:4

The year was 1981, and we were both working at National Cash Register (NCR) in Ithaca, New York. Brad was a mechanical designer, and I was a department secretary, both working in different departments. We had mutual friends who wanted to play matchmaker and set the two of us up. I was having nothing to do with that; I just wasn't interested in him at all. He seemed like a nice guy, but he just didn't seem to be my type, and besides, he was old! I heard later from him that he wasn't at all interested in me either, so at least the feeling was mutual. Both of us were going through a divorce and raising our own child by ourselves; I guess we just weren't ready for each other yet.

Brad had plans of his own that didn't involve any woman, and that was taking a cross-country trip with a buddy, Rick, (with his daughter in the back seat) and backpacking in the Grand Tetons for a couple weeks (now you know why the AT was a dream of his) after he dropped his daughter off at her mother's in Colorado. He quit his job at NCR so that he would have the freedom and flexibility to take this trip. I know many probably thought he was irresponsible to give up the security of a good job and pension, but he didn't care. The mountains were calling him, and he needed to go!

My friend who tried to fix me up with Brad was determined she was going to find someone for me. She eventually did. He was more my age, not entirely my type, but was really a nice guy. We did date for well over a year, but I ended up hurting him and ending it. I just had so much baggage; I wasn't ready for such a commitment yet.

Jump ahead to 1983. I was still working at NCR, and Brad was now working for an engineering and industrial design firm in downtown Ithaca, New York, that had a contract with NCR, so he was back at the plant, working in the same department as he was when he quit. I started to see him again on a daily basis, and something changed where I started to view him differently than I did two years ago. He was looking not so old and just maybe more my type. Maybe his rendezvous out west made him younger looking and more my type. Who knows.

I didn't tell anyone I was now interested in him, which makes this part of the story pretty amazing—what we now call a match made in heaven. It was a Friday morning. I was thinking it would be nice if he asked me out. Remember, I told no one my newfound interest in him. That same night, he called. "Hi, this is Brad Lewis—you know, from N-C-R?" he said, slowly pausing after each letter in NCR as if I might not be familiar with it or him.

"Yes, I know you," I said.

"I was wondering if you wanted to go to the movies with me tomorrow night."

"Well, I guess so, since no one else has asked." No, of course I didn't say that, but I do wonder now how he would have reacted if I had. I agreed. A time was set, and conversation ended, as we were both too shy and awkward to figure out what else to say. Should be an interesting evening.

I remember being so dumbstruck at the fact that he called me when I had just had that thought earlier in the day. It was like someone heard, but I knew I hadn't told anyone.

Our Date

We are headed to the movies at the Ithaca State Theater to see *Max Dugan Returns*, starring Marsha Mason. I have of course doodled myself up and have thrown on dress pants and a dress shirt and added some heels to look extra special and taller. Brad has on a plaid shirt and blue jeans and has even combed his hair for the big occasion. When we arrive in Ithaca, he finds a parking space that is miles from the theater (okay, that is an exaggeration, but when you're in heels, it seems like it!). It was probably a good half mile away though. I remember kidding him that I probably shouldn't have worn my heels. (Never did again and not now either. He hasn't changed; he still parks miles away [like 545 miles] and makes me walk.)

We get to the theater and are waiting in line to pay. When our turn approaches, Brad awkwardly pulls out a roll of quarters and tries to hide the fact that he is paying with quarters for our tickets. He turns to me and says, "You're not supposed to be seeing this."

Okay ... I turn around and look the other way and act as though I have no idea what he is doing. "Did you rob your daughter's piggy bank?" I might as well have fun with it since I did see it. It's funny now, but I could tell he was quite embarrassed about it then.

After the movie, he asks if I want to go for drinks at a bar on the Commons. Sure, why not. I wonder if I'm supposed to watch him pay or look away again. He spares me a second time of awkwardness and finds us a table before he heads to the bar to get us drinks. Before he leaves to do so, I guess he wasn't completely satisfied with how it looked under the table, because he gets down on all fours and starts clearing away debris. What in the world? Thank goodness I didn't decide to wear a dress! I would have thought him a pervert! In his defense, after I realized what he was doing, there was a broken glass under the table, and he was being a gentleman to make sure I didn't cut myself on broken glass. *Okay, so he's not so strange after all.*

We both have quiet personalities, so conversation was awkward at times, but we always had our past marriages and our kids to fall back on during those times.

Upon returning me to my apartment, as we are saying goodbye, I feel this breeze by my face and have no idea what just happened. I found out much later in our relationship that Brad tried to kiss me and missed my face!

Well, that night did not meet any of my expectations! I told my sister I would not be going out with him again. At least he showed his true colors that night. He would make me walk, he is cheap, he doesn't like mess on the floor, he's not a conversationalist, and he doesn't always hit his mark. Other than that, he's a great guy but probably not for me.

Well, I wouldn't have gone out with him again, but he doesn't play fair. The next day, he comes to my apartment with his daughter in tow! She is five years old, adorable, very shy, and didn't say a peep the whole time as she sat there staring at me and my son. I think Brad knew he could use her to win me over. It worked.

His first impression of my son was quite different, I'm sure. I had an active three-year-old who spent the whole time showing off and swinging from door handles. Oh well, he might as well see what life is like with me and my active son. You get the whole package. It didn't deter him. He came back.

It was really hard trying to make it work with two kids who were fighting for our attention and would fight with each other. It seemed a battle that was just too hard to fight to come out on the winning side. I wasn't ready for all that this relationship involved, so I told Brad it was over.

I was pretty strong-willed and determined on my end, but somehow a force stronger than me drew us back together once again. Ironically enough, it was I who proposed to Brad and bought my own ring. (Okay, well, he did pay for some of it, in quarters!)

Sidenote: I must add he did redeem himself. For our twenty-fifth wedding anniversary, he bought me a new diamond and paid for it himself (with discount coupons!).

On November 11, 1984 (same day as my birthday—I do *not* advise anyone to do that; you get ripped off on presents [I know, I was forewarned that he was a cheapskate]; he forgets it's my birthday and thinks it's just his anniversary), we moved everything out of our living room, put in tables and chairs, and had our wedding and reception right at our house, with family and friends by our side.

It wasn't always easy, but it wasn't always hard. A blended family comes with challenges but so many blessings as well, and with GOD's help, we made it work. We're still happily married, the kids turned out to be responsible adults who are still talking to us, and they have both blessed us with amazing grandchildren. I call that success! It turned out to be a true match made in heaven.

Roan Mountain, North Carolina, to Erwin, Tennessee

You will not fear the terror of night, nor the arrow that flies by day.
—Psalm 91:5

Looks like from our side SOBO, North Carolina really isn't too excited that we've arrived (no signs welcoming us to their state). On the other side, if walking NOBO, they are sure glad you're leaving (when we turn to look behind us, there is a sign "Leaving North Carolina"). Hmmm ... I'm sure it's not true, but North Carolina sure doesn't seem too friendly.

Anyway, we're here! Our third state! Happy, happy, happy dance! (We will soon find out that the AT runs along the border, in and out of North Carolina and Tennessee, so we have no idea if we're coming or going—meaning which state we are in. FROG would say we were in the state of confusion until we hit Georgia.)

After a water stop to fill our water bottles with fresh, filtered water, we look ahead to see where the trail will lead. It is a wide-open meadow, so the top of Hump Mountain at 5,559 feet, our highest point today, is visible. Egad! It's two miles away; it seems so far away and so high up! If it took us all morning to climb 1,705 feet, we wonder how long it will take for us to climb another thousand feet elevation. An advantage we have with this climb is, because it is open, there will be views in every direction. That's a huge plus in our books!

We can do this! Let the groaning commence.

Mountains aren't funny; they're hill areas 😂

It is an arduous climb with a lot of stopping (and groaning!), but taking these stops rewards us with great views of the countryside and homes that are definitely out of our price range. Too much house for me. I guess I'll just stick with what we own right now, and being homeless, that is just our tent. It might smell slightly inside, but other than that, a nice tent it is.

I have to say, we are both shocked when we reach the top. We think we are hitting a false summit and that we still have more to climb. There is another hiker here when we arrive, and we both say, "Oh, this is it. This is the top." He looks at us like we have three heads instead of two and nods his head in agreement. We want to stay, eat our lunch, and enjoy the view, but it isn't meant to be. It is a warmer day (even on top of the mountain), but the biting flies and gnats are everywhere and have plans to eat their lunch too, so we have to move on. They need to get their lunch elsewhere, and we'll eat ours elsewhere as well.

Today is so different from past days of hiking. Since we've hit this part of North Carolina, it's been all open—no trees, just meadows and fields. Normally, you are hidden in the woods, not knowing what could be coming up; today you can see the trail for miles and can see what's coming up. Not sure which way we prefer; good and bad points for both.

Coming down Hump Mountain, one mile down is Bradley Gap. Of course, we have to stop and make a big deal about FROG's namesake and get a picture. (Do you think we got one with him next to it? Of course not. Just a picture of the sign! We are so not photographers!)

HOBOS GOING SOBO IN THEIR OBOZ and we never looked back ...

As we are standing here, a young couple stops by to talk with us. It is small talk at first, but the young lady can hardly contain herself and blurts out, "We just got engaged! Right up there on Little Hump Mountain!" She turns and points where she has just been. The young man is slightly taken aback that she just blurted that out but of course is full of smiles. We are so excited for them and offer our congratulations. FROG mentions that we have been married for thirty-six years and it was the best decision he's ever made. Well, if he didn't say that, he should have! My advice ... happy wife, happy life! No, of course, I did *not* say that (but I might have been thinking it!).

Hiking up to Little Hump is hard, y'all! The path is so rocky and wet in places, and with climbing back up in elevation, it makes the walk so slow and tedious. It took all we had and a lot of team effort to help encourage each other. We can do this, and we did; it just took longer than we had hoped! As we're standing on Little Hump, we can't but help visualize the young couple we just met—him on his knee proposing and her jumping up and down with joy. Not sure how it went down for sure, but I'll bet it was pretty close to something like that.

Our plans are to walk another 1.6 miles to Overmountain Shelter. It is an old barn that got condemned in 2019 due to structural weakness that could eventually lead to collapse. Tenting is allowed as long as you stay forty feet from the structure. And guess what? I hear there is a privy there! That, my friends, is good news when you've had to use the woods while traveling through Tennessee. That's a good motivator to walk those last miles. If we can do it, will be a 9.7-mile day of very hard hiking!

We see Overmountain Shelter from a distance and know we are close. Those last steps when you're so tired and worn out seem like forever until you arrive, but eventually, we come to the intersection where the shelter is still 0.2 mile off-trail. There are tent sites right here, so we wouldn't need to go that far to the shelter if we didn't want to. What should we do?

Another couple (who at the time we thought was a couple) arrives at the intersection, trying to decide what they are going to do as well. Since we need water for the night, we decide to head toward the shelter since it is on the way there anyway (oh, and there is that whole privy issue that helps me decide). As we're getting our water, the young lady arrives (minus the young guy) who we just met up above to also get water. She is so relieved that he hasn't followed her. She just met him a few days ago, and he has been so clingy; she's been trying to lose him for some time now. She goes on to say she just got a divorce and set out to hike alone and didn't want his company. She just needs time alone to think about things without distractions. Makes perfect sense to us.

We're not totally sure which direction to go to find the shelter, since there are side trails going in two different directions. We decide to take the trail off to the right, which happens to be a winner! Yay, us! There are already tents set up by the time we get there but still plenty of room for us. The site we choose has a picnic table with it! FROG is thrilled! As stated before, he has such a hard time when all we have is a log to sit on. What a great surprise after a day like today!

My surprise is the privy! Y'all, guess what? This one is noteworthy! A pit privy with a view! Wait till you see the picture. I feel like a queen sitting upon her throne, looking out over my kingdom. What a view of my kingdom it is! (Hands down best privy with a view on the trail!)

The Queen's Throne

Day 22 (Wednesday, April 28)—Autopay

What! In! The! World! It is that same noise we heard on day 20! We peek out our tent to see if we can see anything, but all we see is a field full of tents and no one out and about. It's definitely some kind of bird in distress.

As daylight dawns, we start to hear stirrings around us as hikers are getting ready to start their day. We drag ourselves out of our tent and wonder if we are the only ones who feel sluggish due to lack of sleep from all the ruckus going on around us during the night. Needless to say, it is a slow morning of getting things packed up. We are one of the last few to finally hit the trail.

On our way out, we make another stop at the spring to refill our water bottles and meet up with a hiker who had also camped at the area near the shelter last night. She asks, "Did you hear the owls last night?"

"Is that what was making all that noise?" FROG asks.

"Yes, it is mating season for the owl right now," she responds. Oh my goodness! That is what we've been hearing nights and why there was so much hooting and screeching that lasted for hours last night! They really need to have their fun, get their business done, and let us sleep! This is leaving us exhausted!

Once we get back on the trail and within cell range, we get a message from Verizon that we will have our phones shut off today if we don't make our payment. What? I thought it was set up for autopay.

Oh, welcome back to the reality of civilization! We decided before we left for the AT to get Verizon because we heard it got the best reception out on the trail. Up to this point, we would agree, it has been pretty reliable. We thought before we left the store, we were set up for autopay; I guess that is not the case.

What a challenge we encounter as we try to find just the right spot, on top of the mountain, to make a call to Verizon to get this straightened out so that our only link to the outside world will not be shut off. "This will cost you a seven-dollar-and-fifty-cents administrative fee for me to set you up for autopay over the phone," the representative says.

We are thinking, *Lady, we are on top of a mountain in the middle of nowhere, praying we don't lose reception at any moment. Just set us up!* We *sweetly* respond, "No problem. We are willing to pay. Please go ahead and set us up for autopay." I guess it is a good idea to make sure *before* you leave for an extended trip that you are set up for autopay, especially if it is your cell phone carrier!

Today we are headed to our highest point in the Roan Mountains, the Roan Mountain Shelter at 6,270 feet in elevation (and the highest shelter on the AT), which is 7.1 miles away.

Our first stop is at the Stan Murray Shelter, where we meet up with a young man and his best friend, his furry dog friend. He has just found a damaged tent out in the woods that someone discarded, and he is pretty sure he can fix it, so here he is strapping it to his backpack. It was pretty rude for someone to just leave it, for sure, but man, that's extra weight you will be carrying. Well, he's young; he can probably do it without any problems.

Three other men show up and ask if we've seen their long-haired friend go through here yet. We haven't passed anyone with that description, so now they are wondering if he took a wrong path somewhere. He headed out before they did this morning to get a head start since he's slower than the rest of them. Their cell phones aren't working (uh-oh, wonder if they forgot to sign up for autopay too), and they can't seem to locate him. They decide to hang out at the shelter and wait it out to see if he shows. Not sure how long they waited or if he ever showed up, but we still didn't see anyone who fit that description pass us as we headed in the direction he would be coming.

We arrive at the base of Grassy Ridge Bald, where there is a confusing intersection if you're not paying attention and miss the sign. The AT continues to the right for SOBOs. If you take the left, it is a 0.6-mile side trip up to the summit of the bald, where you can see some tremendous views (we're told), the highest bald in the Roans. We opt to not go up there. I mean, 0.6-mile one way is 1.2 miles more than we want to take, with 3.4 miles yet to go to the next shelter, and we hear they are difficult miles yet ahead. No way! We will just sit ourselves down right here on this rock, enjoy the view looking up at the summit of Grassy Ridge, and eat our lunch before heading to the next bald, Jane Bald.

As we're eating, we see a confused young hiker who's just come down from Grassy Ridge Bald. She comes to the intersection and looks at the sign. I'm thinking she didn't see the sign; as a NOBO, she needed to turn left, but instead, she went straight. She walks over to us, sits down, and confirms my suspicions; she never saw the sign. At the top of the bald, she had met up with a group of older ladies (her words, not mine) who were in a walking group that told her she had taken a wrong turn down below. Back down she went. Now she just needs to take a break before going in the correct direction.

We have an enjoyable conversation with "Clean Plate" and find out she used to work at Walmart and decided she needed to take time off to thru-hike the AT. Her main goals were to lose weight and to figure out what is next in life. She thinks she has already lost at least ten pounds and has walked 382 miles so far. I'm happy someone is losing it if I'm not! (So many we met seemed to have the same goal: find out what's next for them, looking for answers and direction.)

As we're sitting there offering Clean Plate some beef jerky, the "older" ladies have made their way down the mountain. Hmmm … older ladies. Guess I fit in that category as well. They are glad to see that our new friend has found her way back to where she needs to go. They look like a fun group of ladies (I refuse to call them old; call it denial if you must) who have committed to walking different trails together every week.

After about a half hour sitting with us, Clean Plate is ready to head out and says she needs to get going; she's trying to stay ahead of the group that calls themselves the "Dirty Bubble" because she doesn't want to be associated with them. We have enjoyed our time with her and wish GOD's very best for her. We know she'll go far on this journey. She's already gone this far; she will finish. I pray she found the answers and direction she was looking for and has a life full of blessings and adventure.

Time for us to get moving as well. At least for us, the journey is downhill to Jane Bald and Round Bald, where it is an open summit with views of several open balds within the Roan Highlands. The views all around us are spectacular as we try to take it all in.

The Roan Mountains are broken down into two sections by Carver's Gap: the Roan Highlands to the north side, and the south side is called Roan High Knob & Roan High Bluff. (The Roans are most famous for being the largest naturally growing gardens of Catawba Rhododendrons in the world.) Carver's Gap Tennessee / North Carolina has become one of the AT's most popular spots. After hiking through and seeing the beauty of this area, we can understand why.

When reaching Carver's Gap parking lot, we decide to take a few minutes to sit and relax before tackling the second half of the Roan Mountains, the south side. As we unload and plop down next to another couple of hikers, we witness a Vietnam vet offering them the last two sandwiches he has in his car. We learn that he has hiked this trail, so he knows how hungry one can get and is giving them the last of what he has left to offer. We are fine that we missed out, but he is determined he is going to find something in his car for us too. He comes back with an ice-cold Gatorade and offers it to us. (That, my friends, was the best-tasting Gatorade I have ever tasted! His sacrifice in giving us the drink he was saving for himself after his hike meant the world to us.) "Thank you" doesn't seem like strong enough words for how we feel at the moment. He still wants to help us in any way he can, so he offers to take our garbage off our hands if we have any. (What you carry in, you carry out, so we definitely had some.) Getting rid of extra weight at any time is definitely a plus, so we happily hand over our garbage. This is the type of kindness and the people we have run into. It restores your faith in people, for sure!

With a smile on our faces and our bodies refreshed with something other than water, we prepare to climb to the highest point in the Roans, the Roan High Knob Shelter. The 1.5-mile hike

HOBOS GOING SOBO IN THEIR OBOZ and we never looked back ...

through the woods involves a lot of switchbacks, which helped with the increase in elevation but made the walk seem that much longer by going back and forth, changing directions. It is just plain hard! We never felt as though we wanted to quit, but we did question our sanity in doing this quite a few times. With my previous smile gone by now, I may or may not have said, "We find this *fun*?" and "Why are we doing this again?"

> I don't get it. The trail looked so flat on the map.
> —**Boots MacFarland**

After hours of trudging along, this way and that, we *finally* arrive at the intersection. If we turn left and take a steep climb *up* and go 0.1 mile, we will come to the shelter. Going straight ahead and bypassing the shelter, we will start to decline and head out of the Roan Mountains. Although the latter is *very* tempting, our plans all along were to go to the shelter and at least check out the view from the highest point.

Giving each other a butt smack and saying we can do this, we head straight up. With more groaning and encouragement to each other, we eventually see the shelter and head toward it. There are already hikers here for the night, four of them. They are a young, excitable group and are expecting many more hikers to show up tonight. We wonder if maybe this is the Dirty Bubble that Clean Plate mentioned earlier that she wanted to stay clear of. We don't know, and we don't ask. We're really not sure exactly why they choose to go by that name. Do they smell? Because if that is the case, we would all qualify to be in their bubble. Or is it because they don't necessarily play nice and are a rowdy group? If that's the case, I wouldn't want to be associated with them either. (We find out later at Nature's Inn Hostel & Cabins that it was the latter.) I am not sure this is the group, but we decide not to stay and find out.

Well, we're up here. Now where is the view? PUD! Nothing! We might be at the highest point, but view-wise, it's a disappointment! It's an area full of trees with a shelter among them. Okay, well, the shelter is different from all the rest: this one has two floors, fully enclosed with four walls, a door that closes, and it can hold up to fifteen people (which is a good thing since a lot will be staying tonight).

We stay and rest for about a half hour, deciding what we are going to do and how much farther we will plan to walk today. We are already tired, but we really don't want to stay at the shelter, and our hike would be downhill, so maybe we can squeeze in another 1.9 miles and make it a nine-mile day and stay at Ash Gap.

With a new plan, we say our goodbyes and well wishes and start working our way back down to the main trail. It is a gingerly walk down as we maneuver cautiously, trying not to twist an ankle. (That is one of the biggest problems out here with hikers we've run into—so many twisted and hurt ankles due to rocky and unstable conditions. We don't want to be included in the statistics, so we are very slow and cautious.)

We seem to have gotten enough rest at the shelter because our energy level has increased, and we're pumped and motivated to conquer these last miles for the day. The terrain is still rocky and unstable, but we are at least descending instead of steep ascents. This side has plenty of switchbacks as well. We pass many NOBOs (planning to stay at the shelter) and feel sorry for them, as they are now the ones to be trudging uphill. As we watch them though, it seems effortless for them. I'd like to think it's all a show as they pass us, and then once they get out of view, they are struggling just as much as we have been. That's my story, and I'm sticking with it!

Ash Gap is a nice flat area with enough space for about six tents and a water source 0.1 mile off on a side trail. Unfortunately, we need water for tonight. That means we need to walk downhill to the water source, and it will be a steep uphill on the return. Crud! After setting up camp, I volunteer to make the journey as FROG starts cooking dinner. No major mishaps for me this time. I must be getting more stable in my Crocs; no tumbles in the stream to report. Thank goodness! But the walk to and back is eerie. It is so quiet and far away from FROG. My mind starts to wander, fear sets in, and I start to imagine all sorts of noises and wonder if I'm not alone, if a wild animal might be close by. I don't lollygag or dillydally. I fill both water bags and try as hard as I can, with both hands carrying water, to boogie back up that hill as fast as I can. By the time I reach the top where FROG is, I am completely spent! As far as I know, there was nothing out there other than me and *fear*!

> Take risks and conquer your fear.
> —**Unknown**

Dinner tonight is a dehydrated Mountain House meal: spaghetti and meat sauce. And to finish it off, we are rewarding ourselves with two Snickers bars instead of just one! It's been a rough two days, time for some bennies in finishing strong! Ha-ha, okay, for at least finishing.

Oh no! Our spork! Looking through our food bag, we remember that our spork (a spoon/fork combination utensil) had been placed inside our garbage bag so that we could clean it off later. We had inadvertently given it to Vietnam Vet to throw out back at Carver's Gap. What a big loss! Thankfully we still have a spoon we can use, or it would have been "How clever can we be in making a utensil out of a stick?" Note to ourselves: keep our remaining spoon away from the garbage bag!

Day 23 (Thursday, April 29)—What a Side Trip

The Roan (Groan) Mountains kicked our butts and really tested our stamina and endurance. So much up (hard to breathe) and down (hard on knees). Weather went from being really warm to windy, rainy, and so cold! We were challenged from all sides, but we can now say *we did it*! The Grayson Highlands and the Roan Mountains are in the rearview mirror, with only the Smoky Mountains ahead for us.

Passing a local couple today, they give us a tidbit of information on some plants that are growing in the area. (One thing we have noticed: so many people have something worthwhile to share if you just take the time. So often, we as a society have a tendency to be too busy to take the time to listen.) We have been calling one plant a wild onion, when in fact they are really called ramps. They are more of a garlic than they are an onion and will stay on your breath for a week. They are so popular around here that they have ramp festivals annually. We already smell, so to not add to our smell, we don't pick any to use in our food, although we have met several hikers who say they pick and use. The couple also tells us about a unique flower, Gray's Lily, a red flower only native to their area that is not in bloom yet. We were able to see pictures of it but unfortunately never got to see it in bloom, another of GOD's beauties we would have loved to add to our flower photo collection.

Speaking of our flower collection, please refer to our website, HOBOSOBOBOZ.com, for pictures of the simplicity yet magnificence of GOD's beautiful wildflowers that He put in our path on the AT to enjoy at such a time as this. I hope you enjoy their simple beauty as much as we have. I've always enjoyed the beauty of flowers but never took the time to *really* look and enjoy the detail and simple beauty each brings. Walking every day forces you to watch your footing as you take each step, and while doing that, you can't help but notice the beautiful wildflowers that surround you. I know I've mentioned this before, but we just can't get over all the wild rhododendrons growing everywhere! (From where we started in southern Virginia through the northern part of Georgia, endless!) Our only regret was that we never got to see the rhododendrons in full bloom. That would have been amazing! (We were able to see the Mountain Laurel in full bloom, a close relative to the rhododendron family, and they were beautiful!)

Today's goal is picking up our resupply package we had shipped to Greasy Creek Friendly, which is still 8.6 miles away. Because of the distance off-trail, we had hoped to be able to stay there the night and then head back out tomorrow from there. Unfortunately, they are only receiving mail packages and are not opening their hostel up yet for the season due to COVID restrictions. It is 1.2 miles (round-trip) off-trail. That is a lot for just picking up a package (which will also make our packs heavier due to the increase in food). We are not looking forward to walking that far off-trail, but it is what it is.

This part of the trail continues to be full and busy with NOBOs. We decide not to stop at Clyde Smith Shelter once we get to the intersection but meet up with a group that has just come from there. One of them has gotten too much water—would we like some? Well, yes, we will never refuse water we don't have to get or filter ourselves.

A mile up, we come to a fork in the trail (no, it wasn't our missing fork). Off to the left is a side trail that will connect to Greasy Creek Gap Road, which will take us to Greasy Creek Friendly for our package (we think but are not positive). Off to the right will take us to a spring for water, and straight ahead, the AT continues. We aren't in need of water, thanks to our Clyde Smith friends, so we proceed to take the left trail for the 0.6-mile journey for our food pickup.

I think our attitude already stinks at the thought of going out of our way to pick up our resupply package, but, fair warning, it's about to get worse.

Sidenote from FROG: This was probably our worst event arguing and disagreeing and not being very nice to each other. It was 0.6 of a mile off the trail and until we got there, we weren't even sure we were going in the right direction. All of this added up to a very stressful time.

In the beginning, I told FROG that he could be in charge of figuring out where our resupply packages should be sent to. (He did an excellent job at the other seven. This one, not so much! He would totally agree with this statement. The unfortunate thing for him is I didn't know at this time that the other five would go as well as they did since this was only mail drop number three.)

We are warm, tired, and low on energy at this point—three strikes against us. Should have known once you have three strikes against you, get out of the batter's box. Your turn is over. We should have turned back around and just said forget it. Nope, we keep going.

The side trail is windy, and we don't see any connecting road ahead; we're just not sure if we're headed in the right direction or not. We stop several times and argue with each other about where we are supposed to go, like either one of us would really know. We are getting ready to turn around and head back when we see another couple in their motorcycle duds headed our way. Oh good. Maybe they know where we are supposed to go. Nope. They aren't from around here, just out riding their motorcycles and decided to stop and see where this trail went. They did let us know the connecting road is not far away and that they passed houses on their way up, so maybe one of those houses is where we need to go.

When we get to the road, we can go either right or left. Well, the couple said, "as they were coming up the road," so we must go left, which is an advantage for us, as it would be going downhill. Trying not to focus on what that means for the return trip, we proceed downhill, where at first it is very rocky, wet, difficult, and slow-moving.

We pass their motorcycles, so we at least know we are headed in the direction they came from. Hopefully that is a plus. There are no houses or any sign of civilization, which continues to frustrate and confuse us as to whether this is right or not.

In the heat of the moment, due to pure frustration, it turns ugly and we both say things to each other that aren't nice. I lift my hand in a stop position and loudly exclaim, "You are not my best friend right now, it's best if we just quit talking to each other!" I know I have the advantage of walking faster, so I quicken my step to get ahead. This woman can only stand the silence so long before she turns around and blurts out, "You're never again in charge of mail drops!" as she turns back around, stomps away and basks in getting the last word!

After half a mile, we see our first house on the left. With no indication that this is it, we keep going. We pass a few more houses. No signs. If someone was outside, we could ask, but no one is around. We hear a lawn mower going just a bit farther down the road; maybe we can ask them if they know where we need to go.

Our journey thus far has us walking next to Greasy Creek, a really nice, flowing creek that, if need be, FROG mentions we could just camp alongside tonight instead of trying to trudge back up the hill since we are so whipped. I'm still upset with him, so I don't respond to him, but it does seem to give me some bit of hope that not all has been lost by making the decision to go this far out of our way.

We have caught up to mower man, and I, of course, curtly send FROG to ask if we are close to where we need to go. Ding! Ding! Ding! It's a winner! We have arrived at Greasy Creek Friendly!

Meeting CeeCee and Gadget (owners of Greasy Creek Friendly) helps to snap us out of our funk. They are really great people and live up to their namesake, Friendly. They have our package (oh boy, if they hadn't, I'm not sure what nasty thing would have come out of my mouth directed toward FROG), so we go through it and figure out what we need (what we didn't need, we offered to CeeCee and Gadget) and give them money to send a package to the next hostel, Nature's Inn Hostel & Cabins.

With sodas in hand, we spend an hour sitting at the picnic table out front in the warm afternoon sun. It is a much-needed time of respite after a miserable time of getting here. We take time to reflect on our 0.6-mile journey here and wonder why we took it kicking and screaming instead of wondering if GOD had a purpose for us coming here. Why can't we just go with the flow and see what GOD might have in store even if we think it's inconvenient? There might just be a divine reason for that inconvenience.

> **Have a super butterfly day! Which means no rain, butterflies can't fly in the rain and hikers shouldn't have to hike in the rain. CeeCee**

> **Always remember to enjoy the hike and enjoy the beauty, take time to view the beauty. Gadget**

Our return 0.6-mile uphill goes so much better for us after that time of reflection and apologies. Even though we are going uphill, it just seems to fly by with ease. We do take a wrong turn but quickly realize it and get back on track. A second wind must have been blowing through because somehow we have so much energy and are ready to tackle more miles once we reconnect to the AT.

We think we might be able to do another four miles, so our new goal for the day is Iron Mountain. We'll see if we can get that far and then look for a place to set up the tent. If we can make it that far, it will be a 10.5-mile day.

When we reach the top of Iron Mountain, it is so windy that we decide to try to find a place to hunker down for the night in a lower elevation, in an area that might not be so windy. We still have some energy left, but leaving this flat area might have been a mistake. As we head down into lower elevation, we are struggling to find a flat spot where we can set up the tent. Past experience tells us putting up on a slight slant works, but we aren't finding anything acceptable. We are both intently looking this way and that for a spot—nothing. Not wanting to backtrack, we keep saying, "Let's just go a little bit farther. There's got to be something around here." I take a few side trips here and there, looking at what we think are potentials, only to be disappointed that it won't work. After half a mile, we look up off to our right at another potential spot. I decide to run (okay, more like a slow jog) up the hill and see if it flattens out enough to put up our tent. Success! And there is a ready-made fire ring, so I know it's an area used for camping. Excitement at finally finding a place would soon change once GOD turned out the lights. We had no idea the night we were soon going to have!

Day 24 (Friday, April 30)—What a Night!

Let me try to explain just what happened.

Before climbing into the tent for the night, we made sure the footprint was neatly tucked under the tent; FROG has been so good about making sure the tent is securely staked down, so not to have any more fly ups like we had on day 3. We had no idea or advance warning as to what was expected to happen last night.

HOBOS GOING SOBO IN THEIR OBOZ and we never looked back ...

It started about nine o'clock last night and lasted until three o'clock this morning—a torrential wind and rainstorm with thunder and lightning, six hours straight! It was *in-tents*!

At first, it was just pouring rain. Then the thunder and lightning rolled in, and if that wasn't scary enough, the wind picked up and started blowing the tent sideways. FROG had all he could do to hold the inside tent poles in place so that it didn't blow over. The tent stakes must have blown out, and now the footprint we put down was exposed to the rain, so water was dumping down on it and running under the tent, which was causing water to start seeping inside the tent. I was being splashed with water on the sides where the vent holes were, so we huddled closer together in the middle, trying to make sure we stayed on our air mattress so as not to get wet from underneath. It was a long six hours as FROG held the tent poles and I held FROG. GOD heard from us a lot that night as we kept praying for His safety and protection from the storm around us.

Of course, we have experienced storms like this before but have always had the protection of a secure building; it is so different when you're in a tent and feel no security whatsoever. It was a scary night with very little sleep. Once the storm ended around three o'clock, we were able to get a little bit of shut-eye before getting up at six thirty.

(Between all the owl noises at night and now the storms, we are getting cranky from lack of sleep. This needs to stop. We need our sleep!)

We wake to sunshine hitting the top of the tent, and as we are looking up, just above our heads, we see there is a large pool of water that has gathered in a section on top of the tent—directly above our faces! We can't even imagine how awful that would have been to have had that give way during the night. (A *huge* kudos to Big Agnes, who made such a hearty, durable tent! It was expensive but worth every penny in our books!)

Now ... to get up and head out to assess the damage outside. FROG heads out first and makes such an exasperated noise I am not sure I want to even go out.

Our tent has two vestibules (a sheltered area that extends from the front and back of the tent at the doors) that we use as a gear shed basically. Every night, we put our shoes and FROG's backpack under the one vestibule we aren't using for our front door.

I hear him walking about, pretty upset with the surroundings, and as I look out, I see just why. Nothing is as we left it before we went to bed. Things are thrown all over the place, and everything is soaked! The gear we had tucked away under the vestibule is completely soaked and muddy from the stake coming out and exposing it to the rain, which means our shoes and socks are really wet. FROG's backpack is wet, and of course the tent and footprint are soaked and muddy. They will have to get rolled up that way, which means additional water weight for FROG as he carries it all in wet shoes and socks. And the real kicker—a cold front has come through with the storm, so now, being wet and cold equals freezing!

But it was a night of miracles, and that's what we need to focus on. The Lord kept us safe. He kept the two of us completely dry when everything around us was soaked. He kept the water from dumping on top of us, and we're especially thankful for keeping our bladders in check so we didn't have to go out in the middle of the night!

(This won't be the last storm we go through, but it was the worst as far as how long it lasted and the intensity, or rather in-tents-ity!)

Well, the saying "Be bold, start cold" has a whole new meaning today. We will definitely be starting cold but not because we aren't layering. We have every layer we can get on, and we are still shivering! It is just going to be, point-blank, a cold hike today. So, tell me, why are we doing this again?

Passing by some NOBOs has us commiserating over last night's events. As the saying goes, misery loves company. It really doesn't help as a pick-me-up to complain about what we went through, but sometimes you just need to know you aren't alone in it, that others suffered through it as well.

We would very soon get the pick-me-up we need. About a mile from Iron Mountain Gap, some NOBOs are approaching us with

HOBOS GOING SOBO IN THEIR OBOZ and we never looked back ...

huge smiles. They have just come from the road and announced there are bratwursts up ahead. Trail magic! Our pace is not very fast at all, but I can tell you it sure quickened after hearing that news. I'm sure we set a personal record for that mile!

As we get closer, we can see through the trees that indeed there is a couple set up with a table full of food and chairs around a grill. They are looking the other direction to see if any NOBOs are coming, so we surprise them coming SOBO. We meet our trail angels, Fourth Quarter and his wife, Pam, who are trying to stay warm around the hot grill. He is currently a thru-hiker on the AT and is taking a few days off to spend time with his wife, who has driven from up north to meet him on the trail. We feel so blessed that they have decided to use one of his zero days to provide food for his fellow hikers.

They apologize to us that they left the chairs outside last night, so they are wet (oh, don't we know all about that plight!), but if you sit on this sheet of tin foil, it should prevent your pants from getting wet. Clever idea that actually worked! We sit and enjoy conversation with other hikers and our trail angels as we continue to shiver immensely, but who cares? We are having the best-tasting bratwurst sandwiches we have ever had! We fill up on those, bananas, chips, and soda before heading back out on the trail. We are smarter this time and don't load up our backpacks with additional food. Instead, we just grab a couple candy bars to enjoy later tonight. We couldn't thank Fourth Quarter and Pam enough for their generosity. Someday we would love to be able to do that for other hikers as well!

With a full belly and a wet backpack and tent, FROG is struggling some with the weight. In three miles, we plan to stop at Cherry Gap Shelter, and hopefully we can spread some of the wet stuff out to dry. We are in need of water, and from what we hear, there is a great water source there about a hundred yards from the shelter.

A father/son team is resting and eating lunch at the shelter as we arrive. The father (Pinball) has thru-hiked the AT before, and now his son (Strider) has joined him to complete a long section of the trail together (fellow LASHers!). If all goes well, Strider plans to go beyond the section and continue on to Maine, and his dad will rejoin him toward the end. (We would continue to run into several families that were making this trek together, either thru-hiking or section hiking.)

I volunteer to go get water while FROG gets the wet tent and footprint out and lays them over the picnic table to dry out. Thankfully, even though it is still pretty frigid, the sun is shining, so our attempts will prove to be successful.

Again, no bad experiences at the water source to report! It was an easy walk there and back with a full load. Phew! I will definitely take those times when it goes smooth and easy and fear does not follow me on my journey.

Pinball and Strider have just come from Erwin, Tennessee (which is our next stop, where we plan to take a couple zero days). They tell us they stayed outside the town of Erwin, a beautiful spot right on Nolichucky River that is close by Uncle Johnny's. Uncle Johnny's is a popular hostel right on the trail and tends to be very busy and sold out nightly, with mostly young hikers who like to party. They say it might not be a place we would feel comfortable staying. They are right. Our young party days are over.

> **Enjoy your hike to Springer! It was a pleasure meeting you and crossing paths at Cherry Gap Shelter. Strider**
>
> **May your miles be full of smiles. God Bless! Pinball**

We have had plenty of time to dry things out, filter water, and eat our candy bars that we got from our trail angels. You didn't think we would wait to eat those later tonight, did you? Now it's time to climb 1,200 feet in elevation to Unaka (pronounced U-nake-a) Mountain (5,183 feet). We're cold now. I can just imagine how unbearable it's going to be on the top.

A nightmare of rocks! What! A! Challenge! One positive thing is because it is a tough climb up, we actually feel warm enough to take our down vests off. But once we hit the top, they go right back on again. It is so cold and windy up here, and to boot, no view! PUD! You make a steep climb, you at least want to be able to see a view of some sort! Despite that, it really is a beautiful mountaintop to hike through, a land of enchantment forested with mossy pine needles. It might be a nice area to set up our tent, but our thoughts are to go lower where it might not be so windy.

Another half mile, we see a great spot off to the left. It's still cold and windy, but we will just have to make do. It's been a ten-mile day, and we are ready to just end it!

MISSING: trail legs. We've been told from week one that we'd find our trail legs within the first month and be able to walk fifteen to twenty miles a day. Hah! If anyone finds some missing trail legs, could you please send them our way? We are in dire need of them.

FROG is coming down with a cold and wants to get the tent set up so he can lie down. It isn't an easy feat when you're trying to lay the footprint down and instead are battling the wind that won't let you accomplish that simple task. Then add that we're both so tired from not getting much sleep last night—a double whammy! I will lie upon the footprint; you grab the tent bottom, and we'll try to place it and stake it as quickly as we can. Somehow, we manage to make it work as we both crawl into the tent and call it an early night. It's only 5:30 p.m.

Day 25 (Saturday, May 1)—Yuck, Colds!

It was a super cold night! With our head wraps up over our faces, every stitch of clothing we owned on, we were curled up into our sleeping bags in the fetal position, trying to stay warm. FROG's cold is getting worse, and he's low on energy. We are not sure how far we will get today, but our plan is to get to Curley Maple Shelter, which is nine miles away. That will mean a shorter walk into Erwin tomorrow, only four miles.

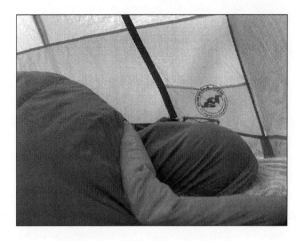

It is a beautiful morning, no clouds in the sky, but there is still a chill in the air. It's hard to get moving this morning, which is reflected by our start time, 9:15 a.m. I feel bad for FROG, as he's wheezing and sneezing and having a hard time of it. We are just not sure if we are going to make it very far today.

We are headed downhill for the first part of our journey, which helps with getting the stamina we need to push on. It is an up and down trail after that, crossing dirt roads, over wooden ladders, and then hiking up to our highest point today, 4,436 feet to Beauty Spot. We are rewarded with panoramic views of the surrounding Tennessee and North Carolina mountains. It is a beautiful spot (hence why it might be called Beauty Spot). There are campsites all around the top, but unfortunately for us, it is too early to settle in, and FROG is feeling like he might just be able to make the trip to the shelter. We stay awhile and enjoy the view and remark on how there must be absolutely stunning sunsets and sunrises from this spot.

A mile down off in the woods, I spot a cross. I've seen a lot just lying on the ground when I walk, but it's unusual for me to spot them in the woods, and this one is a good-sized one. I tell FROG to wait up as I jog in to see what it is. This is a first. The backside reads, "This is a dog, do not call 911, US Forest Service & Unicoi 5.0, 11-19-2020." The front reads, "D's Baby Boy, Adolf," with plastic flowers all around the base. We assume that someone was hiking with their dog, Adolf, and unfortunately, he did not make it all the way to Maine. I can only imagine the heartache Adolf's owner was going through at the time, but I can tell with such a beautiful spot memorialized for him that he was well loved and had a good, long happy life.

Another 2.5 miles brings us to a paved road, Indian Grave Gap Road, which is a good place to eat our peanut butter and jelly tortillas and give FROG extra time to relax before heading to Curley Maple, four more miles away. He is really starting to feel drained from having to farmer blow (he's pretty good at it, unlike me!) so often from his cold, so today our pace is slower by making many little stops along the way. He really is a trooper. I know he is not feeling well but is pushing along to make our journey tomorrow that much shorter.

The last four miles are hard but mainly because it is just so cold out. One-tenth of a mile before the shelter, we come to Curley Maple Gap junction, which has an old house foundation that still exists. There is plenty of room within the foundation to set up our tent for the night, and we hem and haw about doing so, but our lack of water pushes us the last tenth of a mile to the shelter.

When we arrive at the shelter, four other people are already there. They have taken claim to spots within the shelter (it is a double decker, so there would be plenty of room available for us) and mention that we are welcome to stay in there if we wish. I can tell FROG is wanting to stay in there, but you know me, I am not a fan of the shelter, so I say we are probably just going to tent it tonight, but thank you.

We are enamored by this young girl as she is doing yoga positions on a huge log and holding that position while her boyfriend is taking pictures of her doing so. Wow! We are so impressed we ask if we can get a picture. There is absolutely no way we would be able to do something like that, even if we were her age! Good for her! Hopefully age doesn't stop her, and she's able to do it well into her later years.

More people arrive as we are setting up our tent near the water source. They have started a campfire, so we decide to take our dinner up there and sit around it with them before going to sleep for the night. We really enjoy our time with the yoga couple. They are really down to earth and so excited to be out on the trail doing this together. Again, we are impressed with her. She is bound and determined to fix healthy, delicious meals for her and her boyfriend. She has some spaghetti with veggies and a lot of different spices that she has mixed up together. It looks and smells good as we sit and eat our ramen noodles and Snickers bars!

They are trying to figure out how they can make a life of it on the trail and never go back to reality. Life for them doesn't make sense; striving for and having so much seems worthless to them. They are just so happy living with just what they have on their backs, stopping in towns periodically to resupply, and living out in the wilderness. As a young couple, they seem to have figured out life a lot sooner than we did, that it's not about the *things* but about *experiences* and time spent together. I have no doubt they made it all the way to Maine. I would love to know where they are today and what they are doing. I bet she is still doing her yoga, eating healthy, and living off the grid in a tiny home in the woods.

> A simple life is a happy life.
> —**Unknown**

After a while, we can smell what the others are doing in the shelter and decide it is a good time to exit and head to the tent. Let them party on. We made a good choice to not stay in the shelter. (Ahem, *I* made a good choice!)

Day 26 (Sunday, May 2)—Heaven on Earth

Even though there was partying going on last night, by hiker's midnight it was quiet, and all had called it a night. It was another extremely cold night again! We bundled up in all our available clothes and tried to snuggle with each other, which is very hard when you're both in separate sleeping bags! (Some have asked why we didn't zip our sleeping bags together; because of the different sizes and make, it wasn't possible.)

FROG is feeling so much better this morning and more jovial than he has been the last couple mornings. We are still the last ones to leave camp, which is around 8:15 a.m. Even though the others were the ones up late partying, they still manage to get up and out before we do. We feel bad that we didn't get Yoga Couple to write in our journal before they left, but they will forever be remembered in our book.

It's a big day, a nero day! We are so excited that in four miles we will be in Erwin, Tennessee, and taking a couple days off to just recuperate.

After crossing several footbridges, we start to see more hikers headed our way. We must be getting closer to Erwin because as they pass us, we can't help but notice how good they smell. Okay, I know this sounds weird, so I better explain quickly what I mean. Whether they are a day hiker or a section/thru hiker, the closer you are to a town, those you pass smell like a fresh bar of soap, whereas we who have been out on the trail for some time smell like we are in dire need of a bar of soap! You can definitely tell who has spent time in town! Take my word for it; it's the truth!

One of those nice-smelling hikers stops to talk with us because he thinks he remembers us. We're trying to place where we may have seen him, and then it hits. Fourth Quarter! He was the trail angel from two days ago who had set up with his wife, Pam, and handed out those delicious bratwurst sandwiches! He is taking a slackpacking day and will meet up with his wife at Beauty Spot. How cool that he recognized us and we had the chance to meet up with him again!

We just hit our two-hundred-mile mark! It's hard to believe we have hiked that far already! Just 345 miles to go!

We are starting to see the views of the Nolichucky River off to the left, which means we'll head down into town very soon. As we cross the railroad tracks and come out onto a side road, we see the bridge we are to cross that will take us over the river onto the other side, where Uncle Johnny's hostel is. We have decided not to stay there but will plan to stop there to see if we can get a shuttle into town or find out who we should call if they won't take us. We have heard that the Super 8 in town has great hiker rates, so we plan to stay there. We have not made advance reservations, so we are hoping it works out.

Just as we're getting ready to cross the bridge, we see a sign "AT cookout" and an arrow pointing to the left down into a park. We have no idea what this means or even if it is meant for us, so we proceed across the bridge to the other side. As we're standing there contemplating our next move, a lady from across the street yells over to us, "There is a cookout for AT hikers back at the park! Please join us." Oh, that sign is meant for us. It means that we will have to backtrack, but when food is involved, no problem! We follow Marleen, who tells us she was a thru-hiker herself and has started this ministry with the help of local area churches to put on an annual cookout for the hikers every year. There will be a church service, and then afterward will be an all-you-can-eat buffet, a hiker feed. She is speaking our language!

The sermon is short but very uplifting. It encouraged all the hikers to take time to see GOD in the adventure we are on. We agree 100 percent. He is everywhere if you are looking and seeking.

There are six tables of food—six tables, y'all! There is everything you could think of at those tables: assorted salads, beans, hot dogs, hamburgers, assorted chips, fruit, drink, and my favorite, a whole table of desserts! And I wonder why I'm gaining weight? Oops—that's right, I'm not going to talk about my weight until Georgia!

Wow! What a great way to celebrate our accomplishment of two hundred miles! What a feast! One could think they died and went to heaven and are surrounded by the banquet tables. Instead, we'll call it heaven on earth! We did not leave hungry, and if we had, it would have been our own fault!

But truly the best part ... we meet Sandi. Sandi is a member of one of the local churches that is helping Marleen with the cookout. She is currently new to Erwin and mentions that she has walked a section of the AT with her boys, until injury stopped them from going farther. We shared a lot of our stories together that afternoon. In just a short period, she became a forever friend; we are truly thankful that GOD put her in our path. To end our time together, our trail angel prayed the most beautiful prayer for us. (At this point, we didn't know how much our trail angel was going to continue to help us throughout our stay in Erwin.)

> **There are times along the trail (both the AT & the trail of life) where the way becomes hard to see. The blazes are obscured by cloud or fog or darkness but the light of Jesus & the voice of the Holy Spirit is always there to give direction when we look to Him. May your journey be led by HIS SPIRIT—you'll never lose your way. Blessings in Christ—Sandi**

After the cookout, Marleen offers to take us into the town of Erwin to the Super 8. Four miles is not that far away, but when you have passengers in your car that smell horribly, I'll bet she thought it was pretty far away! She drops us off at the door and says she'll wait to make sure there are rooms still available before she leaves. It ends up not being a problem; there are plenty of rooms available. As we head back outside to tell her, she is standing outside her car. How much you want to bet it smells so bad in her car she got out for some fresh air? We don't ask; we don't want to know.

Time to go to our room, turn the heat way up, and take a hot bath. See y'all later.

Think outside. No box required.
—**Unknown**

Our Support Team:

I loved the picture of the privy with a view. Just glad I didn't have to use it. Safe travels and thanks so much for sharing your experience with us. Mary K.

Just loving your adventures—pictures and narrative!!! Keep that sense of humor handy, and I'm SURE those trail legs are just around the corner!! Denise A.

So many hymns coursing through my heart with the beautiful photos—like "For the beauty of the earth." Love your posts! Praying safety and joy on the "downhill miles" which will actually be UP and Down! Hugs! Denise L.

I love the updates! Miss you guys—I have been telling family about your adventures. Everyone is in awe. Keep up the good work. Looking forward to seeing what's next. Diana T.

You are my heroes! Love your pictures and the great way you have of including all of us in your experiences. Can hardly wait for the book to come out! Bev G.

> Some of the best moments are never captured by cameras and are not posted on any social media platform. They are kept in private and are cherished together with the best people.
> **—Unknown**

Erwin, Tennessee, to Hot Springs, North Carolina

> Nor the pestilence that stalks in the darkness,
> nor the plague that destroys at midday.
> —Psalm 91:6

Day 27 (Monday, May 3)—Golden Arches

Sharing is caring! Guess who caught FROG's cold? Yep, now I have a runny nose, am sneezing, and have body aches. I feel fortunate that we are not hiking today, but I wonder, *How in the world did FROG manage to walk as many miles as he did if he felt like this? He's the man!*

"Faith, look what I see." As I peer out the window, there standing close by are golden arches.

"Ahh, sweet!" I reply. "You know what sounds really good right now? A milkshake!" Nothing better in my eyes when not feeling well. We bundle up and walk over, which ends up being a little farther than we thought when looking out the window, but I am anticipating it will be so worth the walk.

As we're sitting in McDonald's drinking our scrumptious milkshakes, the floodgates open up, and down comes the pouring rain! Well, I guess we will just hang out here for a while before heading back. A local customer who comes in daily for his morning coffee is sitting in a booth next to us and strikes up a conversation. He seems intrigued that we are hikers and have a goal of hiking to Georgia and have plans to finish at Amicalola Falls State Park. He lets us know that most people who start there and are walking NOBO reach this spot (Erwin) in about two weeks. Bless his heart, we are not most people, so I'm sure we will not finish our journey in two weeks. (Not even close!)

It has stopped raining, but the skies are still dark, so we decide to make a run for it and try to get back before it starts up again. We catch a slight sprinkle but make it back just in time, right before it starts up again. So very thankful that we aren't out on the trail today and took a zero!

FROG stops by the hiker's box in the lobby to see if there is anything in there that he can put on while we do laundry. He comes back with a huge pair of shorts and a long shirt, both which may have worked before he lost so much weight, but now they just hang like bags on him.

We haven't been able to use the laundry room since we arrived last night, due to other hikers doing theirs, and with only one washer and dryer, we've had to wait patiently for them to be available. It's really not the best feeling to take a shower and then put dirty, stinky clothes back on. It defeats the purpose, but that's what we've had to do, until now. The washer is available. "I'll run back and grab our clothes; you stand here and guard the machine and don't let anyone get it!"

When we were at the cookout yesterday, we found out that Sandi offers shuttling services, and if we want to do any slackpacking, she will make sure she is available to help us out. I am still not feeling 100 percent but am antsy and just ready to get back out on the trail, so we call her to see about tomorrow. We would like to be shuttled eleven miles away, start at Spivey Gap, and hike back to Erwin.

This would mean we will be NOBOs for a day. "Do you need me to bring you any day packs to use?" Sandi asks. "No, we're all set," FROG says.

Our backpacks have a top section that is called a "brain" for extra storage that you can keep on or take off your pack. FROG has a cool feature on his where his will become a day pack. We decide to take his off and use that tomorrow. Do you think we can figure out how to snap it together to adequately use it as a day pack? Of course we can't! We call Sandi back and humbly ask her if we can use her day pack.

Day 28 (Tuesday, May 4)—Oh the Rain

Sandi picks us up at 8:00 a.m. and drives us to Spivey Gap. We decide to meet back up at 4:00 p.m. at Uncle Johnny's, which should give us plenty of time to hike there and even have some rest time before she arrives to pick us up. She can tell I still am not feeling well, so before we get out of the car, she prays for GOD's strength for me and for Him to keep us both safe as we journey through the storm today. And rain, it did! Eight of the eleven miles, we will hike in pouring rain.

After five miles of slopping through the wet mud, we stop at No Business Knob Shelter. We are totally drenched, and our shoes are soaked, so we decide to wait out the storm. Not sure why; we are already soaked to the bone. I guess because there are others there doing the same. It's good to suffer in numbers.

Despite the rain, spirits are high in the shelter. One couple found a chess board in the corner and is playing a game. The other couple is huddled together in the other corner, eating lunch. We sit at the picnic table that is in front of the shelter but under the roof. Two other solo hikers show up and sit down at the picnic table. They all seem to know one another from staying at the same place last night, Nature's Inn Hostel & Cabins (which is our next stop) and have been driven to Spivey Gap to slackpack to Erwin as well. They are remarking about how they all got together last night, pooled their food, and came up with a great feast of assorted items. They were doing things together and forming a tramily.

Being a SOBO, we have discovered has its pros and cons.

Pros:
- No one is traveling south, so we don't feel the pressure to be walking faster or having to get out of people's way.
- We get information from the NOBOs on what's coming up, good water sources, and tips on where to stay.
- We meet so many great people during our stops at shelters, hostels, and towns, but then …

Cons:
- We don't have a *tramily*, a trail family. Those traveling together become close and develop relationships. We meet them briefly and then never see them again. We have each other, which is great, but sometimes you just miss forming bonds with others.

It is still raining and not letting up, so we decide to head out first before anyone else does. They will most likely catch up with us anyway. It proves to be true not long after we start out. One of the couples and the two solo hikers pass us and are going at a much quicker pace than we can go. Because I know there is still one other couple that has not passed us yet, I spend the remainder of the hike looking back over my shoulder to see if they are near so we can get out of their way. For me, it doesn't make it an enjoyable walk, always being on the alert.

As we're heading close to Erwin, we are starting to get great views of the Nolichucky River and the town of Erwin from a distance. Only 0.8 mile left, and we'll be at Uncle Johnny's. It is slow-moving on our descent; from all the rain and mud, it can be slick in places. I'm reveling and feeling a sense of accomplishment that the other couple never passed us. We hiked faster than they did. Fist pump! Okay, so the competitive side of me just came out. That one-upmanship quickly deflates as I start to worry and wonder that something may have happened to them. I really do hope they are okay.

HOBOS GOING SOBO IN THEIR OBOZ and we never looked back ...

Sandi has not arrived yet to pick us up, which is good because we want to check out the outfitter store inside Uncle Johnny's and see if they may have a spork we can buy. We are still just using our spoon, which is working, but a spork is just that much better. They don't have what we are looking for, so we buy ourselves a couple cans of soda and sit outside to wait. One of the solo hikers who stopped at the shelter and passed us on the trail is sitting out front and tells us there is free food (another trail magic!) just around the corner if we are wanting. Of course, we're wanting. It's food, isn't it?

Today's trail magic is sloppy joes. Very nice! We grab a plate and a bun so that our trail angel can slop some joe on it. Ahh, it looks so good! There isn't much left, so we're thankful he is still being generous with our portion. It is as good as it looks!

"Oh no! Look where he is from." There printed on the side of the van, we read "Boots Off Campground and Hostel." You remember them? We haven't forgotten! This guy is so friendly and hospitable. We wonder where he was when we were at his campground. I think maybe today Boots Off redeemed itself from our bad experience. They are forgiven. When Boot man leaves his post, FROG sneaks up and gets himself another sloppy joe. He is caught. Hopefully he is forgiven.

As we're eating our sandwiches, we can't help but think about his marketing strategy in providing trail magic to the hostel here at Uncle Johnny's. Since most are travelling NOBO, they haven't stopped at his hostel yet, which is eighty-four miles away. What a great way to advertise your business! And looking around, this really is the clientele they attract, a young crowd happily drinking and smoking. Sigh.

Oh good! Missing couple shows up! No need for me to continue worrying. Now I can revel in the win. We can finally say we outpaced someone else! Yay, us!

Sandi arrives soon after we wolf down our food. We apologize profusely that we are getting into her car so muddy. It can't be helped; we are a complete and utter mess! Our shoes and socks are soaked. We're cold, we need a hot shower, and we're in need of another laundry detergent pod to wash our clean clothes from yesterday that are now filthy again. Why did we even bother yesterday? Now we have to do it all over again. Well, I guess we can at least say we smelled like a clean bar of soap when we first started on the trail, instead of smelling like we needed a bar of soap like we did when we ended.

Day 29 (Wednesday, May 5)—Dominos

Our original plans were to get back on the trail this morning, but with the forecast looking bleak again today, and still feeling under the weather (like that play on words I used?), we decide to take another zero day.

We were able to get our laundry redone last night, so today will be last-minute things. We'll walk through town to get resupplies, enough to carry us through until we reach Nature's Inn, which is 13.5 miles away, so we really don't need much.

Erwin is a large town, but I wouldn't say it catered to the hiker that much. There is a big Food Lion grocery for resupply, which is very nice, but we were hoping there may be another outfitter store to look for some things (a spork mainly!) but we never found one if there was. We got everything else we needed and decided tonight we are going to splurge. It's going to be a pizza and wings night from Dominos!

It was a lowkey day. It never did rain—just dark and gloomy all day. Our shoes finally dried out. FROG has put his defective brain back on his backpack, and our bags are repacked for tomorrow. We are ready to hit the road, Jack, and never look back! (I know it's "hit the road, Jack and don't you come back," but I was making a funny—or rather, trying to be funny—on our book title.)

> Life is short. Go to the mountains and never look back.
> —**Unknown**

Day 30 (Thursday, May 6)—Act of Kindness

Sandi is a saint! Before returning us to Spivey Gap to hike SOBO, she can tell that I am not feeling quite up to par yet. She asks if I want a fleece-lined pair of sweatpants that she has at her house that no one is using; it might just help me on cold nights. Not having my long johns to keep me warm, I can hardly refuse such a kind and thoughtful gift! (Those warm, fleece-lined sweatpants stayed with me for 207 more miles, and even then, it was hard for me to give them up. What a gift of love!)

She took us back to Spivey Gap to walk the opposite direction from two days ago. We prayed for her today before we left. It is really hard to say goodbye to our new friend. She will forever hold a special place in our hearts. We will see her again, either here on earth or on the other side for eternity.

Our Trail Angel and Sister, Sandi

It is an uphill climb, two thousand feet from Spivey Gap to Little Bald to reach an elevation of 5,153 feet. We climb to the top of the boulder on Little Bald, hoping to catch some sort of view. Nothing! PUD! It is anything but *bald*! I'd call this pretty hairy! There are woods and trees all around. All that work to get here, and then to not be rewarded for it. I guess that is a good example of how it is in life sometimes; you can work really hard at something and not always get rewarded, *and* you shouldn't do something just to be rewarded. That can be a hard one to swallow at times!

There is an option to take a bypass to go around the bald, but we choose not to take it, so it is a challenging descent over huge boulders. The one time we decide to be purists and follow the white blazes and not cheat by taking an easier route—not sure what we are thinking. I guess we aren't thinking; that is the problem.

We reach Bald Mountain Shelter about 1:15 p.m. to relax and eat lunch. We meet Mike, who has also stopped and is eating his lunch. He got caught in the rainstorm last night so is drying his tent out. We know all about it! It's the worst!

He asks us, "Have you run into Nimblewill Nomad yet?"

"No. Who is he?" we ask.

"He's a really interesting man that I met yesterday. He started thru-hiking from his home state of Alabama in February and is currently hiking this section. He's eighty-two years old and will celebrate a birthday by the time he finishes in Maine, which will beat the current record holder who completed it in 2017 at the age of eighty-two," says Mike.

We wonder if maybe we already passed him and just didn't know it. Mike says, "Oh, you would know if you saw him. He's got long gray hair and a long gray beard." We haven't passed anyone with that description and hope we will have the pleasure of running into him.

Mike is traveling alone and hasn't really acquired a tramily. It sounds like it might be his preference since he hikes all day long and sets up camp late at night, then leaves before others get up in the morning. A true definition of stealth camping. FROG asks him if he has a trail name yet. He doesn't. FROG says, "You should take on the name of Stealth Man." (We still refer to him as that and wonder if he decided to use it or not.)

God Bless and happy hiking! Mike (Stealth Man)

As you are well aware, if there is a privy, I would prefer to use that instead of … well, you know what. I follow the arrows to where it says it is, and it's an open-pit privy just like the privy with a view! *Although* this one is run-down, with no view whatsoever! Someone has stripped me of my title and my kingdom. I no longer feel like a queen sitting upon her throne, overlooking her kingdom. Back to a life as a peasant.

Please pardon my silly humor. When all you do is walk eight to ten hours a day, you have to start finding fun and humor in yourself and each other; otherwise it just becomes a boring walk (and story!). We've laughed so much with/at each other over the silliest things, but it's been great!

After saying our goodbyes to Stealth Man, we head south, determined to be observant so that we don't miss an encounter with Nimblewill Nomad.

Almost a mile in, we can see the view of Big Bald in the distance. Looks as though we will not be disappointed this time and will get a spectacular view. It does not disappoint one bit! Views are panoramic and beautiful! Weather is breezy and cool, but we take time to enjoy the view before our descent.

Nature's Inn Hostel & Cabins is still over four miles away, and we know there is absolutely no way we will make it there today, so we call to make reservations for tomorrow night for two nights. We request one of their private cabins, but it looks like they may be filled up, so we have a bunk reserved in the bunkhouse. Not my favorite choice, but it is a bed, and they have showers, so all is good.

FROG seems impressed that I have held out so long today, but actually I think I'm starting to make a comeback and am feeling much better. Watch out, world! I am on my way to normal! *My* normal, that is!

It takes us a while, but we finally find a flat spot to stealth camp. After ten miles of mostly uphill, we are pretty whipped. We are in for another cold night, so once we finish our nightly routine, around seven o'clock, we head in the tent, play our game of cards, and turn out the lights. Well, GOD turned them out for us. Sweet dreams and don't let the bedbugs bite (which has a whole different meaning when you're camping!).

Day 31 (Friday, May 7)—This Will Get Your Goat

A nero day! Cold and cloudy morning, and it rained again last night. The tent and tent fly are soaked, but again, thankfully, we stayed dry and comfortable. The trail is wet, and we are still descending, which means we walk a slower pace to avoid any injuries. So far, thirty-one days in, I've had a tumble but no injuries. Knock on wood (which isn't hard to find, lots of trees around us).

We have less than four miles to go to Sam's Gap, I26 underpass, and then will call for shuttle pickup when we reach there. As we break out to a clearing and walk through a meadow, it starts to graupel or sleet; we're not sure which one it technically is. Some kind of frozen precipitation is happening! It is really cold!

Please, somebody, anybody, if I *ever* mention to any of you that I plan to go on a backpacking trip in April or May again, you have my permission to bop me side the head and remind me how cold it was. Those who know me know I love the *heat* and not being cold! This is nuts! We get to the underpass and feel instant relief to be out of the wet, frozen droplets that are falling as we call for shuttle pickup. We are doing our own special type of dance to stay warm as we wait.

We meet Amy when she arrives with the shuttle van. Nature's Inn is owned by her brother, Taft; he built the cabins and most of the buildings there on the property. She started helping him run the place not too long ago when she realized he was in desperate need of help. It's been quite an undertaking for both of them, but they are doing an excellent job. She has her hands full with all she does: shuttling, check-in, checkout, and cleaning—pretty much running the administrative part of it. We're not sure how she keeps up with it all, but she does it with a smile. We instantly like her.

"Every night, same time every night, about six thirty, if you look up on the mountain, there are mountain goats that appear on the rocky cliffs above the complex," Amy tells us. We make a mental note to try not to forget this to check it out later.

As we pull into Nature's Inn Hostel and Cabins, we notice how quaint, rustic, and inviting it looks. We fall in love with the place and are so glad to be making a stop here. To top it off, Amy says she is able to give us an upgrade, and we now are staying in a cabin! Music to my ears! She has turned the heat on in the cabin, and it is ready for us. Happy dance to the music in my ears!

Our first stop is the common area, where she will check us in. We walk into the warm, cozy room that has a bunch of couches surrounded by a woodstove. The TV is on, and the other side of the room has tables and chairs with a kitchen that has everything a hiker would need to fix their meals. Off to the back is a resupply room with all sorts of trail food, pizza, ice cream, and frozen meals, where they work on a self-serve honor system. If you take something, you are responsible for writing it down on your tally sheet. We wonder how honest people are, but she quickly adds they have never had any problems with the system. We are so glad to hear that.

She lets us know we are in Creekside Cabin #1. Ah, nice, really close to the bathrooms. As we walk up the steps to our cabin, we first walk onto a screened-in porch that is open to the flowing stream below, Sam's Creek. It is a gorgeous setting. On the porch are a couple Adirondack chairs and a hammock. If it wasn't so cold, it would be a perfect place to just sit and relax. (We were bummed we never were able to sit out there due to the rainy, cold weather.)

When you walk in the cabin, there is a built-in bunkbed with a comfy mattress, pillows, and blankets for us to use, as well as a space heater. A heater that is supposed to be working—it is *cold* in there! Are you starting to see a pattern with heaters in our cabins? Flashbacks to Black Bear Resort and the trouble we had with our heater when we first arrived. Brrr! Back up to the common area we go to let Amy know and to hang out where it is warm!

Amy immediately goes to check it out, and indeed, it is not working. She will run into town and get us a new one. Before she leaves, she gives us our mail drops, two boxes, one with our resupply of food, and the other is our bounce box.

Nathan was in the right place at the right time. When we go through our boxes, we come up with a whole slew of food that we don't think we will need and ask him if he is interested. His face lights up, and he takes all of it. This is what it's all about! Giving always brings joy to the giver and receiver!

Amy has returned and says we have a heater set up in our cabin that is working now. It shouldn't take long to heat up the small space that will be our living quarters for the next two nights.

We're slackers! Setting up and taking down a soaked tent (while you're soaked) is not much fun, but if we're able to work it out on a rainy day where we can slackpack, we're all in! There's nothing like carrying a day pack and returning wet to take a hot shower and get in a warm bed after walking in the rain all day. Tomorrow is expected to be raining again. It's been quite a stretch of rain lately. We have made plans to slackpack tomorrow, starting at Devils Fork Gap and returning back to Sam's Gap, 8.5 miles.

Speaking of a shower ... Can I just tell you, this place by far has the best showers and bathrooms! Whoa! I can't vouch for the men's bathroom, but the women's bathroom is stocked with toiletries and fresh towels and has big shower stalls with lots of hot water and flush toilets! Oh, the joys of modern-day conveniences! I know I mention this a lot, but when you don't have, you are so thrilled when you do have!

Our cabin is toasty! The only problem with being in here a long period of time is that it doesn't have any windows, so you feel like you are in a box, so we spend more time up in the common area than we do in the cabin. If it had been nice out, as I stated before, sitting out on our porch and listening to the water trickling down over the rocks would have been our preferred choice. (Maybe if we go back for a visit, we'll make sure to schedule it during a warm spell and not a cold, rainy spell.)

As we head up to the common area to fix a frozen pizza before bed, we see people standing outside looking up. Yep, it's 6:30 p.m., just like clockwork, and there are the mountain goats! They are quite a distance away, but you can see movement and tell they are goats. It is a good thing there are people outside looking up, because do you think we remembered on our own? Of course we didn't.

Day 32 (Saturday, May 8)–Moye Family

"Have you run into Nimblewill Nomad?" asks Amy. We are in the van headed to Devil's Fork Gap to slackpack back to the hostel. There's that name again.

"No, we haven't yet, but we're really hoping to," we respond.

"He stayed with us a few days ago. We really enjoyed having him. What a great guy." Somehow, we have missed him again, and it doesn't look like we will get to meet him. One of us must have been off-trail when our paths would have crossed. We are feeling really disappointed that we missed out on meeting him.

Arriving at Devil's Fork Gap, we make plans to call when we arrive back at Sam's Gap, and Amy will come and pick us up at the same spot as yesterday. We will be traveling as NOBOs again today, so I will feel compelled to constantly look over my shoulder to make sure we are not in anyone's way.

It is a sunny but very cold day. Forecast is calling for precipitation, but so far it looks like we'll have a good day of hiking. Maybe the rain we had earlier this morning will be all we have today. When packing our day pack today, we made sure to include our rain ponchos just in case of a change in the weather.

Wildflowers! I've become so obsessed with the trilliums; they are everywhere, all different kinds and colors. The fields are full of many different wildflowers: reds, greens, pinks, purples, whites, all glistening from last night's rain, having left rain droplets on their petals, which makes them sparkle as the sun shines on them. It is a sight to behold! And then there is the rhododendron tunnels. I will never tire of seeing those! I am feeling so carefree and light footed (might have something to do with not having a heavy pack on too!) as we stop and marvel over all the beauty.

Water is flowing abundantly at Sugarloaf Branch, a rocky

brook that has a nice little waterfall to enjoy as we stop to filter water. Just as we're getting ready to leave, I look down and, on the ground, there are some sticks shaped as a cross, and right next to it looks like a large nail. (This was not staged. This is exactly as we found it.) I immediately think of Jesus and his being nailed to the cross for me, for us. (Check out the picture and see what you think.)

What Do You See?

Gravesites for Dorothy Shelton Hensley, May 8, 1865–April 30, 1965. Joe Riddel, May 16, 1877–July 9, 1967. We tried to do some research to learn more about these gravesites but were unable to obtain any information. (I was able to learn that they are related to the Shelton's who also have graves, which we will see tomorrow.)

We don't usually go off-trail unless we really have to, mostly for getting water or going to a shelter, but we break our rule this time and take a short walk into High Rock to check out the view. So glad we went! A beautiful cliff-top summit that dead ends right at High Rock for a spectacular view of the surrounding area. Not only are we blessed with a view, but we are showered with ice pellets from above. Yep! More graupel (sleet)! It doesn't last long, but we got it nonetheless. Well, there is our precipitation for today. Hopefully that is it.

We make a stop at Hogback Ridge Shelter, another short distance off-trail, but hey! They have a privy! And a picnic table to sit and eat our lunch. Will be well worth the walk. And it is. As we sit at the table and think upon our day … it has been quiet—just us, GOD, and nature. I am truly thankful that we have a day like today to go slowly, to really enjoy the views and our surroundings, to be reminded of all that GOD has done for us and given us. We are enjoying the solitude.

The first and only hiker we encounter for the day has come up behind us and stops to ask us if we know how he can get in contact with someone to shuttle him to the nearest airport; he has just learned that a family member has passed away, and he needs to get home. We give him the number for Nature's Inn and suggest speaking to Amy or Taft to see if they may be able to help or if they know someone who could shuttle him. (We found out later that Taft took him to the nearest airport so that he could get home. So glad that we were in his path to help.) What a reminder that life is continuing outside of our quiet hiking bubble.

We are almost done for the day when we come upon a monument, MOYE REST, placed there by the Moye family, with this on the plaque:

> **As this natural bowl of springs, creeks, meadow, and forest passes from our family to the U.S. Forest Service, Jim, Sarah, Mike, and Jim Moye, Jr., of Atlanta, Georgia, recognize this part of the Appalachian Trail as a manifestation of the glory of Christ Jesus, our Lord (Romans 11:36). As GOD nurtured our "strong love for Jesus," we had personal encounters with Him regarding this unique property. It is our prayer that the Moye**

tract on the trail will be a place of inner peace and gentle rest.

It is no wonder that we felt a strong presence of the LORD today as we walked this section. We felt that inner peace and gentle rest that they hoped we would feel. We saw and felt GOD everywhere—the wildflowers, the sunshine, the rhododendron tunnels, the panoramic views, the cross and nail, the water/waterfall, the sleet, the picnic table to sit at, and even providing me the privy! If you seek Him, you will find Him, I guarantee it!

Within ten minutes of our call, Amy is there to pick us up at Sam's Gap. We tell her about our day of going slowly, enjoying all that was around us. It was a good day, no falls and no injuries. We return to her in one piece. Amy proceeds to tell us about a group of three hikers who had previously stayed at their place and were slackpacking for a day. She received a call from one of the hikers that one of the girls in the group was hurt badly. Could she shuttle to a certain trailhead and be there by such-in-such a time? Amy knew this was not something to take lightly, but not knowing how serious it was, she brought all sorts of medical supplies and had her van parked right up at the beginning of the trail so they didn't have to walk far and she could be lifted up into the back easily, if need be. She waited for hours for them to get off the trail, and once they did, the group was laughing and acting like nothing happened, and the girl who was supposedly hurt badly only had scratches on her and wasn't really hurt at all. Amy said she was pretty upset, understandably so. (They were part of the Dirty Bubble we've heard about!) I don't blame her one bit for feeling like she was taken advantage of. People like that make it harder to believe those in the future who really might be hurt and need medical attention. Like the boy who cried wolf!

It is a very cold day but nothing a hot shower won't fix! And some ice cream from the store! Okay, almost sounds like an oxymoron, but believe me, they do go together!

We get our bounce box ready so that Amy can send it on to Hot Springs, North Carolina, where we will pick it up at the post office.

It will take us a few days (thirty-five miles to go), but all depends on the weather and terrain. Hot Springs will officially be our halfway point. Already looking ahead and wondering how we will celebrate that momentous occasion!

Day 33 (Sunday, May 9)—Mother's Day

> Thank you, FROG and Faith for staying with us @ Nature's Inn @ Sam's Gap! It has been a pleasure to serve you. Please come back when you're not hiking & stay awhile. Happy Trails! Amy

Up early to catch the shuttle back to Devils Fork Gap and walk south this time. Will be good to be SOBOs again. It is a sunny, warm day to start, which is a huge change from the weather we have been having. Well, happy Mother's Day to me!

Our goal today is to make it to Jerry Cabin Shelter, 9.3 miles away, set up camp, and celebrate Mother's Day with a dehydrated meal and dessert: lasagna and cheesecake. We've been saving this just for today.

Heading out today, we run into a pastor and Sunday school teacher, both from the same church. The pastor is on sabbatical for six months to walk the trail. FROG asks if he is planning to thru-hike to Maine, and he responds, "I have to. I live in Maine. It is the only way I will get home." What great material and stories he will have to share in his sermons when he returns! They are a lot of fun to talk to, and if we had been hiking NOBO, I'm sure we would have become a close tramily with them.

The terrain so far is pretty favorable. It's been uphill but a gradual climb up. Stopping off at Flint Mountain Shelter for a quick snack, we run into two guys also taking a break. Normal conversation starts with finding out where everyone is from and of course our usual, "Upstate New York," putting emphasis on *Upstate*. FROG interjects his standard line: "Not the city—you can have that!" It just so happens they are from the city. Whoops! Great way to make friends by dissing their city! Now I think it's a good thing we are heading south and they are going north. I leave FROG to bail himself out of that one and whisper to him that I am headed to the privy, to please look out and make sure no one heads that way since there is no door on it. He must have recovered from his slipup because when I return, he is deep in conversation with the guys, and another has joined as well. The point I need to make here is that he is *not* looking out to make sure no one shows up at the privy while I am in there. Anyone could have come in from the other direction. No! He is too busy digging himself out of the hole he made to look out to see that no one saw me using the hole! Humph! I really am not upset, but really, he's supposed to have my back—or in this case, my front!

Three miles up, we come to Shelton Graves. It's a short walk in, but we decide to go in to check it out. We did some reading up on it, and they are the gravesites of an uncle (David Shelton Jr.) and nephew (William Shelton), Union soldiers who were ambushed on this spot while visiting family, along with Millard Haire (thirteen-year-old Shelton relative) by Confederates during the Civil War. What a somber moment to think we are standing on the exact spot where these three people took their last breath in such a tragic way. So very sad.

After two miles of feeling the heaviness of sadness for what their families must have endured, we know we need a pick-me-up to get out of this mood. Disclaimer: silly humor coming up. Remember, we have to find things to laugh at, or we'll go bonkers out here.

We are just told by some NOBOs to avoid climbing up Big Butt (interesting name)—not much view to see, so take the bypass. You'd think if it is a *big butt*, there would be plenty to see!

Speaking of which, I have to say FROG has literally walked his butt off! Poor guy. He has lost so much weight he has to keep his drawers *hiked* way up (like that pun?). It reminds me of Urkel on *Family Matters* (I'm sure I'm dating myself on that one). Yep ... that's my husband and his drawers! (Don't feel too bad for him. By the end of the day today, he will have grown a big *butt*. It's one of those you *had* to be there to find the humor in it. You'd have thought we lost our minds with how much we were laughing about it. Okay, it was really mostly me laughing since he couldn't really see his backside wiggle.)

Another gravesite:

> Howard E. Bassette, age 83, died Nov 9, 1987. Hiked the AT 1968. Ashes on this spot 4/88.

At least this one is not as sad as the earlier gravesites. Howard decided he wanted his gravesite here with his ashes; the others certainly didn't choose their gravesites.

> Sidenote: We have seen a lot of graves on the trail lately. I'm wondering if we should be concerned!

It is starting to rain as we near Jerry Cabin Shelter; many tents have already gone up around the area, but FROG wants to get to the shelter to see if there is any room there, so as not to have to put the tent up in the rain. There are a lot of people gathered around the shelter, but no one has taken claim to any spots. The floor in the shelter is curved downward, and I'm pretty sure FROG's feet will hang over the end if he stretches out. But there is a really cool-looking fireplace inside; at least it's got that going for it. We sit at the picnic table to contemplate whether we will stay or not. I am not interested in the shelter (I'm sure you already knew that!), but if he wants to put up the tent, I am all for it. Of course, a disagreement ensues; FROG wants to stay but in the shelter. Ugh!

We get distracted from our debate by a couple that is planning to stay the night in their hammocks, but it's not just them; in tow is their three-year-old and their youngest, not quite a year old. We are so intrigued and amazed that they not only are carrying backpacks but are most likely carrying their children and extra things needed for them, then sleeping in hammocks with them nightly, in cold, rainy weather. I can't even imagine how much of a challenge this must be, but they are all smiles. They are looking at this as a great adventure for their family. I am pretty sure by now, if it were me, I would have thrown in the towel and wanted to go home. We are not sure how many nights they were out, but they for sure deserve some sort of award for their courage and bravery!

We still haven't made a decision about what we will do, but at least our attitudes have changed, and we are more agreeable with what the other wants to do. FROG decides to ask a hiker who has just appeared and will be staying in the shelter what the conditions of the trail are up ahead now that it has rained some. He warns us that Big Firescald Knob is coming up, and it's very rocky, and due to wet conditions, it may not be safe if we take that route. He recommends we take the Bad Weather Bypass to avoid taking the tricky trail up. It would normally have great views going that way, but because of the rain and fog, we won't be able to see much anyway. He reminds us the three hundred mark is just up ahead. What? We totally forgot about that! Now, we both are motivated to hit that milestone, so we decide to keep hiking. It has stopped raining and looks like it may hold out for us. We've walked just over nine miles and have had enough rest to push on. We will have earned our lasagna and cheesecake today!

We have a heads-up this time where to find the milestone marker and know it is close to the Bad Weather Bypass for Firescald Knob. We can see the sign ahead—and yep! There off to the left just before the sign is "300" written with sticks on the ground. Someone has taken the time to lay them out. The ground is dry enough, so I lie down beside them for a picture. Three hundred miles to go! We've walked 245 miles, so close to our halfway mark!

HOBOS GOING SOBO IN THEIR OBOZ and we never looked back ...

Three-Hundred-Mile Mark

Taking the bypass is most likely a good idea to avoid climbing up over wet boulders with a cliff to our left, but even going this way is really tough walking! It is a really rocky and hard-moving 1.4 miles that seem to go on and on and on. And to top it off, it starts to rain again. A light mist, so it gives us time to dig out our Frogg Togg ponchos to get them on over us and our backpacks before it rains any harder.

You know when you get so physically tired that you start saying and doing goofy things and can't stop laughing? It happens a lot with kids when they tire at night, but hey, we're still kids, aren't we? This is one of those afternoons for us. I had been remarking earlier in the day how FROG had literally walked his butt off, to find it hysterically funny that now that he has his poncho on over his backpack, and it looks as though he grew a butt! A *big butt*! Walking behind him and watching his backside jiggle up and down is just too much for me to keep silent and not roar with laughter. Again I will date myself, but it reminds me of the movies, *Big Momma's House, Mrs. Doubtfire, Madea* ... you get the picture. I know. It's one of those *you had to be there*, but you would have found it pretty humorous, too, if you had been there!

A Big Butt!

We are in desperate need of water and just can't find a place to camp for the night. We have almost gone fourteen miles today, and we're exhausted. We find a good-sized log to sit on to relax and check our Guthook app to see what is coming up. Not wanting to fill up too much because we have a great meal planned for later, we share a power bar. Guthook indicates just ahead is Jones Meadow Camp Creek Bald, location of a cell tower. It also says, "not worth the walk in and you can't camp there, it is off limits to the public." Well, my goodness. What kind of camp is that if you can't even camp at it? Fine! Just a quarter mile away is a piped spring with flat sites available; we will head there.

"Can you help me up?" asks FROG. I reach out to take his hand, and I guess the power bar hasn't kicked in yet. Neither one of us has enough energy, and instead he falls backward off the log. You ever see a turtle on his back, struggling to get back on his feet? Yep, that is my FROG with his twenty-five-pound backpack on. (So wishing I had gotten a picture of that for y'all to chuckle over!) We're still in our silly, tired, laughing mode, so that makes it doubly hard to figure out how to get him back up. FROG figures I'm not much help anymore since I am laughing so hard at his predicament. He rolls himself to his side, grabs the log, and pulls himself up. Don't go thinking that it is a quick process he does all that in. Oh no, it is somewhat pathetic, and a video would have been much better than a picture for y'all to see!

We finally find a spot next to the spring and filter our water. As soon as we get the tent set up, the heavens open up, and it comes down in buckets. I make it in just in time—FROG, not so fortunate. But frogs like the rain, don't they? Not so much for this frog. Our silliness has ended at this point. He is so wet, and so now it's wet inside the tent.

Remember that wonderful Mother's Day meal we had planned? Instead, it is another protein bar and water, not quite the celebration we had planned. Happy Mother's Day to me.

Day 34 (Monday, May 10)—Mickey and Minnie

It rained all night. Woke up to rain. We lay inside contemplating whether we should just stay the day in the tent or at least wait it out for a while before heading out. Looking out, we see that it's really foggy and doesn't look like it will let up anytime soon. The thought of taking everything down while it's still raining is not appealing at all, but I guess the push to get to Hot Springs overtook because we decide to get up and get moving. (We would soon find out that this decision was due to divine intervention and would be full of miracles and blessings!)

It isn't a very chipper morning for either one of us. Actually, we are in a downright ugly mood. Packing up wet gear is hard enough, but doing it while it is still raining is miserable! It makes for two not very happy campers!

FROG's shoe is coming apart at the toes, where it is literally flapping as he walks, waving to all the passersby each step he takes. Although it's nice to have a friendly shoe, it adds to his misery.

Our plan today is to stop at Little Laurel Shelter to eat breakfast and get more water, and then onto Spring Mountain Shelter, a total of eleven miles for the day.

We are the first to arrive at the shelter; we take our packs off and take claim to the free space available by spreading our things out. FROG is starting to complain about his ankle really hurting from his flapping shoe, so this is a much-needed break to give his ankle some rest. We just hope we'll be able to make it with those shoes for another nineteen miles until we can get to Hot Springs and get new ones.

Privy breaks are needed as well, so I get the pleasure first. I walk in there, and I kid you not, the contents are up to the rim. It is horribly disgusting! This is the first privy that we've encountered that we have to make sure we do not accidentally lower ourselves too far down, or we just might wear the contents. That would stink! Yes, of course you need to know all this. I promised to keep it real for you! When I return to the shelter, I don't tell FROG what to expect. I just warn him to be careful. (I am happy to report no mishaps!)

While FROG is using the privy, another couple arrives at the shelter. I move our stuff out of the way so they can sit down and spread out their things. They are having a time of it and are on their last legs. I feel so bad for them; nothing is going right, and they have just about had it with the weather. I agree with them about the weather and totally understand why they are feeling depressed; we were feeling the same way this morning when we started out. Rain every day can sure bring you down. His wife had previously gotten hurt, they were spending way too much money when off-trail ... they were just ready to call it quits and get off. FROG is back now and is getting the drift of the conversation. We remind them of the saying, "Don't quit on a bad day." They agree but ask, if they're not enjoying it, should they really continue? That's a really good point. Conversation changes, and they tell us that up ahead in three miles is trail magic! Now you're talking good, positive stuff! We are not sure we will make it in time before they take down, but we will try to up our step, though with FROG's bad shoe and ankle, it might not be possible. They share another great tip: make sure we make a stop in Helen, Georgia, when we are close by. It's a small German town with Alpine food and drink; they tell us we will not be disappointed. It seems like an eternity before we will get there, but we'll keep that in mind. (We really hope they continued on. After walking through Georgia, I wish I could congratulate them on what they had already accomplished. Those 295 miles they had just endured when we met them were tough ones, and they had made it! We'd give them a huge high five!)

We need water, so we head to the spring before trekking on the three miles to hopefully get some food! We're trying to remain hopeful, but it's most likely not a possibility that we will make it in time.

FROG's shoe is still flapping, and his ankle is really hurting by the time we make it to Log Cabin Road. We can hardly believe our eyes. Trail magic is still set up on the road, and there sit the trail angels. They are looking the other way, not expecting SOBOs, so when we come up behind them, they are surprised and delighted at the same time. We learn they are called "Mickey and Minnie," SOBOs who thru-hiked the trail in 2016. Fellow SOBOs!

They have been sitting here for quite some time without anyone coming through but kept thinking they would wait it out and see if anyone showed. They only have a quarter of a sub left, but we don't care. We share it between us along with a banana and some chips and wash it down with sodas. We are satisfied and delighted! They are the neatest couple and share their experiences on the trail, where he proposed to her while hiking. We tell them of our experience with the couple we met on the trail that also got engaged. So many romantics we are meeting!

FROG is starting to tell them about his shoe and how his ankle is really hurting. He hopes that we can make it another 16.2 miles, which would be two more days for us. I am so doubtful and think he is just going to hurt himself more by walking on it. There is a hostel on this road somewhere, but they tell us it is closed due to COVID; they can drive us into Hot Springs tonight if we want to go. They need to go pick up something for dinner anyway so will gladly take us there. *Really?* We don't hem and haw about an answer. Yes! Please and thank you!

They are ready to close up anyway and will leave the cooler with drinks there for anyone who happens to come by. Mickey is going to take their dogs back to the cabin, and Minnie will run us into town. Had we stayed at Jerry Cabin Shelter last night, we never would have made it here today. If we had stayed in our tent all day and waited the rain out, we never would have met them. We truly believe it was divine intervention that worked it out so that we (or they) were at the right place at the right time.

We are on our way to Hot Springs—our halfway point!

> **So glad to meet some fellow SOBOs! We've had a great time doing trail magic this weekend and happy to give you a ride to Hot Springs. Hope your ankle heals up soon. Happy Trails! Mickey and Minnie SOBO '16**

Our Support Team:

You write a great travelogue! And great pics. I wish it was easier. But you're more than half way!! I think your trail legs are just around the next bend. Linda M.

Thanks for your interesting notes and beautiful pictures. What an adventure! I am glad to hear but not wanting to participate! Praying the next half gets better and you find those trail legs! Nancy K.

We were just talking about how great it is that you are able to do this hike at your pace and take time to smell all the beautiful wild flowers along the way. Again, thanks for sharing your hike with us. I am so enjoying your journey. Stay safe. Mary K.

HOBOS GOING SOBO IN THEIR OBOZ and we never looked back ...

He Loves Me!

With such rocky terrain, we keep our eyes down a lot to make sure we don't inadvertently step on a rock wrong and twist our ankle. It is slow-moving when it's so rocky, like it is today. A lot of times, we spot a lot of crosses, but today ... I get to see a heart-shaped rock. I wish it isn't so heavy. I would love to take it with me. I love those reminders that GOD is with us and continually shows me His love for me. But I didn't always know of this love ...

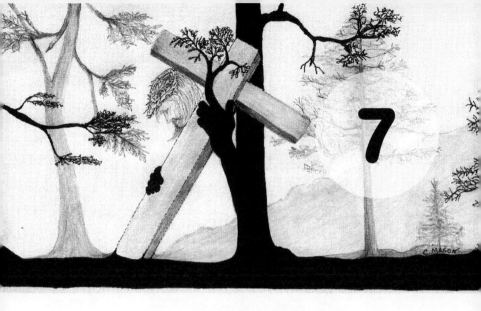

Lori's Glory Story

> A thousand may fall at your side, ten thousand at
> your right hand, but it will not come near you.
> —Psalm 91:7

I have always been shy, quiet, and introverted but never thought it a problem until I hit my awkward preteen years. I grew up in a family where my parents, brother, and sister all loved to be around people and loved to socialize. For them, they looked forward to getting in the car and going to visit people I didn't know; me, I just wanted to hide in the car.

Throughout my childhood and now as an adult, I have had and continue to have those close friendships where people have taken the time to build a relationship with me, have waited for me to open up, and have learned to love and accept me just the way I am. They are the ones who eventually see the real me. I will forever be grateful for these special friends. What is hard for me is meeting someone new and trying to make small talk, not having the time to build that relationship so that I can trust them enough to open up to them and then let them see me for who I really am. Some people are just made to socialize without that trust or relationship first—this was how it was with my family—and because I wasn't like that, I was what I would call the black sheep of the family.

My family became my definition of what *normal* was supposed to look like, and because of this, I started to believe that I was different and something was really wrong with me. I desperately needed to hear that I was loved and that I was okay just the way I was, but instead, my worst fears would soon be confirmed.

I remember it vividly. It was during a family camping trip where I had just spent the day struggling with insecurities and wishing I was able to make new friends at the campground as easily as my brother and sister. Because it didn't come easily for me, I spent the day walking around alone, feeling sorry for myself, comparing myself to them, wishing I could be just like they were.

That evening when they thought I was asleep, I overheard my parents say they wished I was more like my brother and sister. *There it was*—validation that I *was* different, that I was not okay just the way I was, and that something truly was wrong with me. Those words cut deep; if my parents thought this way about me, it must be true. (I now believe this wasn't what they meant, being a parent myself. I now think their reason for saying this was more that they felt bad for me and my struggles. No parent wants to see their child suffer. But it was not how it was taken when I didn't understand this at twelve.)

I buried my head in my pillow and cried myself to sleep. I felt so alone, misunderstood, unloved, and certainly not lovable. How could anyone possibly love someone like me?

That night changed everything for me, and because I was so young, I didn't know how to process or articulate these feelings, so I became a very hateful, angry person who started building imaginary, protective walls so that no one could get close enough and I had a place to hide from the hurt. Instead of seeking positive attention I craved from my parents, I started getting a lot of negative attention. What's ironic is, outside of my home, I was quiet, but inside, it was my mouth that got me into a lot of trouble. I never knew when to close it and was determined that I was going to have the last word. I was very defiant and sassy. I'm pretty sure I became the teenager every parent hopes not to have.

When I was growing up, we did attend the Methodist church in Candor, New York, on a regular basis, so I was raised to believe in GOD. I do remember reading Bible stories and singing "Jesus Loves Me" and "What a Friend I Have in Jesus," but I never really understood who this Jesus was and why in the world He would love someone like me and want to be my friend. If He really knew me, He wouldn't choose to love me; I was just not lovable. Either it was a lack of teaching or I just wasn't interested, but I never understood why we went to church. It just didn't make much sense to me. I don't remember learning an awful lot; it just seemed to be a place to go for my parents to socialize and another area I felt uncomfortable.

We stopped attending regularly after my mother died of leukemia when I was fifteen. I was glad to not be going to church anymore, but now I had a whole new set of problems. How does a fifteen-year-old deal with the loss of her mother when her father has pulled away due to his own grieving? Who was there to turn to? Who would understand?

I thought maybe I would have the answers to these questions if I could find a guy who would love and accept me. Relationships came and went. This journey of seeking love led me to two teen pregnancies. The first resulted in an abortion at sixteen, and with the second, I delivered a boy at just eighteen years old. Right before Ryan was born, I married his father because I thought this was the right thing to do—not because I loved him. At this point, I had no idea what love was. With so much anger and hatred toward myself, I did not know how to love myself, let alone others. We divorced after a year of marriage; I was now a single mom at nineteen. I was convinced yet again that I would never find someone because I was so unlovable.

I think this was the first time I didn't use my shyness as an excuse that my life was messed up. I came up with a new excuse: it must be because I am so fat and ugly that I can't keep a relationship. I never had a weight problem until I convinced myself that I did. This started me on a roller-coaster ride of obsessing over my body, constantly exercising and dieting, but the more I obsessed, the more weight I gained! Then I had what I thought was a brilliant idea! What if I ate all I wanted and then forced myself to throw up afterward? I could literally have my cake and eat it too (and then get rid of it later). I thought this was the solution to my gaining more weight. I was wrong! It was worse. I started gaining even more weight! I was out of control and hated myself so much. I was really good at hiding this from everyone, and when Brad and I started dating, he had no idea how deep I was in it and how much damage I was doing to myself.

Our relationship in the beginning was based solely on our similar circumstances; he had gone through a divorce and was raising a child by himself. So, after a year of dating, we decided that Ryan and I would move in with him and Miranda. We came up with so many excuses why this should be a good thing, but never once was it because we were in love. I started feeling uneasy about our decision to live together, so I suggested that maybe we should just get married; so, six months after moving in, we got married.

It had been a couple of years of my binging and purging and was getting to where I was doing this several times a day, still hiding it from everyone. Before we did renovations in our house and knocked down walls, our main floor had walls everywhere. The kitchen was enclosed, so it was easy for me to hide away in there and stuff myself with tons of food and then get rid of it all without being seen. It was there in my closed-in kitchen that my life changed dramatically a few months after we were married.

It was a day just like any other day; I had just forced myself to throw up again, but this time, after I had finished, I realized how badly I was out of control. I started crying hysterically and knew I needed help. I fell to my knees and cried out, "I can't do this anymore! Jesus, I need You!" I still wasn't sure who Jesus was. I just knew at that moment that I needed Him and He was the only one who could help me. Even though I didn't know exactly what had just happened to me, I did know that something wonderful had changed within me. I felt free and hopeful, and somehow I knew my life was headed in a different direction.

In that moment, I was healed completely of bulimia. I never had the desire or felt the need to binge or purge again. I didn't know at the time, but later I found this scripture verse that was written exactly for my conversion and healing:

> They loathed all food and drew near the gates of death then they cried to the Lord in their distress he sent forth his word and healed them; he rescued them from the grave. (Psalm 107:18-20 NIV)

Thank You, Lord Jesus, for rescuing and healing me!

In the Bible, in the book of Matthew it talks about the woman who reached out to touch Jesus's garment and was healed of a twelve-year disease. Although our diseases were different, I, too, knew that Jesus was my only hope that I needed Him—and Him only—to help me. So indirectly, by faith, I reached for his garment and received His power and was healed.

I wish I could say that every area in my life changed at that moment I was healed and cried out to Jesus, but I continued to struggle with seeing myself as GOD sees me and had many years of struggle with body image and loving myself. I still struggled to want to look like those beautiful women in the magazines who had the most perfect bodies: they were so thin and toned, they had big chests, beautifully tanned skin, hair and makeup that looked just right, nice clothes … you name it, I wanted to achieve it as well. (I know, I know, they are photoshopped and airbrushed to look that good, but I still wanted to look like that no matter the cost.) I wanted to be perfect, so I strived for it, for years. I even went so far as getting breast implants and had them for sixteen years until I started having constant itching and esophageal spasms on a regular basis. It took many doctor visits, but I finally discovered that I had Breast Implant

Illness due to foreign objects being in my body. Since I have had the implants removed, the itching and spasms are completely gone.

We started attending church as a family, and now church had a whole new meaning. It wasn't boring, and it was starting to make sense. I was learning more about who Jesus was, and the most exciting part was He wanted *me* to spend time with Him and to talk to Him as I would a friend. *Wow! Me!* He wants to spend time with *me?* Is He actually choosing me as a friend to spend time with because He finds me lovable? Were the childhood songs "Jesus loves Me" and "What a Friend We Have in Jesus" actually true? I still was not able to grasp the full meaning of Him loving me, so I still questioned it. Okay, maybe He loves me, but does He really like me? I think it's very possible to love someone but at the same time not really like them. I realized His love for the world, but I just couldn't grasp the idea or notion that if I was the only one on earth, would he still have died just for me? I found out that if you truly seek answers to your questions from GOD, in time, He will answer, and to this particular question, my answer would soon come.

The day Jesus became real to me, it seemed as though my eyes were open to how truly blessed I was to have children. Don't get me wrong. I loved Ryan and Miranda before that day, but because I didn't care at all about myself and wasn't taking care of myself, I wasn't the best I could be for them. Now the love I felt for them was overwhelming, and I wanted to do everything with them. I started to be involved in things they loved to do. They became my everything. I became very close to them and further from Brad.

All this changed for me Miranda's senior year of high school; it dawned on me that she would be leaving me soon, and although this was a good thing for her to move on, it filled me with so much sadness. She was going to leave, and then very soon after, Ryan would be leaving. What was I going to do without them? I was so involved with their lives that it seemed I didn't have a life outside of them, and I certainly didn't know what my role in life would be after they left. I lived with Brad, but I didn't really know him. I had spent years keeping him at a safe distance, hiding behind my walls. I couldn't let him get too close, because if he really knew me, he might just leave me.

It was a rocky time for us. There were many times when the word *divorce* came up and we wanted to just end it; it would be so much easier to walk away and not deal with the problems anymore. But being Christians, we knew that was not what GOD would want for us, so we decided that it would be best to see a counselor, someone who could help us sort out some of our past issues. We found a really good Christian counselor who took turns pointing his finger at each of us, forcing us to both see our problems and own up to them. It was during one of my finger-pointing sessions that I was to be given the answer to my most burning question: but does Jesus really like me? Now, I must say, I don't believe we were talking about that particular question in our session. I recall I was asking the counselor about my shyness and why I was that way. Our counselor then opened the Bible and started reading scripture that literally came alive for me. At that moment, what I thought of myself changed completely. The scriptures he read were:

> Before I formed you in the womb, I knew you, before you were born I set you apart. (Jeremiah 1:5 NIV)

> For you created my inmost being; you knit me together in my mother's womb, I praise you because I am fearfully and wonderfully made; your works are wonderful, I know that full well, My frame was not hidden from you when I was made in the secret place. When I was woven together in the depths of the earth, your eyes saw my unformed body. All the days ordained for me were written in your book before one of them came to be. (Psalm 139:13–16 NIV)

Wow! Before I was even formed in my mother's womb, He knew me. That must mean I was planned by Him before my parents even thought of me. Every single detail about me was planned—how I would look, what my personality would be, my body size, its structure, my talents, the course of my life, and how long I would live. So, if He planned every detail about me and knit me together in my mother's womb, my shyness was not a mistake. He created me this way on purpose! Words cannot express the joy and happiness I felt that day. I was walking on cloud nine (holy ground.) The only way to explain it is found in the Bible in Ephesians (3:18–19): I was able to grasp how wide and long and high and deep is the love of Christ and to know this love that surpasses knowledge. I was filled to the measure of all the fullness of GOD.

At that moment, it literally felt like He reached down from heaven and wrapped His arms around me and said, "I love you, and you are okay just the way you are." The words I craved to hear all my life! I felt the magnitude of His love and knew beyond a shadow of a doubt that He really liked me and would have died just for me. This day was pivotal and changed so much for Brad and me—because I experienced a love and acceptance so deeply I started to see myself differently. I was starting to love me. My whole outlook on myself changed dramatically, and with GOD's help, I started knocking down those imaginary walls that wouldn't let Brad get close. I realized how much I was holding back from him by not letting him get close. I love Brad deeply and know that I am a very blessed woman to have him. We didn't love each other when we got married, but now we know it was truly a match made in heaven. GOD had handpicked us for each other because he knew how in love we would be someday.

As I stated earlier, our house had walls everywhere. A good friend brought it to my attention how symbolic it was that as we started renovations to our house, knocking down walls, I was also starting to knock down walls I had built inside of me. We hadn't thought much about this before, and I don't believe in coincidences, but the first wall we knocked down was our closed-in kitchen where I had spent many a day hiding behind, and then where life truly began for me. I have learned over the years that I am not what the world calls normal, but I now know that I am loved, accepted, and cherished for who I am, and that makes being different an okay thing to be!

I don't struggle with body image like I used to. Time and maturity have changed that. I let my hair go gray, I have wrinkles, I have age spots, my skin is losing elasticity, I hardly wear any makeup, I wear glasses instead of contacts a lot of the time, my weight fluctuates ... but you know what? I am happy to finally be free to be the person GOD made me to be! I wish I could tell the younger me to stop trying to achieve perfection; it's a waste of time, and you will never find it!

I have to admit though I was really hoping that hiking the Appalachian Trail, I would lose weight and tone up, but GOD in His great wisdom didn't allow that. My journey and adventure wasn't supposed to be about that, and had I lost weight, I would be striving to achieve it every time and only walk for that purpose. He's got better plans for me than for me to focus on that.

My story ends for now, but my journey continues. I will continue to have life's struggles, but I know that I can do all things through Christ, who strengthens me to do whatever He calls me to do. And one day, on that final day He has written for me, I will return to Him, and just like in the fairy tales ... I *will* live happily ever after!

> But in real life, happily ever after is just the beginning. It's where life really starts.
> —**Kay Hooper**

> Frankly, there isn't anyone you couldn't learn to love once you've heard their story.
> —**Fred Rogers**

Hot Springs, North Carolina, to Hartford, Tennessee

> You will only observe with our eyes and see
> the punishment of the wicked.
> —Psalm 91:8

The honeymoon period is over! Our first two weeks now seem like a walk in the park compared to what we've experienced these past two weeks. It's just been plain *hard*! We both came down with colds, which sapped our energy. FROG hurt his ankle and blew out his shoe. The weather continues to be rainy, windy, and so cold (hailstorms!), and we still can't find our trail legs. We're still loving our time out here, but reality has definitely set in!

> We're loving every wonderful, horrible minute of this.
> **—Unknown**

Minnie has dropped us off at Iron Horse Station in Hot Springs to see if they have any vacancies. They sure do, and the room FROG has reserved for us has a clawfoot bathtub. It is extra to get that room but well worth the increase! He is thinking of me and the joy it will bring. He may not romance me with flowers or secret rendezvous, but bringing me to a clawfoot bathtub speaks to my heart!

We try to give Minnie money for shuttling us, but the true trail angel that she is, she refuses. Our regret is that we never got pictures of them to share with you. Our sincere thanks to you, Mickey and Minnie, wherever you are. We hope to be able to someday spread that same love and generosity to others on the trail.

Tonight, we celebrate our halfway point (we will make up some of the missing miles in a couple days) with a huge dinner and a shower and a bath. We prepare for our big day tomorrow. FROG needs new hiking shoes!

Day 35 (Tuesday, May 11)—To Be Humbled

Zero day! Don't tell FROG, but I think I hike just to have these days to enjoy!

First things first. We need to dry out our tent. Okay, although that is true, first thing is really a nice, long, hot bath! (Why I felt you needed to know this tidbit of information is beyond me! I guess because I'm dirty more than I am clean I felt this to be big important news to share with y'all. I'm finally going to smell like a clean bar of soap!) But anyway, back to the tent. It's still soaked from two nights ago. It has finally stopped raining for a while, so we can lay it outside. Hopefully it dries out before it starts raining again.

Right next door from our inn is the outfitter store, Bluff Mountain Outfitters. FROG leaps in and hops back out with a new pair of Oboz! Guess what I ended up getting while in there? A new spork! "Life is complete once again for the Hobos," she says, while holding her spork high in the air!

Because we're planning a slackpack day tomorrow to make up for some of the miles lost due to coming to Hot Springs early, we also buy a day pack that rolls up really small and weighs about three ounces. Since FROG has a defective day pack (remember, the brain of his backpack can be removed and used as a day pack, but the snaps don't work properly), we need to buy something.

We head to the post office to see if our two boxes have arrived; we are expecting one from our daughter and family and our bounce box that was sent from Nature's Inn. The box from our family has arrived, but nothing yet on our bounce box. We will need to hold off on laundry until we get that. Sorry to those around us who have to endure until then!

It's Christmas again as we open up the resupply box from our daughter and family. Nuts, peanut butter, instant potatoes, chicken packets, applesauce, brownies, protein bars, candy bars, fruit roll-ups, beef jerky, and a beautiful card of encouragement. Great resupply! We will thoroughly enjoy every bit of it! Good choices, family!

Miranda also included a memorial rock for us to place somewhere on the trail for her friend and former coworker, Deb C., who recently lost her battle with breast cancer. She had always wanted to go to the East Coast but never made it there. I will carry it with me until I find that perfect spot to place it. What a beautiful tribute to her friend!

FROG decides he is going to take his defective day pack over to the outfitter store and talk to them about how the two snaps are of different sizes, so there is no way to connect it together to carry as a day pack. He wants to see if they might have some idea how we can still use it.

Less than ten minutes later, he is back, laughing and humbled. The only thing defective is us; his backpack brain is smarter than our two brains put together. Neither one of us knew to look under a flap to pull the other snaps out that would connect the straps together so that you can use it as a day pack. Are we smarter than a fifth grader? Apparently not.

It is a good zero day; a lot was accomplished. Our tent got completely dry and aired out before it started raining again.

Doesn't matter. We are inside. Let it rain all it wants! Now, time for another big, juicy hamburger with lots of fries at the restaurant downstairs.

Day 36 (Wednesday, May 12)—Halfway Point!

FROG made plans yesterday with Jason to shuttle us to Hurricane Gap, and we'll walk back to Hot Springs, a 9.1-mile day. It is cold and pouring out—surprise, surprise! The weather has nothing on us today, as we gladly strap on our new day packs, put on our ponchos, grab our trekking poles, and head out to wait for Jason. We know that no matter how wet we get, we can come back to a warm room, a hot bath, and a comfy bed! Bring it on! (Hah! You shouldn't say what you really don't mean; the challenge was accepted, and it rained the whole time!)

Jason arrives promptly at 8:00 a.m. to take us to the trailhead. His shuttle is nice and warm, and when we arrive, it is hard for me to just jump out the way FROG does. He is ready to try out his new Oboz. This is officially our first day that both of us are wearing our Oboz, our namesake—HOBOS GOING SOBO IN THEIR OBOZ. I never had any issues with mine; we are really hoping that is the case with FROG as well.

Jason is either very polite, or it may have been that we haven't had a chance to wash our clothes yet, but he is promptly at my door to open it and let me out. I'm going with his southern charm and believe he is just very polite. A part of me wonders though, *What if I ask him if we smell? Would he be honest and tell the truth?* What would you do?

FROG is definitely going to find out how good his shoes are today as we dodge mud puddles and wet spots. It doesn't take long for our socks and shoes to be completely soaked. For some strange reason, we didn't think we would need our gloves today and already have frozen hands. Sometimes I have to wonder if we do lack brain cells. We've been out here for over a month now, and we still can't figure out it is *cold* out here! You should not feel sorry for us; we aren't helping ourselves out at all. That *hot* bath is sounding so good ... only 8.7 miles to go! Sigh.

For fun, I ask FROG what trail name he would give me if we hadn't already come up with one before we left. Without any delay in thought, out pops "Miss Privy!"

I immediately respond, loudly, "*What? Why that?*"

He says, "It's because you are always asking if we'll run into one." Oh, I guess that is true. I'm just so thankful he didn't respond that it is because I smell like one!

We have a gradual climb up to Rich Mountain Camp, which would be a great place to camp if we needed to. Not tonight, folks; we have other plans. We do make a quick stop to enjoy a wet snack on their wet benches. To just have a bench to sit on is such a bonus we can't let slip by.

The rest of our hike today will be downhill, but due to the wet terrain, we will have to watch our steps not to slip on any rocks or roots. So far, we have seen no one as we journey south. I guess we're the only crazies out here on a day like today.

We cross over many roads and streams to arrive at an old, dammed pond with stagnant water. As we walk through, it looks serene and harmless, but a recent report has some saying there are strange things happening in these parts of the woods. "Unrecognizable animal sounds and big movement happening in the brush ... something weird is going on here. Keep moving, y'all." Don't have to tell me twice as I quickly move onward!

We are starting to break out to see some views of the town of Hot Springs as we approach Lover's Leap Rock. We find this section confusing as to where the trail really goes as we gingerly make our way down over wet boulders. The view of French Broad River and surrounding mountains would be really spectacular on a day that isn't so foggy and rainy, but what we do get to see is still pretty nice.

The story we hear is Lover's Leap is named after the tragedy of a Cherokee love triangle. Mist-on-the-Mountain was the daughter of the Cherokee chief, Lone Wolf, who was chief over the Hot Springs region of the French Broad River. He had hoped that his daughter would marry a powerful Cherokee, Tall Pine, but she was in love with Magwa, a handsome visitor to her village. Tall Pine was so upset that she was in love with Magwa that he attacked and killed him on the cliffs of Lover's Leap. Mist-on-the-Mountain was so enraged and distraught by his murder that she fled from Tall Pine, who found her at Lover's Leap. It is said Magwa's spirit called to her, and she leapt to her death to be reunited with him. Soon after, a panther attacked and killed Tall Pine.

I truly hope this is not true. I look down from Lover's Leap and say, "I love you, FROG, but I am not so sure I would jump off this rock for you." That's a long way down! And it would hurt. A lot! Who knows though what you would do if you really were put in that situation. Easy to say I wouldn't now, but if it had happened … glad I don't need to find out what I would do.

The walk down along French Broad River is really nice. We see a lot of tents set up as we walk by. Many probably have been there all day and just decided to stay put. We start to see more people walking the trail headed our way; more adventure seekers coming out to brave the elements, I guess.

We have made it to the halfway point! We have gone 275 miles and have 275 left to go! By our calculations, we should finish on day 72? We will see.

Overall, so far, it's been a great adventure, and we are so glad we are on it. We have learned to hike our own hike and not worry about what someone else is doing or what they say we should be doing, how fast we are going, or how many days we take off.

Full disclosure: there were times this first half when we didn't always enjoy the journey; we complained, we whined, we argued, and it was really difficult. We were just wanting the journey to be over, to just be at our destination. I think that is so representative of how life is. When we are going through trials and hard times, we just want it to end, but instead, we may miss what there is for us to learn each step we take as we venture on this journey. You will reach that destination, but take the time to learn and grow from the obstacles that are in your path.

HOBOS GOING SOBO IN THEIR OBOZ and we never looked back ...

> Hiking is a bit like life: The journey only requires you to put one foot in front of the other ... again and again and again. And if you allow yourself to be present throughout the entirety of the trek, you will witness beauty at every step of the way, not just at the summit.
> —Unknown

Day 37 (Thursday, May 13)—Hot Mineral Springs Bath

The Smoky Mountain Diner is the place to eat! The AT goes right through town, and the diner is just a few steps off the trail. We've eaten here a few times since we've arrived and would say it is definitely as good as the diner in Damascus. We will be telling all our hiker friends to stop here as well. When you first walk in the diner, there is a mural on the wall of different sections on the AT. It brings tears to my eyes to see the end, what will be our end anyway, and know that if all goes well, in 275 miles, we will be standing in that archway of the Approach Trail at Amicalola Falls State Park. We are so filled with emotion and excitement that one of us spills our drink. My trail name for him if he hadn't already had one would be Klutz.

We received our bounce box yesterday, so today is laundry day! You can bet everyone around us is as glad as we are for this big event! The place where we are staying even offered to do it for us. Such southern hospitality!

As we're finishing up last-minute errands, we see a sign in the window at the gas station "OUT OF GAS." Since we've been on the trail, we really aren't up on the latest news, so we inquire. Someone has hacked into the Colonial pipeline and shut it down and is asking for a ransom to open it back up. Confirms to us that we really are not missing what is happening in the news. Although we are sorry that this small town is suffering because of it.

We mail our bounce box to Gatlinburg, Tennessee, get our

backpacking permits for the Smoky Mountains (we will be there in three days), buy a lift for FROG's shoes (he loves his Oboz, but one of the shoes will fit better with a slight lift so it doesn't rub his big, knobby heel), and now—when in Hot Springs, do what the Hot Springers do—get a mineral bath!

Off we go!

I have been waiting for this day since we arrived. We signed up two days ago and knew this would be a good way to finish our stay here. We were told to bring our swimsuits, but I ask you, what is a hiker to do when they don't have a swimsuit to use? We are assuming it will be well enclosed and private where they take us, so it shouldn't be a problem wearing our birthday suits since that is all we brought with us. I guess you should never assume.

As they take us down to our building that holds the hot tub, it looks as though it will be enclosed, private, and quiet. As we round the corner and enter, it is open in the front with a beautiful setting and view of the river, so it's not enclosed, but at least we get to enjoy the view as we soak.

We are told that we have five minutes to change (won't take us that long) and get into the tub, and then we have an hour to soak. Five minutes before the hour is up, you get a warning bell, and then immediately after those five minutes, the water will start draining out. Okay, let's do this!

As we climb into the tub with our birthday suits on, what to our horror do we see? A road just across the river that has cars periodically going by. Then my husband casually says, "What would stop a teenage boy from standing over there with his binoculars?" Tell me, how is a woman supposed to just sit back and relax after a comment like that? Not only do we get to enjoy the view, someone else may also get to enjoy the view as well!

We had a great four days in Hot Springs. It just might be pretty difficult to leave this place tomorrow. Maybe I can convince Brad we need to take a ZEEK!

HOBOS GOING SOBO IN THEIR OBOZ and we never looked back ...

Our Support Team:

Lori, keep a towel handy for those spa days. Sandy L.

Just do your happy dance and jump in!! My kind of hiking. Love your travelogue!! Claude M.

Love hearing about each and every stop and adventure along the way. Especially the hot tub escapade. You both look pretty lean and fit! Bev G.

I bet this felt AWESOME!!!! Denise A.

I would soak forever!! Tracy M.

I love your journal and photos! Enjoy that mineral soak. Once you are in the tub, there's only your smiling face to see, even with binoculars. What a lovely setting. Penny C.

Day 38 (Friday, May 14)

We leave Iron Horse Station at 8:30 a.m. and take our first step together to signify the start of the second half. We are officially on the flip side.

The weather is cool but *no* rain! This is a huge plus. We walk in silence through Hot Springs and silently say our last goodbyes and recount the time we have spent here. I couldn't convince FROG to stay any longer, but in all honesty, I didn't try very hard. We are both ready to get back on the trail.

It is an easy stroll through town, and once we hit the outskirts, we see the turn we need to take that will lead us deep into the woods once again. We pass a huge rock that is a welcome sight to those arriving to Hot Springs (for us, it is our goodbye). It has a plaque on it: "The Golden Anniversary Celebration Appalachian Trail 1937–1987—Carolina Mountain Club. A beautiful tribute by the local trail crew in honor of the AT's fifty-year existence. We wonder how many people during those fifty years have passed by this exact spot we're standing at.

It is impossible to know that exact figure since not everyone does a thru-hike and many only do small day hikes or small sections, but I was able to do a bit of research on some facts. More than two thousand hikers attempt to do a thru-hike yearly, but only one out of four actually completes it. Since 1936, more than twenty thousand thru-hikers have been recorded by the Appalachian Trail Conservatory as completing the entire 2,190-mile trek. As far as day hikes or short backpacking trips, it is estimated that three million people hike a portion of the trail each year. Interesting facts.

Well, guess what we've run into again, in the middle of nowhere. Gravesites! I wonder if anyone is keeping track of how many we've seen so far. All I know is it's been a lot, which is pretty concerning, to say the least. These are the gravesites of husband and wife, George and Eva Gragg. Eva passed first in 1940, so there is handmade a gravestone (presumably carved by George) for her that reads, "Eva Gragg, Oct 8, 1882–Nov 3, 1940, Absent but not Dead." Hmmm … now I really do feel concerned. Of course, this conjures up a bunch of questions. Did she just up and leave him, and he can't find her? Is her spirit just floating around up here, or is she absent from here but alive in heaven? Maybe he meant to say, "Gone but not forgotten." His choice of words is a good conversation piece, and maybe that was what he was going for. With his passing, a modern tombstone was put in with his name, "George W. Gragg, Feb 29, 1881–May 12, 1966. Departed but not forgotten." I'll bet that is what he meant to say.

As we move onward, we start our climb up. As you recall, that is the way it is out of every town, up and more up. We have mentally prepared for it, but physically, it is hard. It is an increase in elevation of 3,300 feet, so you understand the climb. We are thankful for switchbacks and distractions.

We hear our distraction before we actually see them—so much excited chatter and laughter headed our way. It's a large group of older men out for a section hike this weekend. They are on their way to Hot Springs and then will continue on north. They notice I have Crocs attached to my backpack and are upset with themselves that they didn't think about bringing extra footwear. They didn't think about the fact that after you've walked eight to ten hours a day, your feet need a break from the hiking shoes. I am thankful that FROG did his research and we came prepared. I can't imagine not having them to put on at the end of the day. I gather they must not be seasoned hikers, because whenever you stop at a shelter for the night or are in town, you can tell the hikers. Everyone is wearing Crocs, of all different colors, so the email has gone out; they just must have missed it. Regardless, they are a fun bunch, and they will figure out something. There is always the Dollar General in Hot Springs if need be. Don't forget to stop at the diner!

As we continue up, we see the most beautiful flowering bush we have seen yet on this trail. It is a bright orange flower. We don't know a lot about different flowers, but we do think it is in the family of the azalea. We will have to find out. It's absolutely stunning! We tell the NOBOs we see to make sure they look for it—and to stop at the diner. The diner is already on everyone's radar. They can't wait!

We meet another NOBO on the trail, bending down and taking pictures of a flower. We have seen these blossoms before but aren't sure what they are. He tells us it is called a Lady Slipper, an orchid. He is from Minnesota, and this is their state flower. It's beautiful and very unusual. We tell him about the flowering bush we saw and show him a picture since he seems knowledgeable about flowers. He also believes it is an azalea of some type but is not sure.

The top of Bluff Mountain is a PUD! There is no view unless you call a pile of rocks a nice view. We stop to rest at the top and look forward to the journey downhill until we rest for the night.

I feel the stone in my pocket that I am carrying that Miranda made in memory of her friend. I still have not found just the right spot to lay it. Maybe something will speak to me tomorrow. In the meantime, Deb C.'s memory travels along with us as we walk through the woods of North Carolina.

We can't quite make it to Walnut Mountain Shelter and stop just before at Kale Gap, which ends up being a 12.5-mile day for us. Not too bad for taking some time off. I guess we didn't get too soft from our mineral bath!

Day 39 (Saturday, May 15)—Max Patch

The sun is poking through the trees and is hitting the top of our tent. The birds are chirping and singing their morning songs. It's time to rise and shine. By all accounts, it looks as though today is going to be a glorious day of sunshine. It was a dry night, so no packing up a wet tent. *That* is a welcome treat that we haven't had in quite some time. With the memorial rock securely in my pocket, we head out to seize the day.

Walnut Mountain Shelter is only 0.8 mile away, so we feel there really is no reason to stop since we just started out; besides, report is it's been taken over by bees. We'll just keep buzzing along …

There will not be a shortage today of water sources. We are to pass thirteen available spots, all within a short distance from each other. A lot have footbridges, some you need to cross over on foot. After we cross Lemon Gap Road (saw no evidence of lemons anywhere), we run into two guys filling up at one of the streams. They have just left Max Patch this morning after camping on top of the mountain. The sunset picture they took is one of the most beautiful sunsets I have ever seen. There is a whole clan in the picture, all whooping it up, looking like they had a wonderful night of partying together. They mention if it works out for us, we should plan to stay tonight on top of the mountain. It's only about five miles away. I'm not so sure we will be ready to stop then, but we'll see. We've heard a lot about Max Patch and the views. We can hardly wait!

Unfortunately, it's easy to get disoriented and start walking the wrong direction on the trail if you stop to take a break. We are so excited to have someone come up behind us who is walking SOBO like we are (since we haven't run into anyone yet going south.) "Oh, you're walking SOBO too?" we ask her. A blank stare. "No, I am walking NOBO," she replies. We hate telling her she is walking the wrong way, which means she isn't as excited to see us as we are to see her. She doesn't get mad or upset, just laughs, turns around, and heads back the way she came. Poor thing. I wonder how long she has been walking in the wrong direction. Good thing we were there, or she could still be going in the wrong direction!

As we pass a small stream and round the corner to head away from the stream, I can't help but stop and turn around and look back at that spot again. Something tells me to go back. I tell FROG to stop, we need to go back. Yep, this is the spot to place Deb C.'s memorial rock to rest. It is a beautiful spot under a flowering purple bush, next to a bubbling stream at the base of a mountain. Now her memory lives on in the mountains of North Carolina by a peaceful stream and beautiful flowers.

Lunch stop at Roaring Fork Shelter. The walk so far today has been favorable with pleasant temperatures. Not too cool but not too warm either. It's a Goldilocks kind of day—just right. We're still two miles away from Max Patch, so we know we're headed for some uphill. Good to take a little extra time to rest up. We kind of think our excitement to see what all the fuss is about will negate the challenges the climb might make.

"Do you like butter?" FROG plays my childhood game with me by putting a buttercup flower under his chin to see if the under part of his chin turns yellow. It does, but I recognize his need to shave more than I do the color. He doesn't plan to shave until we finish the trail. I will have me a modern-day Grizzly Adams (minus the grizzly bear companion! I've shaved!).

After a stroll through a rhododendron tunnel path, we turn the corner to start heading up the mountain, doing some switchbacks to get there. We are starting to see views of the top of Max Patch, which is less than a mile away now. Off to the left side of the trail, we see a rarity. I know it is a rarity because our friend we met yesterday said it was and to look out for it. And maybe because I want to believe he was telling us the truth. We come upon the Lady Slipper flower again, but what makes it rare is there are two white ones standing by themselves, and then below them are more pink ones. My understanding is that it is rare to see white ones. I wonder how many people have walked by here and not even noticed them. Thankfully, we aren't one of them.

We're starting to run into a lot of people now. This part of the trail is really busy with hikers. It is one of the most popular peaks in the southern part of the trail. The majority are not backpackers, more like those who are out for just a day hike—you know, the ones who smell really nice. We have no idea what to expect, so when we reach the very top, we are surprised to see tents set up all around and people everywhere. But what really takes our breath away is the stunning 360-degree panoramic views all around us of the Bald, Unaka, and Smoky Mountains of North Carolina and Tennessee. I try to capture it on video, but I know I can't do it justice; it really is something you have to add to your bucket list and see for yourself. And the bright side of that is you don't have to walk the AT to enjoy it. There is a nearby parking lot that allows you to drive here, park, and take a short walk up the mountain to enjoy it for yourself.

HOBOS GOING SOBO IN THEIR OBOZ and we never looked back ...

Max Patch

There are kids and families all around, enjoying the views, playing Frisbee, playing ball, and picnicking. FROG is curious about camping here, so he asks a couple who are in the process of taking down their tent and getting ready to leave. They have enjoyed a couple nights here and say that the sunsets and sunrises are spectacular, but the nights are freezing. I've had enough cold nights, so I am not interested in another one if I can help it. We won't stay the night, but we hunker down and sit against our backpacks to enjoy the view before we head below the mountain, where it's not so windy.

Word on the mountain is to watch out for the raccoons! Seems we have some kleptomaniacs on the loose! A group of hikers had some food stolen, and two of the hikers each had one of their boots stolen. They report, "If you see a raccoon with two different hiking boots on, they are the enemy!"

Update on Max Patch: As of July 1, 2021, the Forest Service's Appalachian Ranger District announced a two-year ban on camping in the area. Due to garbage and human waste strewn all over, they have implemented strict restrictions at the summit.

It's really unfortunate that it's come to this. It can't be humans who have done this; it must be those rascal raccoons that are walking around with hiking boots on, causing all the problems!

We hesitantly decide it's time to move on. We are in need of water, and we know just down below we will come to some. As we are descending from the summit, a sparrow lands right next to us on the pole as a reminder that our Lord is with us and will take care of our every need. Luke 12:7 says, "Indeed, the very hairs on your head are all numbered. Don't be afraid; you are worth more than many sparrows." As we take one last look around, we can't help but thank GOD for all He made for us to enjoy.

> Commit your path to GOD, knowing that if he cares for the sparrows, He will care for you. You don't have to have the whole road map ahead of time as long as you trust that GOD does.
> **—Unknown**

Stopping at the next water source allows us time to talk to fellow hikers who have recently come from the Smokies. This is our first time hearing that the first shelter we will stay in (Cosby Shelter), in the Smoky Mountains, is closed due to excessive bear activity. We are hoping that by the time we get there, it will have reopened and the bears will have moved on. They had not encountered any bears, but they know of people who had. I am not fearful but of course am hoping we are the ones who don't encounter any.

As we continue our journey to find a place to camp for the night, I ask FROG if he thinks we'll see any bears in the Smokies. "No, there won't be any," he says.

I laugh and reply, "Just like there weren't any in the Blue Ridge Mountains when we hiked there?" He laughs, knowing what I'm referring to.

Soon after we were married, we took a trip to the Blue Ridge

Parkway and hiked through the mountains. I was worried that we'd run into a bear and asked him if we'd see one. "No, there won't be any," he says. "Don't worry." Not knowing any better, I believe him because he's the experienced hiker, and if he says we won't, then he must know. He is leading, as is our custom; he sets the pace. All of a sudden, he stops quickly, turns around, pushes me out of the way, and continues to push me until I am behind him, and he heads in the direction we just came. All the while, he keeps saying, "There is a bear." I look up and see the tail end of a bear headed in the other direction to get away from us. My husband who is supposed to be protecting me just pushed me *toward the bear*! I am thankful the bear is headed the other way, but he just pushed me *toward the bear*! He was going to let the bear go after me; he had no idea that the bear had skedaddled the other way. He was too busy getting himself away to know. I have *never* let him forget this story. So now when he says, "No, there won't be any," I don't fall for that again; I will most likely be seeing one. (FROG says this has become a "fish tale" story, and he has a slightly different version of this episode. I am right.)

We are really tired now and ready to find a campsite. We've walked another 2.7 miles, making it a 10.5-mile day. So, when we arrive at Brown's Gap, we are ready to put the tent up and call it a night.

*If a bear is chasing you, does that mean you
are running with a bare behind?*

Day 40 (Sunday, May 16)—Snowbird Peak

Our plans today will be to walk 13.6 miles and stop just outside Smoky Mountain National Park entrance at Davenport Gap. We will put our permit in the box, and tomorrow we will officially start our trek through the Smokies. We are so close now to the area that we had worried about going through during bad weather. Looking ahead on the weather forecast for the next six days, it looks like the weather is going to be pretty good for us—no snow or cold temperatures.

We heard so many stories from NOBO hikers about their

experiences while in the Smokies of waking up to frozen socks and boots and trying to put them on in the morning. Some forgot to sleep with their water filter or cell phone and woke up to a frozen filter or phone that had been exposed to the extreme cold, and now they couldn't use it. We hadn't known that it was possible to have your filter or phone freeze, so nights that were cold for us, we made sure we slept with them, just in case. It was a good tip and something we didn't want to experience since we relied heavily on both.

It's a warm sunny day, and the fields are colorful, with different arrays of color as we traipse through and up, climbing to an elevation of 4,257 feet. It seems an endless walk today, 5.5 miles to reach Snowbird Peak. This is one of those journeys that you just want the destination to arrive much sooner than it does. It seems to be a never-ending story. Going on and on and on and never comes to an end. Apparently, this is the route our parents took to school every day, there and back, uphill both ways. Now I understand their pain.

> When everything seems like an uphill struggle.
> Just think of the view at the top.
> **—Unknown**

And the view is spectacular! To look at the surrounding mountains and landscape before us is worth the struggle! Just beyond that on a grassy bald is an alien-looking building, an active communications facility.

> The strange looking communication unit sitting on top of this peak is actually called a VOR (which stands for very high frequency, Omni-directional range.) It's used for aviation navigation. It sends out two independent frequencies. One frequency will display this particular facility and the other frequency displays which radial an aircraft is from the station.

> Additionally, most of these facilities have DME associated with them which stands for "distance measuring equipment." DME allows pilots to know how far they are from the station. Comment on Guthook by a hiker going by trail name, PraiseTeam

We decide this is a good place, next to the communications facility, to take a break and eat our lunch. As we're resting on the ground, in comes a four-wheeler. Two gentlemen jump off and leave it just sitting there, right in front of us. Hmmm … our getaway vehicle! "You distract them while I throw the packs in. Then you run and jump in. Let's get outta here!" We kid with the driver how tempting it would be to just take off with it. He says, "Good luck," as he dangles the keys from his hand. The word is out on us tired hikers! Well, I guess we have to continue walking; no free rides for us today.

As we're leaving, there is a huge AT sign along the trail. "Just stand there, Faith, so that I can get your picture." It is not made for short people, so I stretch as tall as I can, standing on my tiptoes to put my face in the big A. FROG doesn't do anything quick, so my expression is of pain as I hold my stance waiting for him to take the picture. "Smile pretty," he says.

"This *is* pretty!" I say as I grit my teeth and scrunch my face.

As we're a couple miles down in elevation, we hear, "Have we got good news for you!" coming from in front of us. There is a couple headed our way with big smiles on their faces. We are all for good news. "What's that?" FROG asks.

"Your journey is all downhill for the next three miles." That is good news, but unfortunately, we don't have good news to share with them. Their next two miles will be all uphill. We felt the struggle when we were walking on the other side; it was really a rough walk, so we know exactly what they're feeling. At least she is trying to be pleasant about it and knows eventually she will reach the top as well. We tell her once you come to the AT sign, you are almost there. She is so excited because she knows once they reach the top, she is done for the day. They are going to camp at the peak near the communications facility.

We feel the effects of the hard walk this morning and start to think that maybe we aren't going to make it as far as we thought today. We are seeing more of those beautiful orange blossomed bushes that adds excitement to our walk, but we both admit we are just not having fun. If we're not having fun, we need to stop. Our plans at this point have changed; once we hit Green Corner Road, we will find the Standing Bear Hostel and see if they have room for us to stay there tonight.

Our original plans were to stay at Standing Bear Hostel and to also have a resupply box sent there to help supply what we would need for the Smokies, until we could reach Gatlinburg. We heard such negative comments about staying there that we had changed our plans and told Sheila to hold the box and give it to us when we see them in Gatlinburg.

Once we reach Green Corner Road, there are no signs for which direction we are supposed to head for the hostel. (Again, it was labeled for the NOBO and not the SOBO.) It's either right or left. We choose left. About a quarter of a mile down the road, there is finally a vehicle coming up behind us, so FROG flags him down. "Could you tell us where Standing Bear Hostel is?" He points behind him and indicates we are walking the wrong way, and it's about 0.3 mile the other way. Not music to our ears! We are beyond exhausted and now mad at ourselves for going the wrong way. It doesn't make us too happy with each other at this point. Best just to walk in silence. I am so tired and frustrated I don't even try to get the last word in this time. We are both silently upset.

When we approach Standing Bear, we are pleased to see a staff member sitting out front and seems to be waiting for people to arrive, so we don't have to try to figure out where to go. It is a nice, inviting place. Maybe some of the negative reviews were just people being picky and it's not so bad here. There is room in the bunkhouse; the private rooms in the tree house are filled up. I am disappointed, but at least there is space available where we can lay our heads tonight. And they have a shower! Only one, but it will be worth the wait in line.

We pick our bunks; they are side by side, so each of us will have a bunk mate above us this evening. We get ourselves set up for the evening, take our shower, and decide to sit around the campfire to get to know some of the others who will be staying here tonight with us. Most are young, but there do seem to be others more our age. This is a popular, iconic hostel, so many try to plan a stop here on their way through.

They have come around asking who would like to participate in the cheese enchilada meal that they are making for the guests tonight. Sounds pretty yummy to us, so we sign up. Will be twelve dollars a plate, but if we don't have to cook it, we're in! It is nothing compared to our thirteen-dollar breakfast we had at Mountain Harbour, but it is good. Two enchiladas with a lot of rice, with a tiny lettuce salad next to it with sour cream. It hits the spot.

Sitting around the campfire, we hear from those just coming from the Smokies that Cosby Shelter is still closed. They have ridge runners who make sure you are staying in the shelters or near the shelter each night while in the Smokies. Since this one is closed, we don't know how strict they will be if we camp in an undesignated spot. We decide we need to come up with a plan B.

It's okay if you have to go with plan B. This week is supposed to be a big week for us: the start of backpacking in Great Smoky Mountains National Park! We are all set with a permit and know that we are required to only sleep in the shelters while traveling through the park. What we haven't planned for is a shelter being closed down due to heavy bear activity. What this means for us, going south, we will have to go fifteen miles to reach the next shelter, Tri-Corner Knob, and over half of that is a steep climb to get there. As you know, our trail legs have yet to be found, so there is just no way we can possibly do this. The change we feel we have to make is to eliminate those miles and start hiking from the only other accessible road into the park, which is about thirty miles south from where we would have originally started. I think things like this happen for a reason and believe in divine intervention. It's possible we are being saved from potential harm or we just need to be somewhere sooner than originally planned—learning to FROG, fully rely on GOD.

Hannah, a solo hiker who recently got hurt on the trail, is sitting around the campfire and has just decided with the help of her husband to get off the trail and head home to recover. She will be taking a shuttle in a couple days into Gatlinburg and then will get a shuttle to the nearest airport. We ask her if we can join her in her shuttle into Gatlinburg. It won't be until Tuesday morning at eight o'clock, but that works out perfectly; we can slackpack on Monday into Davenport Gap, put our permit in the box, walk back, and be ready on Tuesday to head out.

With those arrangements made, we head to the bunkhouse to get ready for bed. FROG notices a scale, so he excitedly steps on it. He's lost sixteen pounds. I *refuse* to step on it and head to my bed. I don't want to know!

This is where our view of Standing Bear changes. As we're lying in bed, we hear the conversation going on just outside the bunkhouse. It seems to be a one-upmanship between some people on what drug they are on and how much they take. It centers mostly on mushrooms and the drugs they are able to get right there at the hostel. I am disappointed that I am a part of this and feel so sorry for those who feel they need drugs to enjoy this hike. I think the hike itself is a high. I certainly don't understand the need to go outside yourself and not be present with the spiritual experience you can have naturally. I know they are on a journey to find happiness and meaning. I pray they find *Who* I know they are searching for.

It saddens both of us that this place promotes that type of lifestyle and benefits from it. If we could have left tomorrow, I would not have argued. And to top it off, my bunk mate is strange. I mean *strange*. It took him forever to get in his bunk above me, and I caught him staring at me for a long time. Oh, Lord, help me! It took me a really long time to fall asleep. I was too afraid. Not sure why I didn't crawl over there with FROG. I should have! (Found out the next day he was just as uncomfortable as I was. But as far as he knew, he didn't have a man staring at him, so at least he didn't have that to be uncomfortable about.)

Day 41 (Monday, May 17)–We're Official!

We found the staff member that checked us in yesterday to let her know we need to stay one more night and to ask if there is any room to stay in the tree house for the night. The thought of spending another night in the bunkhouse is not appealing in the least, but if we have to, we don't have any other choice. Fortunately, there is a room available, so at least we have a night where we will not know what is going on and will be off by ourselves in seclusion.

Today is a short slackpack day to Davenport Gap to drop off our permits in the box just before the Smokies. Even though we will miss the first thirty miles, we still need to deposit our permit and let them know we will be in the Smoky Mountains and that we have paid our fee to overnight there.

It is a nice day for a short walk. It will only be 5.2 miles round-trip, so we take our time and don't feel rushed at all. We need to find a spot that has great Verizon reception to call Sheila and let her know of our new plans and that we will be in Gatlinburg sooner than originally planned. We had talked to her before we headed out on the AT about meeting us in Gatlinburg when we got this far. At the time, it seemed so far away, but it is here already. Time flies when you're having fun! Newsflash: it flies even if you're not having fun! Time just flies!

We will arrive in Gatlinburg on Tuesday, but they aren't able to meet up with us until Thursday due to previous plans. That works out perfectly for us; we will plan to slackpack the day before they get there and walk some of the trail. Then we will visit with them for a couple days before we head back out on the trail. It will be so good to see family and have some down time to enjoy with them.

As we head down to Interstate 40, we have to take a long stone staircase to get there. It's a little tricky going down, and I am thankful for the railing and no heavy packs on our back. Normally we would only be going one way and not have to worry about these steps again, but since we are traveling round-trip today, we will have the challenge of climbing them on our return to Standing Bear Hostel.

We cross Pigeon River Bridge, and off to the side of the road is a van with two people sitting there. I don't really think too much about it and am not really looking for it to be trail magic, which is a good thing. It isn't—at least it isn't for us. It is a van that is waiting for a group of ladies who are supposed to be coming out of the woods today. They had met them a week ago and were waiting to surprise them with food and resupply so they could continue their journey with enough food. What a wonderful surprise for them—their own personal trail angels! (We never did see this group of ladies. Not sure if they got sidetracked or met up with those infamous bears at Cosby Shelter, but they didn't come out of the woods that day. She said she was going to just camp there and wait to see if they came out tomorrow. I hope she's not still waiting.)

We make it to the box to drop our permit and turn around to head back the same way we came. We will spend our last night at Standing Bear Hostel, hiding in the tree house, away from the drugs and staring eyes, and will sleep peacefully knowing we are officially ready to hike in the Great Smoky Mountain National Park.

**Campers in sleeping bags are like soft tacos in the bear world.
(Thanks Dan & Dorothy)**

HOBOS GOING SOBO IN THEIR OBOZ and we never looked back ...

Our Support Team:

Congrats on half way! Cathy L.

You got this! Love your pictures, determination, spirit, and grit! Shelby S.

Amazing journey!! Thank you for keeping us posted & a few laughs. Can't wait to hear the rest of the story. Elaine F.

I LOVE IT AND LOVE YOU TWO! I can't believe you are almost done!! We will miss your stories. Maybe you should continue on so we can continue to be entertained?? Lol! Tracy M.

You two are so amazing. I am loving your stories and updates; makes me feel like I am on the trail with you but not doing all the hard work; missing the incredible views and got the easy part of this journey by just loving and supporting you with prayer. On the home stretch now kiddos! Wow! What a celebration that will be. So proud and happy for you! Bev G.

Truly fabulous adventure! Tammy T.

Thanks for the update! Coleen B.

Love your photos, stories and abilities! Yes, you two are amazing! God bless you as you finish your journey!! Linda R.

What an amazing journey! Those heights and sights and all the miles you are killing! That lush vegetation is beautiful! Anja T.

Dear HOBOS, going SOBO in your OBOZ ... you are my INSPOS. Thank you for sharing your journey! I think you need to write a book of your adventures, mis-adventures, and thoughts along the way!! Linda H.

> Your time is limited, so don't waste it living someone else's life.
> —Steve Jobs

Gatlinburg, Tennessee: Newfound Gap to Clingman's Dome

> If you make the Most High your dwelling—
> even the LORD, who is my refuge.
> —Psalm 91:9

Day 42 (Tuesday, May 18)—Culture Shock

Our morning doesn't start out as we had hoped. We wait with Hannah for our 8:00 a.m. shuttle ride only to find out our shuttle driver has gone to the wrong place and will not be coming to get us. Plan B has now become plan C.

    FROG does some quick thinking to come up with a new plan and asks the owner of Standing Bear Hostel if they know of anyone who can shuttle three people to Gatlinburg. She does some searching and is able to find Mike, who will take us, but it will be at least another half hour until he can get here to take us. We are fine with that; we don't have any plans to go anywhere, and Hannah can only hobble, so she's not going anywhere. We'll just sit right here on this here front porch and wait.

The hostel has a lot of action in and out, all day, all the time. It is interesting watching people come and go. It isn't one of our favorite hostels, but for the most part, they did take care of us and served our needs. I may not agree with their practices, but GOD did use them to provide a place for us to stay for two nights when we most needed it. (They did redeem themselves with finding us a shuttle at such short notice and for their comfortable bed in the tree house! Ended up being the most comfortable of all the beds we stayed in.)

Mike arrives but seems confused with just what he is doing here or who he's picking up. Oh boy ... we're off to a good start! We work out the details and give him the agreed-upon money, and hopefully we are headed to Gatlinburg.

It is normally a thirty-minute drive, but our driver, who I am renaming "Jeff Gordon," drives like he is in the Indy 500, so we arrive there in record time, *and* he drove with all the windows wide open. Let me just tell you, it isn't warm enough to have all the windows wide open! Of course, you start to wonder if we smell really bad and he is just in a hurry to get rid of us!

Our smelling bad is confirmed when we check into our hotel in Gatlinburg. The front desk clerk says it is too early to check in, that our room isn't ready yet; we'll have to wait to get into our room later in the day. The manager quickly appears and whispers something to her—and waala! Our room is ready! I guess smelling bad does have its advantages!

It has been forty-two days of living on the trail, so when we first arrive in Gatlinburg, what a huge culture shock! There are people everywhere. It is so busy, and everyone seems to be in such a hurry. I have to admit, at first we are uncomfortable and feel so out of place after living so long in seclusion. It does take us a couple days to adjust back into society, settle in, and enjoy our time.

I would advise not sending a resupply box to Gatlinburg post office (which is about three miles outside the downtown congestion) if you don't have a vehicle to go and pick it up. We take the trolley, which I might add is confusing! You have to figure out what color trolley you need to be on and then what direction you need to go.

We have the color right but the direction wrong and end up riding all over the city until we finally get there ... forty-five minutes later! It didn't cost us anything but our time, so it really is a good way to see the city.

Is there still a coin shortage going on? We check three places to get quarters to do our laundry, and each place says they don't have any coins. At the last place, all I can figure is he feels so sorry for this homeless couple carrying all the smelly clothes they own in a grocery bag because he magically comes up with quarters to give us, even though he said he didn't have any. Again, smell has its advantages!

What is all the fuss about pancakes? There is a pancake house on every block, and the lines are very long to get in. I mean I like pancakes and all, but waiting hours to get in to get some? I don't think so. Same thing for moonshine—long lines and on every corner. I guess I can kind of understand about the moonshine since it's something unique to the area, but pancakes?

We are ignored! We go into one of the Mexican restaurants for dinner on the strip, get a seat, get some chips and salsa—and then *nothing*! Eating salty chips really makes one thirsty, so after twenty minutes, I designate FROG to go and inquire, and no one knows who is supposed to be helping us, so we ask how much for the chips (which are free) and leave. If I wanted to wait a long time, I would have stood in line for pancakes! And just a sidenote because I'm sure you're wondering: we had showered, but now I wonder if we would have gotten service if we had smelled—just to get us out of there!

Day 43 (Wednesday, May 19)–Highest Point on the AT

We had walked yesterday to Nantahala Outdoor Center (NOC) to see if they could help us with shuttle names since we were hoping to slackpack today from Clingman's Dome back to Newfound Gap, 7.7 miles. Since we have another day before our cousins arrive, we thought it a perfect opportunity to get some miles in.

They did provide a big list of names, but the only one who returned our call was Mike. Oh no, not another Mike! But I'm happy to report this Mike drove responsibly and not like a madman at all! And he is a hoot! FROG and Mike are two peas in a pod! They joked back and forth and were quite entertaining.

He said he would drop us off at Clingman's Dome and would wait at Newfound Gap for us to return. We are his priority, but if a job arose while he was there, he would make sure that it would work out with our schedule. We tell him we're not fast hikers, so definitely do what works out for him.

Both Clingman's Dome and Newfound Gap are always busy with tourists, so by the time we arrive at 9:30 a.m., the parking lot is already abuzz with people and cars everywhere. It is a long walk up to the dome but an enjoyable one as we meet up with "Vegas"; he is taking two weeks off from work to see some sights on the East Coast and is hoping he will get a good view from the top once we get there. It is the highest point on the AT at 6,612 feet and has a large observation tower at the top that provides great views if you're fortunate enough to see the mountains.

We are not. It is very foggy when we arrive, so distant views are not to be enjoyed this morning. We aren't totally disappointed because in 2019 we had been here and had fantastic views of the surrounding mountains. We know what we are missing but feel bad for Vegas that he doesn't get to experience such beauty his first time.

We wish him the best in his adventures, and then we take off as NOBOs for the day. As I mentioned, this is a very busy section of the AT with tourists, so we expect that a lot of people will be on the trail today. And there are. I spend a lot of time looking over my shoulder to make sure we stay out of people's way and let them pass. But we have a first: we pass another couple! Do I have to mention that she is walking with a limp and he is a gentleman for walking her pace? Okay, I won't mention that. We passed some people, and they never caught back up to us! Yay for us! We're so fast! (Hah! That never happened again!)

One of our passer-byers, we will call him "Old School" (he is carrying a backpack with an external frame and an old-style aluminum folding chair that our parents/grandparents had back in the day), is out walking with his son-in-law. We take turns passing each other, but the only reason we ever pass them is because they stop to take periodic breaks. Old School would stop and take his folding chair off his pack and just sit right along the trail. I know FROG is jealous of that chair! That was one thing I had asked him a while back, what he missed the most out here, and his reply was immediate, a chair with a back. Me, I miss clothes and shoes ... different choices of clothes and shoes. I am tired of the same two outfits and shoes. I hope someday to have a campfire and burn these clothes and never see them again.

Passing over Mount Collins, there is a slight view. It's still quite foggy out, so not much to really enjoy. There seem to be side trails throughout, but we focus on only the white blazed trail; no side or spur trails for us. We don't even stop at Mt. Collins Shelter for a break. We are so thrilled that we are in the Smoky Mountains, and it's a beautiful warm day. Quite a difference from the weather reports we've heard from those who have already passed through here. Now, we are just praying we don't see any bears while we're hiking through here next week!

Mike has notified us that he had some business and took some people into Gatlinburg but is now back at his post at Newfound Gap, waiting for us with Brett, another hiker who is going to wait patiently for our return so he can also be shuttled back into town.

After crossing over wire fences that are put there to keep wild boars out, we eventually make it to the parking lot at Newfound Gap. It is here, two years ago, that I told FROG to walk along the path of the AT because this was going to be his only chance to do so. "Wait a sec, Mike. We need to take a picture of us standing here at the North Carolina / Tennessee state line. This spot is pretty momentous."

HOBOS GOING SOBO IN THEIR OBOZ and we never looked back ...

Tennessee / North Carolina State Line

Our ride back to Gatlinburg is just as fun as our ride here. Mike is full of adventure and stories to keep us in stitches. Now we have Brett to share in the fun. He is a young, twenty-something hiker who is looking to take a day off to spend in town to get a good night's sleep, a shower, resupply, and a good-sized meal. We understand totally! We recently learned that if you go to NOC, they have rooms reserved for hikers at a discounted price at a local hotel. Had we known before we got our room at Microtel, we may have gone there ourselves. Brett checks into it, and they have one room left; he nabs it. We are so glad it has worked out for him.

May your feet always make you laugh. (Mike)

It's hard to say goodbye to people who instantly become friends. I've only had a handful of those in my life, but FROG is able to find that common bond quickly with people, and today is one of those days when it is hard to say goodbye. They have a bond that is pretty strong. Mike thought his comment would make us remember all the laughs we had because we met him while hiking. We will never forget, Mike—never. You are pretty special!

On our walk back to the hotel, we notice there is a church on the strip sitting in between a CBD store and a pizza/bar joint. We're not sure what to think about that and ask a lady on the street what she thinks. Her response brings laughs and makes you wonder if there may be some truth to it for some. "Maybe they go to the church to ask for forgiveness for going to the other two places." Hmmm.

Tomorrow, our cousins arrive. We're really looking forward to seeing familiar faces and spending the next two days with family!

Days 44–45 (Thursday, May 20–Friday, May 21)–Nothing Like Family

Let me introduce you to our very own trail angels: Sheila and Randy, who just happen to be family. Sheila is FROG's cousin (their moms are sisters), and Randy married into this family because he knows a great woman (and family) when he sees one! They have been there for us from the very start of this journey, and to have them show up in the middle of it seems only appropriate!

We've come a long way from when they dropped us off at the bus station forty-four days ago—spiritually, physically, mentally, and emotionally. Looking back, we are not the same people who started out, full of fear and trepidation, asking ourselves all those questions: *What in the world are we doing? Can we really do this? Are we ready for this?* We found out we can do it and we are conquerors! We have grown exponentially.

> It is not the mountain we conquer, but ourselves.
> —Sir Edmund Hillary

We know they are close as we wait outside in the parking lot on a bench by the road. We recognize the vehicle as it pulls in, but it is the huge smiles and big waves that are such a welcome sight. Family is here at last! What a sweet reunion!

This time, they are the ones full of questions, and we have the answers. Reliving our last forty-three days and all we've seen and done both exhilarated and overwhelmed us. I am very proud of what we have accomplished so far, and GOD willing, we will finish this journey in Amicalola Falls State Park, Georgia, in two hundred more miles!

Their hotel room isn't quite ready yet, so we tell them they can put their things in our room until it is ready. When they step in our room, they politely suggest we might want to consider opening our window. Gotta love family and their honesty! We may have smelled better, but our room certainly did not with all our smelly gear! We tell them the story of being able to check in right away because we smelled so bad; maybe they should have considered not showering for a few days before they got here so that they could have had that same service. Not a chance, they say.

We decide to take a trip to Pigeon Forge to look around and have dinner at Applewood Farm Restaurant. We ate there before but forgot how much food they give you. It is so good but way too much food. This would definitely be a hiker's dream to eat here, but maybe because we haven't hit the hiker hunger yet, we left stuffed and hurting and couldn't even finish.

So not to hang out in our rooms (pew! ours, not theirs), we decide to go to a nearby park and visit for a while before we settle in for the night. We choose a picnic table close to the stream, a beautiful spot, nice and quiet—so different from the craziness of just a half mile away in downtown Gatlinburg. As we're sitting there sharing our latest news, Randy stands up and says, "There's a bear!" We all jump up to see, and he isn't kidding; walking across the park is a big black bear. We have traveled forty-two days on the trail, and we never saw a bear, but now we see one in a park in Gatlinburg? Who would have thought that would happen? It is far enough away but close enough to recognize it is huge! We are thankful to see one but much more thankful that there is distance between us! What a great way to end a spectacular day and evening!

Our last full day together includes a trip to the post office, a day trip to Cades Cove within the Smokies, and a final walk around downtown Gatlinburg.

Sheila and Randy have brought our resupply box that we had set aside at their house that was originally supposed to be sent to Standing Bear. We have now gone through it and filled our food bags with the food we will need for another four nights on the trail. The remaining food will be included in our bounce box that we will send to our next stop, Fontana Dam, North Carolina.

Randy has volunteered to take us to the post office so we don't have to take the bus again. Even after doing it once, I'm positive we still would get the color or direction wrong again. I hope someone else out there thinks it was as confusing as we did! Just give us white blazes to follow, hah! We could still mess that up—and we have!

Then it's off to Cades Cove for the day. It is an eleven-mile driving loop within the Smokies of a settlement established in the 1800s by European settlers that includes churches, cemeteries (more gravesites!), log cabins, barns, and a gristmill. A lot of history and very interesting to go back in time! While we are driving, we see four different bears within the loop. So happy to report none of these sightings happened while we were hiking on the AT but safely inside a vehicle. That is my way to see bears!

Dinner is in town. Then a last-minute walk through downtown and an ice-cream cone to end our day! Sweet!

> **Brad & Lori aka FROG and Faith—Thank you both for allowing us to be a small part of your AT experience! We've crammed in a lot in the past two days and it's been great being with you here in Gatlinburg, Tennessee. (In spite of your stinky room!) With less than 200 miles to go on your journey, we will look forward to seeing you next month in Georgia. Safe travels. We keep you in our prayers and know GOD has been with you**

HOBOS GOING SOBO IN THEIR OBOZ and we never looked back …

> every step of the way! GOD Bless, Sheila & Randy.
> We love you guys!!

Sheila and FROG, even though cousins, didn't grow up knowing each other very well due to distance. It was years later that they reconnected, and she played a major part in the change that happened in his life … see Chapter 10.

Our Support Team:

You both are amazing. I would burn the clothes too! Ann P.

My biggest fear is bears!! Glad you're safe!! Tracy M.

Glad to see you still have your sense of humor! Diana T.

I'm trying to wrap my mind around you stinking like that. I just can't imagine. Louise S.

Sitting here chuckling!!! I just love reading your adventures!!! Stink free!! Denise A.

Great updates and I, too, enjoy your humor! Take care! Denise L.

You two are amazing! … even if you do stink! Michelle E.

Lori, that must be awful for you, having only two pair of shoes! I feel bad for Brad without a chair, but really terrible for you! Sandy L.

> God loves each of us as if there were only one of us.
> —Augustine

My Journey to GOD / Brad's Life Song

(Written by FROG, a.k.a. Brad)

> Then no harm will befall you, no disaster
> will come near your tent.
> —Psalm 91:10

How many of you have ever wrestled with GOD? Unfortunately, I have made a habit of it. Since I've done it so much, I thought I would check out the Bible and see what there was about wrestling with GOD and see what I could learn.

There was a guy named Jacob, and he was wrestling with a stranger who turned out to be GOD. Before GOD let go of Jacob, He touched the socket of Jacob's hip and wrenched his hip, and he walked with a limp after that (Genesis 32; 22-32). Well, here's the problem. I have had both of my hips replaced. I concluded that I better stop wrestling with GOD because I have no more natural hip sockets left.

The first thirty-three years of my life, I wrestled with the idea that GOD was actually real. GOD was a fictional story, and He wasn't alive.

And for three and a half years, I have wrestled with this moment. You see, during the time when I was driving to work, I would listen to the second CD by the group Casting Crowns. It was their *Life Songs* album. As I'm listening to the songs, I'm realizing that this is a story of my journey to GOD. Then I felt GOD say to me, "Yes, it is, and I want you to share your life song with others." Well, I said no.

But this moment just wouldn't go away. So, for three and a half years, I have gone through times of feeling guilty because I didn't want to do this, and then there were times when I felt I was being prideful because I really did want to do this. I have questioned my motives. Did I want to somehow bring recognition or glory to myself? Then, a while back while driving to work, it was finally revealed to me why I am doing this. So, in an effort to keep you awake through this, I'll let you know the reason at the end.

My Life Song (Testimony)

I was born and raised in Trumansburg, New York—actually, in a little town outside Trumansburg called Waterburg. It was a neat place to grow up as a kid. There was a huge creek that ran through the community, so in the summer, we swam all the time, and in the winter, we were always ice-skating and playing hockey. It was difficult to get into trouble, although we still found ways.

As a kid, I went to church. We went to the Methodist church in Trumansburg. But I don't remember anything about GOD being real. There was no existence of GOD outside of church; there was no applied GOD in the everyday, real world.

There are two things that stand out to me from my childhood about church and GOD. Being a kid, I don't know the events that led up to this, but a large number of people left the church that we went to, including us. Friends and families who used to go to one another's homes didn't speak to one another anymore. Even as a kid, this didn't seem very church-like.

The second thing was going to my grandparents' house. My experience with Grandpa was that he wasn't warm and cuddly. Every time we would get ready to leave after visiting him, he would get out the Bible and start waving it around. He would pound the table, raise his voice, and start quoting scripture. I hated it! The first chance I got, I snuck out the door and hid under the bridge. There was a bridge connecting the road to my grandparents' property, and I would go under there and wait until my parents were headed for the car. What I discovered was that I continued to hide under that bridge (metaphorically) for about another twenty-five years.

So, by the time I was in the seventh and eighth grade, I didn't go to church very much. And when I was in high school, I hardly ever went to church at all.

In the ninth grade, I met my buddy Mike. He moved into our school that year, and we instantly hit it off. We played sports together, hung out with each other, and did everything together. In the eleventh and twelfth grades, we had another common bond: we partied, and we drank.

As graduation time was fast approaching, I had no idea what I wanted to do with my life. It seemed like everyone else knew exactly what they wanted and where they were going to college. So, I ended up going to the same college as my older brother, Mohawk Valley Community College (MVCC) in Utica, New York, and took the same course that he did, mechanical technology. But the neat part was that my buddy Mike was going to college with me.

In college, Mike and I continued with our common bond, but now we could find a lot more people to do it with. But after ten weeks, he said that college just wasn't for him. He packed his bags, moved out, and went back home.

On weekends that I went home, I would look Mike up, and we would go out and do what we do. Then one weekend, I came home and went to his house, and he didn't want to go out. He started using words like GOD, Jesus, the Bible, sin, forgiveness, grace, and mercy.

All I could think was, *What happened to my buddy?* We quickly drifted apart and didn't see each other for about fifteen years.

Well, I finally graduated from MVCC and went on to live the American dream. I got a job as a mechanical designer at a company called National Cash Register Company (NCR) in Ithaca, New York. I designed parts and mechanisms for printers that went into point-of-sale cash registers. I was making pretty good money. I married my high school sweetheart, bought a house, sold a house, built a house, and had a beautiful baby girl, Miranda. I thought we were happy, but through those seven years of marriage, there was no GOD, no church. I don't even remember anyone in our lives who talked that way.

After my divorce, the only thing that kept me sane was that I had the blessing of raising Miranda on my own, so I needed to try to be the best I could be for her. This was going to be hard for both of us, and we needed each other.

Soon after, I quit my career job in engineering. You see, I had schemed this great idea of traveling cross-country and backpacking in the Teton Mountains in northwest Wyoming. A guy I had gone to high school with, Rick, had bought a house right next to my parents, so when I visited my parents, I would go over to visit him. Well, he thought it was a great idea, so he quit his job too. This was the first summer for my daughter to visit her mom, so we stuffed her into the back seat of my former in-laws' Datsun hatchback, between our backpacks and all our bags. I knew I was searching for something, but I just didn't know what it was. There was an older song by the group U2 with a line in it that goes, "And I still haven't found what I'm looking for." The whole time we were backpacking in those beautiful mountains, the Creator was staring me right in the face, and I didn't even know it. My friend was into Buddhism and the martial art of tai chi. Fortunately, that didn't seem to make much sense to me. So, after almost four months and 12,000 miles, I got back home with no job and no money and a four-year-old to raise.

My second brilliant move involved my social problem, trying to escape the hurt of rejection and the bitterness I was building up.

I was driving home one night from a bar (I should not have been driving), and I drove right through a T intersection. I smashed up my car. As I was walking down the road trying to find some help, a police car drove up behind me. The officer was kind enough to give me a ride to the police station. He gave me a ticket for DUI, which is a nice acronym for drunk driving. I would like to say that this was the first time I drove like that, but I'd be lying. So, I had no car, I lost my driver's license, my insurance shot way up, and I had to attend AA (Alcoholics Anonymous) classes. Life was not going well. I've often wondered why GOD spared me the consequence of another car coming through that same intersection and how that would have changed lives forever.

Through all of this, I was very lonely. Conversations with a five-year-old aren't very in depth. Out of the clear blue, I started writing to my cousin Sheila in Atlanta, Georgia. We had never been really close, and the last time we had seen each other, I was twelve, and she was seventeen. But I knew that she had been through a similar circumstance, so maybe she would understand. We instantly connected, and the letters flowed. More recently, when she and I got together, she reminded me that there were times when I was writing her two letters a week. Then I got a letter that had words in it like GOD, Jesus, the Bible, sin, forgiveness, grace, and mercy. (*Wow, it's the same alien that got my buddy.*) Well, I stopped writing, and we drifted apart.

It had been two years since the separation, and I hadn't been dating very much. There weren't a lot of women beating down my door to go out with me. (I know it's hard to believe!) I was working for a small design place in Ithaca, New York, and I was also doing some consulting work at my old job at NCR. There was this beautiful secretary, Lori, working there, and I finally worked up the nerve to ask her out. All she could say was no, and others had done that. She said yes, and we went out on a date. It was very awkward at times, especially when I pulled out the roll of quarters to pay for the movie. But we had one thing in common: she was a single mom raising a three-year-old boy, and I was a single dad raising a five-year-old girl. So, when times got quiet and uncomfortable, we had that to talk about.

We dated for about a year, and then we made a financial decision. Lori and her son moved in with us, and soon after that, we got married. It was a simple ceremony in the living room of our house, with just our immediate family and a few friends.

It was a rough beginning, and there were many times we just wanted to call it quits. We both had baggage from our first marriage and some real communication problems. We really didn't love each other, let alone ourselves.

One evening when I came home from work, Lori started saying words like GOD, Jesus, the Bible, sin, forgiveness, grace, and mercy. I was simply overjoyed and thrilled (that was sarcasm). I was ticked, I was mad, I was confused, and I just didn't understand! Why couldn't she just take care of the problem herself? Lori said she had a problem she had been dealing with for a couple years (I just figured it was me), and she just couldn't handle it any longer.

Lori wanted to start going to church, so we went to the Presbyterian church in Spencer, New York. I could do this, and church seemed pretty safe. You get a program, an agenda, when you go in, and I could always tell how much time there was until it was over. Sometimes the preacher would get a little longer winded (oops, sorry), but most of the time, it went well.

Then Lori wanted to go to a church service at Youth Challenge. Youth Challenge is a Christian drug and alcohol rehabilitation center, and there was one just outside the village of Spencer. I remember walking into the building, and it wasn't quiet. There were a lot of people, and there was a lot of noise. Right after the beginning of the actual service, they had an invitation to go forward for prayer, and Lori immediately shot forward. I should have known at the time something was going on because that just isn't like her to take off on her own. I shot out the back door of the building. I was outside, stomping around in my bitterness and confusion. I remember looking up to the sky, because if there was a GOD, that's where he would be, and saying, "If You really are real, You must really hate me right now."

GOD has revealed many things to me by revisiting my journey to Him, but this experience is beyond the words I have in my vocabulary, so I will do the best that I can. Right after I said those words, I was in the presence of something, someone. I felt forgiveness, peace, love, understanding, compassion. I felt this presence say to me, "Brad, I knew you were going to do this, and it's okay. I still love you." All of my bitterness and confusion absolutely melted, and I bawled. Not just one of those with tears, but the nose is running, and the breathing gets all messed up, and you can barely breathe. I wanted so badly to be able to explain what was going on, but I couldn't. After a while, I got myself back together, and I met Lori back at the car. I didn't dare tell her what had just happened because I didn't know what just happened.

At the time, I didn't understand the significance of what happened outside of Youth Challenge. I lived a scripture in the Bible! I experienced GOD's living words in His book. There is a story in the Bible where Jesus is presented as the shepherd of a flock of one hundred sheep. It says that Jesus would leave the ninety-nine just to save the one (Matthew 18:10–14). GOD loved me so much that it seemed as though He left all those people in that church to spend time with me, because I felt His presence and I didn't even want Him there. That is incredible love!

I was doing a lot of running at the time. I was running twelve to fifteen road races a year and doing weekly thirty to thirty-five miles of training runs. Running was a very important part of my life, maybe too important. But I had this time, so maybe I'd try this praying thing and see if I made contact with GOD. So, I would start out with "Dear GOD ..." but after a short time, I would drift back to monitoring my running. How is my stride? How is my arm position? Is my upper body straight? I tried a number of times, but I just wasn't getting anywhere. It was a pathetic attempt, but I was trying.

Then one night I was awakened by a slap in the face. I remember sitting up and looking over at Lori, and she was sound asleep. So, I did what most guys do well. I fell right back to sleep. I really didn't think much more about it.

I'm not sure how much time had passed, maybe two weeks. I was out on a training run, and I started with "Dear GOD ..." and the usual was still happening. Finally, I kind of threw my hands up and said, "This just isn't working out. If You're real, GOD, then You're just going to have to come down here and slap me in the face." The next words that came out of my mouth turned out to be the truest words I have ever spoke. I said, "Oh! You already did. You are actually real!" I was jumping around and just couldn't believe this was real. By the time I got home, I had talked myself out of that experience, and once again, I didn't tell my wife.

There finally reached the point where I had to accept the evidence and make a decision. I recently bought the *Case for Christ* DVD by Lee Strobel. He was an investigative reporter for the *Chicago Tribune* and set out to explore the scientific evidence to prove if there was really a GOD. He didn't believe in GOD and basically was trying to prove he was right. What he did in the process was prove that GOD did indeed exist. He weighed the evidence and ended up accepting Jesus Christ. But he didn't want GOD to exist because then he would have to be accountable to someone other than himself. I kind of felt the same way. There was my high school buddy, my cousin, my own wife, Lori, the experience outside Youth Challenge, and finally the slap in the face.

So, at the beginning of a training run, I stopped on the side of the road on top of Dawson Hill Road in Spencer, New York, about thirty-six years ago, and accepted Jesus Christ into my life. I wasn't quite sure what that meant, but I was convinced that was what I was supposed to do with my life. There were no fireworks, no choirs singing, and no fanfare. It was a quiet, humble moment.

What changes? What does it look like to accept Jesus Christ? How do you know that you are different?

The first example is through my wife, Lori. I said that when she accepted Jesus, there was a problem that she had been dealing with (and I thought that problem was me). Well, she had an eating disorder that she had been trying to overcome for the past two years. At her moment of salvation, she was instantly healed. The temptation, the problem, was gone. Something that she couldn't do on her own was taken care of by Jesus.

Our marriage was totally transformed. GOD put two broken, rejected, and lost people together and created a marriage of joy and happiness. We were convinced we weren't going to make it, and the world has already proven that 85 percent of second marriages end in divorce. The Lord used Lori to help me learn to communicate much better and to learn to listen because she needed to talk through issues (James 1:19). GOD began to bring down the protective walls that Lori had built to protect herself from hurt. GOD allowed us to learn how to love and be loved. There were years that I dreaded coming home, and now I can't wait to get home to be with this woman GOD has blessed me with!

My job took quite a turn of directions. I never really enjoyed engineering, but the money was good. GOD let me run out of work, and I went back to college at the age of thirty-eight to become what I really wanted to be, a teacher. I am now retired from that profession.

While teaching, I had the privilege of leading a prayer group at school and being able to pray with many teachers at school. One evening, I was working late, and a teacher came to my room, totally depressed and in tears. This teacher was ready to quit. To be honest, I was scared and at a loss of what to do. Then I had a brilliant idea (sarcasm again)—pray with her. So we prayed, and in my weakness, GOD was great (2 Corinthians 12:10). She came in the next day and began by saying, "You won't believe what happened last night." She went on, telling me all of the great ideas that came to her and all of the insights that were given to her. Praise GOD!

I had the blessing of praying with another friend of mine who just found out he had lung cancer. On the day of his surgery, I intentionally planned on getting to the hospital after he got into the operating room. But GOD had other plans! When I got there, he was still in the room, and the room was packed with family, many who didn't know the Lord. He asked for prayer, and most of his family joined us. He is now cancer-free! I praise GOD for my weakness.

On a Saturday morning, the Lord led a young man down my driveway at home. This young man was going through some serious personal issues. He talked, and I listened for a few hours. He commented that he had seen a positive change in my life, but he hadn't seen a positive change in his father's life. So, I proceeded to tell him the reason for that change. He ended up accepting Jesus on the front porch that day.

In conclusion, I would just like to share a few thoughts.

To those of you who already know the Lord, I think we need to go back to that moment when we first found Him once in a while. We need to revisit that moment when Jesus first became real, when we first fell in love with Him. We need to rekindle that love, just like in a marriage. And we need to cherish those GOD moments that we encounter. During those difficult and dry times, we need to cling to those. I write mine in the back of my Bible. We also have to remember that people are watching us and observing our actions. They want to see that we are different in a good way.

To those of you who don't know the Lord, I'm here to tell you that He is as real as you and I are. GOD doesn't just exist in church. He will leave the church to meet you anywhere, no matter who you are or what you've done. The GOD that I met will hug you, will smile, and won't raise His voice at you. GOD loves you! And that love is a free gift given through Jesus Christ. All we have to do is accept that gift and ask for His forgiveness (John 3:16).

To those of you who are married and may be going through some tough times, GOD wants much more for you. GOD designed marriage as a shelter from the world. No matter what the world does to you during the day, you should be able to come home at night and be accepted and loved without judgment. My most important job as a husband is to build my wife up, and I'm still trying to get better at that. I've seen too many marriages where all the energy goes into cutting each other down. The differences that exist between you and your spouse are there to make your marriage stronger, not to cause division. My wife is a planner, and I'm spontaneous. If we were both like me, our lives would be chaotic. Don't let your differences divide you.

And to you young people, don't spend a lot of time away from GOD. What happens is that you end up having experiences that GOD never intended you to have. Yes, GOD will make good out of bad, and many times He will heal you of those experiences, but sometimes He leaves them there as a reminder of how much we need Him.

Oh yeah, I almost forgot. Why did I finally decide to do this? It is my gift to GOD for what He has done for me. If He decides to do something more with this, it is totally up to Him.

> Don't worry about hard times because some of the most beautiful things we have in life come from changes and mistakes. Live with no regrets because everything happens for a reason.
> **—Unknown**

Great Smoky Mountains: Clingman's Dome, Tennessee, to Fontana Dam, North Carolina

> For he will command his angels concerning
> you to guard you in all your ways.
> —Psalm 91:11

Day 46 (Saturday, May 22)—Two Hundred Miles to Go

Early-morning breakfast at seven o'clock at Log Cabin Restaurant so that we can get on the trail early. Guess what we have? Well, pancakes, of course! We get there early enough so we don't have to wait in line. They are good but not wait-in-line good. We had to see what the fuss was about; we never did figure it out.

Thank you, Sheila and Randy, for a wonderful break from the trail. We will see you soon at the finish line in Georgia! We promise to take a shower or two before we meet up with you. Thank you for helping us with whatever we needed. You two are the best!

We had a bit of home by seeing family, and now it is time to go to our new home—the only home we know right now. We are missing it.

> Going to the woods is going HOME.
> —John Muir

We arrive back at the parking lot at Clingman's Dome to continue our hike going SOBO. Saying goodbye is a lot easier than it was at the bus stop. I don't need to hang on longer than needed out of fear of the unknown. I am still not exactly sure what lies ahead, but I do know whatever it is, with GOD, I will be able to conquer it. This has already been proven.

We repeat our half-mile trek up the hill to Clingman's Dome but will take the bypass since we already walked up to the dome observation tower three days ago. Right before we get to the entrance to the ramp, we turn left and head into the woods. We are officially on the AT again. Ahh, home at last!

It is a beautiful, warm morning. We have both decided to wear shorts, so you know for me to be doing that, it has to be pretty warm out. The views at this height are phenomenal! I guess, had we decided to walk back up Clingman's Dome before we cut into the woods, we would most likely have had a great view of the surrounding mountains this time. We were just too anxious this morning to get back into the woods to revisit the observation tower again.

Today is a big day for us! Somewhere right around this spot should be the two-hundred-mile marker. We look on trees, rocks, and the ground and find no sign that we have crossed over the two hundred mark. I'm not sure if we missed it or there just isn't one, so I come up with the idea of making our own. I get out our playing cards and find a 2 and two Qs and stand there holding the cards up for a picture. It's official—2QQ more miles to go!

HOBOS GOING SOBO IN THEIR OBOZ and we never looked back ...

Two-hundred-mile mark

Our first stop for the day is at Double Spring Gap Shelter, where we meet up with two men and one woman (all young) in the Air Force. They are on leave, staying in Gatlinburg, and decided to do a day hike since they have never been in the Smoky Mountains before. They seem impressed with what we are doing, but honestly, I think they are more impressed because we are *older* and doing it. They are so polite and respectful and don't come right out and say that, but it's my story, so I'm sticking with that version. I guess it is impressive, but I think so many could also do it; they just don't think they can, or in some cases, don't really want to.

As we're eating our snack, a guy in a kilt shows up carrying his pack with moonshine. He thought it would be a good idea to reward himself with some white lightning later when he settles in for the night. He still has a way to go, and his pack has become heavy with that and extra food he got in Gatlinburg. I wonder if he has pancakes to go with that moonshine. Seems to be the thing.

This isn't the first time we've seen a guy hiking in a kilt, but it might be the first time FROG has come right out and asked someone how he likes it. I'm thinking if he's wearing it, he must like it, or he wouldn't be wearing it. Of course he responds, "I like it. It's very comfortable." What did you think he was going to say? "My pants were dirty, and this is all I could find in my backpack to wear"? He leaves before we do, so maybe we'll see him later at the shelter since he is walking SOBO. Our first official SOBO!

Just ahead is a family with two very young kids. It reminds me of the young family we saw one hundred miles back, out doing the same thing. It amazes me how these families with very young kids have decided to just go out and spend weeks backpacking, especially in the Smokies where you know there is an abundance of bears. They have just met up with Gram and Gramps on the trail, who have hiked in to meet them with their next week's resupply of food. The kids are jumping around and joyful that their G&G are here! Ahh, what a sweet reunion for them! Makes me miss my grandkids. I try to imagine them out here backpacking, and I'm just not sure they would find it fun, at least not now at their ages. Maybe someday they will try this or something like this.

> There is no Wi-Fi in the forest, but we promise you will find a better connection.
> —**Unknown**

Our walk over the peak of Silers Bald is beautiful. The summit isn't totally open, but you get many different views of the mountains in each direction. We are so fortunate to have such a nice, clear day to see the many rolling mountains. Splendiferous!

Not far from the summit is Silers Bald Shelter, and guess who we run into? Kilt-man! (My name for him.) He has only gone another 1.5 miles and has decided he is stopping for the night; his pack is just too heavy. He is in the process of setting up his hammock in the shelter. I ask him if he's gotten into his moonshine yet, and he says that he hasn't; he needs to get his chores done first. Then he can enjoy his wares. We eat our lunch and decide we'll stop at the next shelter, Derrick Knob Shelter, another 5.7 miles away, for the night. (Although Kilt-man was traveling SOBO, we never ran into him again. It can't possibly be because we were faster; makes me wonder if his drinking moonshine had anything to do with not seeing him again.)

We hike 10.2 miles today and reach the shelter about 4:30 p.m. We are met by the park ranger (called a ridge runner), who checks our backpacking permit to make sure we are legit. She tells us since we don't have reservations, we aren't allowed to stay in the shelter (oh, boohoo!), but we can put a tent up anywhere in the area near the shelter. She also mentions that if someone cancels their reservation, we will be able to stay in the shelter tonight. FROG is quick to indicate his interest. I stay numb. (The rule in the Smokies is you must stay in the shelter unless there are others who have previously made reservations; then they get first dibs. Blows my mind that someone, anyone, would actually make reservations to stay in there!)

As it turns out, there are two who cancel their reservation, but you know me—I tell FROG I am not interested. If he wants to stay in the shelter, he is welcome to. I want to stay in the tent. He doesn't see the logic in that (there wasn't any). We stay in our tent with many others all around us in their tents. I am not the only one who prefers their tent over a hard floor with mice (and probably snakes too) crawling all over them.

Day 47 (Sunday, May 23)—Our Last Views in the Smokies

We woke early this morning to try to get an early start. By the time we get around to leave, it is no earlier than any other day. I'm not sure why, and I've said this before, but it is usually FROG who delays us in getting on the trail early. For men to say it's usually their wives they are waiting for is *not* the case in our situation as we hike.

This morning, it is to take time out to talk to the ridge runner. She is very interesting, so I agree, it is worthwhile to have taken that time to ask her about the snorting and squealing we heard last night. We know the wild boar weren't close, but it sure sounded like they were right outside our tent. Noisy things, they are!

She mentions that there are a thousand wild boars in the park, and they kill up to seven hundred of them yearly to keep the population down to the one thousand. They do so much damage while eating. They rutt up and devour rare native plants, so they have no choice but to kill or trap them to relocate them. A bit of news I like hearing is that they have a keen sense of smell and can smell a human fifty yards away, so they don't get close. I am so glad we stink more than the average human; maybe for us they can smell us a hundred yards away! Feeling good that we smell so bad, we head on our way. Maybe that will keep the bears away too.

Hiking through Sugartree and Starkey Gaps is easy and not so bad—and then bam! We are hit with an all-out climb that is extremely difficult. Climbing up Thunderhead Mountain is right up there with the Grayson Highlands and the Roans. It is throw your poles kind of *hard*!

I finish taking a picture of FROG climbing up a steep rocky section, and when I put my phone away, I look up, and he's rolling down the hill. Well, the timing of that stinks! What a great picture that would have been, or better yet, video. Of course, I'm just kidding! I run up the hill to try to stop him from rolling any farther and make sure he's okay. One of our fears is when going uphill that we will fall backward, I guess that is what happened. He leaned back too far, fell over, rolled a couple times, and ended up with his face down in the dirt. I know he's lying there trying to figure out what just happened and if he's okay and can move. "Are you okay?" I ask, trying to catch my breath from exerting myself from the run up. I hear a muffled "I don't know." I reach down to try to help him move to see if he can get up. He is able to get himself up on all fours, and then I am able to help him to a standing position. He seems to not have any aches or pains and can walk. I think the shock of it is worse than the fall was, thank GOD! (I think he was more upset because he fell so hard, and he didn't at least have a couple bruises to show for it.)

The very summit of Thunderhead Mountain is a PUD! We climbed so hard to get up here, even falling, and then *no view* whatsoever! That's just not right! It is overgrown with rhododendrons; this is not a place to have the rhododendron tunnels! We want a view! We eat our lunch at the top, but we should have walked just a bit more downhill. We would have had a slightly better view of the surrounding mountains while eating.

But the most exceptional views come when we arrive at the summit of Rocky Top, a half mile later. Wow! The view of the rolling mountains in all directions is breathtaking! We see views of Fontana Lake in the distance and are told this will be our last view within the Smoky Mountains for the next twenty miles. Knowing that once we arrive at Fontana Lake/Dam, we are done hiking in the Smokies, we decide to hang out here for a while longer and enjoy the view.

As we're sitting there, we hear, "Look at all these trilliums. GOD is just showing off now, isn't He?" We hear the comment before we see two ladies who have just climbed to the top. We agree wholeheartedly. GOD has reason to show off His design and creativity; all we're seeing is just out of this world!

The last bit of advice given to us before we leave the summit is to make sure we stop at the marina at Fontana Lake. Not many people know that if you walk the pier to the marina, they have all sorts of drinks and goodies available there to purchase. Sounds like a mighty fine plan to us. We will plan on it.

It is a lot of down and up, repeat, as we head toward the next shelter, Spence Field Shelter. Nothing is ever just flat in these parts. A comment made to FROG: "You go right, you go left, you go up, you go down." That about sums up our whole hike of the AT. As we near the next shelter, it is a 0.2 mile walk off-trail to get there. We stand there at the intersection trying to decide if we are tired and need to stop or we can make it another three miles to the next shelter, Russell Field. Right now, we have hiked six miles, and most of that was pretty difficult. It ends up that neither one of us likes the idea of walking off-trail, so if we're going to walk, we want it to count. We head SOBO.

When we arrive at Russell Field Shelter, we are greeted by two other guys, brothers Hiku and Randy. There is no ridge runner here monitoring and looking at permits. I know we're supposed to stay in the shelter, but we set up our tent near the bear cables, and the brothers set up their hammocks out behind the shelter. The shelter was empty all night. Shh! Don't tell! We're rulebreakers again!

FROG is otherwise preoccupied, but I see our first sign of wildlife—deer! Three harmless deer graze near our tent site. By the time he shows up, they are gone. They really were there, I promise, but I have no proof; I didn't get pictures.

Day 48 (Monday, May 24)–Tennessee No More

Following the dream. 1st overnight in a loooong time. Tired legs, happy mind. Nice running into you. Good luck on the journey. Hiku

Spent a nice overnight at Russel Field. Thanks for the inspiration. Randy

Lots of wild pig rutting last night! Another noisy night. Not sure who's noisier now, the owls or the pigs!

We get back on the trail about 8:30 a.m. and hike 3.3 miles in one hour and fifty minutes to Mollie's Ridge Shelter. Not too bad for us slow folk. We sit to eat our breakfast, and another newly engaged couple stops by. Well, he arrives first, and then she trudges in several minutes later. I hope this is an arrangement they have; otherwise I'm not sure if I would have liked being left alone to walk by myself in bear country. They are a cute couple, taking a section hike through the Smokies. We wish them many happy trails as they venture this new journey together!

> Marriage is … Sharing life with your best friend, enjoying the journey along the way and arriving at every destination … together.
> —Fawn Weaver

The days have become warmer. We no longer have to bundle up and even have zipped off the bottom part of our pants to make them shorts. It seems good to be hiking in warmth and no rain.

I have a love/hate relationship going on with my trekking poles. I thought it would get better over time, but here we are close to our seventh week, and I have the same issues! We get along fine when we're walking together (and they've saved me from quite a few mishaps), but once we stop and I need to stick them in the ground to get something, they fall to the ground almost every time. To pick up poles that have fallen to the ground is not an easy task with a full backpack on. I am planning a breakup when we reach the end, but in the meantime, breaking up is hard to do!

FROG has had both of his hips replaced, so doing this hike brings some struggles for him. He's not very flexible, so climbing and bending can be difficult, and he sometimes has trouble lifting his foot high enough to avoid tree roots sticking up. Although I can't fault him totally on the roots, they can be brutal, and it's easy to get your foot wrapped up in one or stub into one. I've already had a tumble because of one. Today is his day. Poor guy—his second day in a row of falling and landing with his face down in the dirt. He is fine, just shook up, and again, no bruises to show for it.

We don't see any bear as we trek the trail through the Smokies, but we do see evidence of them. Why is it that they decide that right in the middle of the trail is an okay place to poo? Thank goodness FROG didn't take his last tumble and have a face full of you know what!

When we hit the intersection of Gregory Bald Trail (mile 174), we have officially left Tennessee (no more in and out between Tennessee / North Carolina) and are exclusively hiking in North Carolina until we hit Georgia. Woohoo! Two states down! Two to go!

We have gone 8.5 miles today and decide to stop just off-trail at Birch Spring Tent Sites. There is room for several tents, and we are the first to arrive. After walking past tent site number one, which reeked of urine (oh my goodness, no thank you; I wonder if, it being so strong, it was that evidence of bear again), we finally find a really good spot that is up on a platform that overlooks our water source and smells very nice and woodsy, thank you very much. By the time we call it a night, several tents are set up throughout the campground. Just an FYI—no one is set up in tent site number one.

Day 49 (Tuesday, May 25)—Tailgate Party

Short hike today and all downhill! We could take a side trip to Shuckstack Tower, only 0.1 mile off-trail (uphill), but we are just so anxious to get to Fontana Dam. I'm sure it is worth the trip with great views, but I hear sodas and food calling our names! So, down the hill we go!

As we get closer, we start to see views of Fontana Lake and can hardly contain our excitement. This means two things: we are almost out of the Smoky Mountains, and we're so close to a nice, comfy bed, showers, and food!

Just before we exit the woods, at the trailhead is the permit box for the NOBOs. We are officially out of the Smoky Mountains. We did it! Four days in the Smokies, thirty-five miles. We stand next to the Great Smoky Mountains National Park sign and attempt to take a selfie in front of it. How is it people can do this and smile at the same time? We just don't have this selfie-taking down at all!

Our sorry attempt at a selfie

It is a long walk over the dam to the visitor center, but we don't care. It is a beautiful walk. We take our time to take pictures and take in all the beauty. We can't. It is overwhelmingly breathtaking! Fontana Dam is the tallest concrete dam (480 feet) east of the Rocky Mountains. Surrounded by the Great Smoky Mountains National Park, Nantahala National Forest, and deep river gorges, it ranks one of the most beautiful dams in the world. We can attest to that!

Fontana Dam/Lake

We know there are showers at the visitor center, but we decide that we will wait until we get to the lodge at Fontana Village to have that luxury. But first, we are going to take the advice we were given a couple days ago and go to the marina and get some ice-cold sodas and some food. Now, how do we get there?

We see a shuttle driver pull up, so FROG goes over to see if we can catch a ride. He is looking to shuttle someone else and not going to the marina, but maybe he can work it out and shuttle us both. Another man (with his wife and mother) overhears that we need a ride, so he offers to give us a lift. FROG warns him that we just got off the trail and aren't smelling too good. He says, "That's okay. You can sit on the tailgate." We laugh, thinking this guy is pretty funny. He pulls up with his truck, gets out, opens the tailgate, tells us to throw our packs and poles in, and then points to the tailgate. "You can sit here and hold the side." We thought he was just kidding when he said we could sit on the tailgate; he was dead serious! A half mile isn't a long ride until you're sitting on a tailgate holding on for dear life! Sorry, no pictures. Neither one of us dared move! (Now I wonder if we should have taken that shower at the visitor center!)

We arrive at the marina sporting the wind-blown look but thankful nonetheless for the generosity extended by our tailgate party friends. He gets out and points in the direction of the marina, waits for us to grab our gear, and shuts the tailgate. We say our thanks and goodbyes, and off they go. As we're walking to the marina, we can't help but belly-laugh the whole way about how we thought he was kidding and how we were humbled because he wasn't.

When we walk into the marina, there are several coolers with drinks and aisles with snacks and microwave meals to choose from. Out back is a sitting area overlooking the lake, with boats in dock blocks. It's a warm, beautiful, sunny day, so after we figure out what we will eat and drink, we head out back to enjoy the view and the sun. The couple that told us about this was right; it is a well-kept secret, so there aren't a lot of people back here. It is quiet and peaceful. We have found that coming out of the woods where it is completely peaceful and hitting a lot of noise and people is so overwhelming, so this is nice to have a gradual break into reality.

We are not sure when the shuttle from the village arrives to pick up hikers, but we are through with our soda and hamburger (we even grabbed an ice cream, because, well, why not?), so we head back up the pier walkway to check out front by the bathrooms to see if there is a sign of shuttle times. Just as we arrive at that spot, the shuttle arrives. Well! This is great timing, if I must say so myself! The shuttle van is full, but they say they can squeeze in and make room for us. We warn them that we don't smell very good, and they reply, "None of us do! C'mon aboard!" The poor shuttle driver!

On our way to the village, we hear from another hiker, "It is a good thing you were right there waiting for the shuttle, or you would have had to wait another three hours for the next one." I call that GOD's timing for sure!

HOBOS GOING SOBO IN THEIR OBOZ and we never looked back ...

We have plans to stay only one night in the village at the Fontana Lodge, where we'll have a good night's sleep in a soft bed, take a shower or two (or three), do laundry, eat a big dinner, and get our resupply box from our friends from Arizona. That's a lot on our plate (always thinking of food!) for one night, but we can do it!

The lodge is *fancy*! Not your typical hiker destination at all. I'm not sure if we are going to know how to act, but we will try to act dignified and civilized.

Our room is really nice, and I'd love to just jump in the shower, but it's off to the post office we go. As we're leaving our room, a huge group of bikers arrive for a motorcycle convention, called Blue Knights. They are retired law enforcement, correction officers, or anyone involved in law enforcement from all over the country. The guys staying next to us are from Upstate New York *and* from a town only thirty-five miles from where we used to live, Elmira, New York. It is so neat to be able to talk about an area we are both familiar with. Small world!

A huge shout out to our trail angels from afar, Tracy and Walt! Thank you so much for the *two* boxes of goodies you sent! You totally spoiled us with dehydrated meals, chicken packets, fig bars, trail mix, candy bars, tuna with crackers, ramen noodles, propel electrolyte packets, granola bars, and cookies. We will enjoy all of it and think of you when we do. You two rock! (We have to admit, the cookies were gone soon after we opened the package.)

We made the decision to not open our bounce box and to just send it forward to our next stop, NOC in Bryson City, North Carolina, thirty miles away. The postman in town told us if we didn't open it, we could forward it for free. (You know FROG and his being a cheapskate, I mean *frugal*.) I guess we just figured since we were staying only one night, we really didn't need it. You will soon find out why that decision wasn't one of our better choices.

We have taken our showers ... uh oh! The reason for the bounce box is we have clean clothes in there to put on so that we can wash *all* our dirty clothes—and we absolutely need to wash our muddy, filthy clothes! I have a few pieces of clothing that aren't so bad, so that is what I throw on. FROG decides he will wear his birthday suit with his rain poncho on to cover himself. Not quite the look I think he should go with, so I tell him to put a towel around his waist first and then the poncho. I am hoping the whole way there that no one is at the Laundromat to see this. No such luck. There is an older couple (older than us and definitely not hikers) doing their laundry when we arrive. I have no idea why FROG chose the next words he did. After greeting them and letting them know we are hikers, he says, "I have nothing on under my poncho." Seriously? Why would you let anyone know this? I wish I could hide from the embarrassment I feel right now. They laugh but probably because they are in shock and don't know what else to say or do. So much for our acting dignified and civilized!

> The truest test of civilization, culture and dignity is character and not clothing.
> **—Mahatma Gandhi**

Note from FROG: Two regrets that I have so far, and they are both within the Fontana Dam area. Hiking into Fontana Dam, we were tired and just wanted to get there, so we didn't take the 0.1-mile side trip to Shuckstack and the fire tower. The views there would have been beautiful. And we also didn't see the Fontana Dam Shelter (because we took the ride on the truck tailgate instead and missed it), also known as the Fontana Hilton. What makes this a Hilton is there are indoor flush toilets and showers next to the shelter with USB ports, iPhone cables, a water spigot and fountain, garbage cans, and benches with a nice view of the lake.

> I chose the road less traveled and know I don't know where I am.
> **—Unknown**

HOBOS GOING SOBO IN THEIR OBOZ and we never looked back ...

Our Support Team:

Good job. Don't hurt yourselves. I felt a little nervous you guys spent 3 nights in bear country. God bless and be safe. Allen S.

So proud! Continued well wishes for this week's journey. I look forward to your stories and pictures. Stay safe and on your feet (Brad!) Maryann V.

I so enjoy your stories! Very informative and written with a sense of humor. Hope Brad will continue to remain upright and know he doesn't need bruises to prove this has been a challenging adventure ... we see your pictures! Praying for a safe finish! Hugs! Michelle E.

Love reading of your adventures as well as your wry observations!!!! However will you fill your time when this adventure is over??!? Denise A.

Great to hear of all your adventures ... does this mean you won't try to do other parts of the AT in the future. I know you haven't convinced me to try it! Nancy K.

Great update! Stay safe and loved! Hugs across the miles!! Denise L.

Wonderful to hear from you! Keep up the amazing spirit! Shelby S.

Wow—what an adventure—you are brave souls! Wishing you a wonderful journey! Truly fabulous adventure! Tammy T.

Very nice I love to hear all that you are seeing and doing each week you two are amazing. God be with you the rest of your trip. Milt K.

Love your stories and adventures! Big UP! All respect due! One Love! Georgene C.

Love your storytelling! You should plan to write a book. Pat T.

> God never said that the journey would be easy, but
> He did say that the arrival would be worthwhile.
> **—Max Lucado**

Fontana Dam, North Carolina, to Franklin, North Carolina

> They will lift you up in their hands, so that you
> will not strike your foot against a stone.
> —Psalm 91:12

Day 50 (Wednesday, May 26)—Guys Just Don't Get It

Leaving Fontana Village after only a nero day is different for us. It's usually a nero and then we take a zero to enjoy a full day of rest before heading back out. I think what makes it okay is FROG has made reservations for us to stay at NOC on Friday night, where we will stay two nights in their dormitory-like room. We will enjoy a longer break then.

We catch the 9:00 a.m. shuttle back to Fontana Marina to start hiking where the shuttle picked us up yesterday. The plan is to hike 11.5 miles to Brown's Fork Gap Shelter. It's a huge goal, and we're not sure if we'll make it or not.

We know that when we leave a town, it is an uphill jaunt for a time before we flatten out. Today, it's three miles of steep switchbacks. It is extremely rigorous, and we have to stop so often just to catch our breath. We thought by now our endurance level would be better, but these hills get us every time! Today, we had another butt-kicking day!

On our way up, we meet "Oneida" (our name for him since he is from Oneida, New York, about 1.5 hours from where we used to live). He is a young guy, I'd say very early twenties, who is attempting to hike from here all the way to Springer (that would make him a SOBO!) and doing it in five days. That is 164 miles, which means up to thirty-three miles a day. (By our calculations, it will take us up to three weeks to accomplish that!) We can't even imagine! This uphill climb has him stopping quite a bit due to cramps. He says he is stopping at every stream and cameling up to try to combat the cramps, but it's just not working. We take turns passing each other along the trail until we get to Billy Goat Gruff Memorial Bridge, and then we never see him again after that. Our guess is that the cramps got the best of him, and he turned around and went back to his car. This is the second SOBO we met up with this week that we never saw again.

I promise you we did not do anything with either of them!

As we get to Walker Gap, we meet a couple on the trail that tells us about Cheoah Bald, that the view is spectacular but watch out for the rattlesnake that has taken up residence there. Oh great! The new thing to fear now on the trail. We've heard from a lot of people lately to watch out for the rattlers; they are out in full force. So now every tree root we see looks like a dreaded snake! I think I'm more afraid of encountering them than I am a bear. They say you will be plenty warned by the rattle, but we have no idea what that sound is. All we ever had in New York were harmless (but ugly!) garter snakes. Will I really recognize a distinct rattle?

It isn't long after we were warned about the snakes that FROG stops quickly in front of me. Bam! I run into him as he slowly pushes me backward. I don't hear or see anything. He whispers, "Snake." Just off to the side of the trail is an ugly black snake about three feet long, not moving at all. It seems completely paralyzed, but I assume he is just sunning himself and not caring that we are here. We care that he is here and take a *wide* detour around him. I have a hard time thinking these are magnificent creatures that GOD has made. I just don't like them, harmless or not!

Ewww!

We have another nice sunny day today, so the distant view of Santeetlah Lake is simply beautiful as we stand admiring the mountains and the shimmery lake in the foreground. I have always been intrigued by this type of landscape. If we had known the grueling trail just ahead for us, we probably would have called it a day. But we have no idea what's ahead, so we push forward.

Our last mile is full of twists and turns, with climbs up and over boulders going this way and that. It almost seems like it will never end; we think the shelter should be coming up around the corner, and it just isn't. It is getting late, and we've never arrived at our destination this late before. We are hoping there is still room there for us since it's almost seven o'clock. We're usually in bed by this time!

We finally arrive at the intersection. Left will take us to Brown's Fork Shelter, and right continues you on the AT. We happily take the left and are soon greeted by a growling, teeth-showing, tiny beagle. He is not happy that we have decided to make a stop at his shelter. After what seems a long time of this dog growling at us, the owner finally retrieves her dog, and we are able to make our way to the shelter.

There are six other people here already, and they have taken claim to all the flat spots around the shelter with two people sleeping in the shelter. The only good flat spot left is smack-dab between two hammocks. One is occupied by a guy, the other by a gal. The guy (and FROG) find nothing wrong with us putting our tent up between them. The gal, you can tell, is not fond of the idea, as I am not either. I understand the importance of sleeping on a flat surface, but women just need their privacy!

It is a battle between husband and wife for a while out behind the shelter (we might just be taking separate vacations after this!). FROG either wants to set up between the hammocks or stay in the shelter. Neither idea is one I can agree with. "I am not going to sleep between the two hammocks and you know I don't want to sleep in the shelter. We need to find something else."

"Well, you need to go find us a spot then," says FROG, as he motions for me to go out ahead of him and find something. It doesn't look promising but I am determined I will find something. I end up finding a nice, slanted tent site (past experience says sleeping on a slant works just fine!), and we will just have ourselves some nice, slanted privacy! Thank you very much! Why is it sometimes guys just don't get it?

After we set up our tent, we decide to go to the shelter to eat our dinner. FROG is confronted with an upset beagle again, but eventually we are able to get ourselves to the shelter. The owners of the dog keep saying he's the nicest dog ever and he will eventually warm up to us. He never did. He hated us the moment we arrived and the moment we said our goodbyes in the morning.

Day 51 (Thursday, May 27)—Ultimate Hiker

As stated before, flat ground is overrated! We had a great night's sleep! I'm sure it had more to do with the fact that we had traveled 9.5 hours yesterday and were dog-tired from pure exhaustion, but to win my argument, I'm going with the slanted ground theory.

As we come out of our tent this morning, the "nicest dog ever" comes charging at us, growling, wanting to eat us for breakfast until he is taken away by his owners. They were the first to leave, and I have to admit, we are glad to see their furry monster go. I'm not sure why he disliked us so much. Neither one of us had any fear of him and tried to be nice, but he just wasn't having it.

Right before two of the ladies leave, they tell us to walk carefully out of here; they encountered two rattlesnakes on their way in yesterday. What? I wish I hadn't heard that. Now I am afraid to leave. It's usually FROG, but this morning it is me delaying our departure. We are the last to leave. I can't help but walk gingerly, looking this way and that, in fear, hoping our family of rattlers hasn't decided to make an appearance yet this morning.

> I knew that if I allowed fear to overtake me, my journey was doomed. Fear, to a great extent, is born of a story we tell ourselves, and so I chose to tell myself a different story from the one women are told. I decided I was safe. I was strong. I was brave. Nothing could vanquish me.
> —**Cheryl Strayed**

I am all these things because I know GOD is with me every step of the way, and He was. I make it out of there with no signs of any intruders.

The hike this morning seems easy and manageable as we head down to Stecoah Gap on Highway 143. We are high enough up that we can see the parking lot below—and there are picnic tables! I know this gives FROG an extra boost as he anticipates sitting and leaning back against the table. We arrive late morning and take the unoccupied picnic table. We notice there is another hiker at the other picnic table, doing what hikers do best—eat! We sit at our table and do the same, in complete comfort!

The weather is again sunny (but somewhat cloudy) and warm. We are finally getting into warmer weather, and *oh* it feels so good! As we're sitting here, we watch two women environmentalists looking at something in the nearby woods. Of course, FROG is curious as to what they are looking at, so when they come out, he asks. They are looking at different types of species of plants and animals living in the nearby Nantahala National Forest. He then asks, "Do you know what the bush is that has the bright orange flower?" I quickly look through my pictures to show them what we are asking about.

"Yes, that is a Flame Azalea." We finally have a name for the flowering bush that is our favorite. I think it's the brilliancy of color that draws us to it every time we see it in the midst of all the green trees and bushes. Stunning beauty!

The hiker at the other picnic table has finished his food and is standing up to pack his backpack to head back on the trail. We can't help but notice the sign on his backpack, "Key West to Maine." FROG, who is so full of questions today, gets up to go and ask him about it. He started his hike on January 1 in Key West, Florida, and his goal is Mt. Katahdin in Maine. We have no doubts that he will make it there. He seems focused and determined, and look how far he's gotten already in five months.

Ultimate Hiker

We can't get over the variety of wildflowers we are seeing out on the trail today as we continue our hike up and away from Stecoah Gap parking lot. They are everywhere. Purples, yellows, reds, and white. One of the white flowers, we are not sure what it is, looks exactly like one of Snow White's seven dwarfs, maybe Grumpy. What do you think? Do you see the face? We need to entertain ourselves out here somehow!

Grumpy Face

Our goal is Sassafras Gap Shelter, which is still 6.8 miles away. Even with our delay getting out this morning, it's still early, so we think it shouldn't be a problem to reach that goal. What we didn't know is the hike would be a lot like it was yesterday afternoon, full of twists and turns going this way and that as we start our ascent to Cheoah Bald. It was *tough*!

> The best view comes after the hardest climb.
> —Unknown

But the *views*! Oh! My! Goodness! Panoramic views of the

west. We stand there in a trance as we look out over the bald. Astounding!

We would have stayed here, and after that hard climb, I think we are both ready, but I don't forget that we were warned days ago about a rattlesnake that has taken up residency in the area. That is enough to convince both of us to boogie on down the road—or rather, trail. There is another 1.2 miles until we reach the shelter, but it is all downhill, a seven-hundred-foot drop in elevation. We can do this!

> Trust that the path you are on goes somewhere and wherever that is, GOD knows. Walk in Faith.
> **—Unknown**

We make it to Sassafras Gap Shelter and are greeted by Long Sleeves and Beans, who have taken up room in the shelter. They do say we can stay in there if we wish, but we let them know we will stay in our tent (shocker!). There are plenty of tent spaces to choose from, but we stay close and put our tent up behind the shelter.

FROG is jealous of Long Sleeves when he sees that he is sitting in a lightweight chair that he carries with him so that he is always able to sit comfortably when he stops for the night.

It is a warm evening, and the blood-sucking vampire gnats are out in swarms! They are horrible! Usually a covered building gives you some relief but not tonight; even sitting in the shelter, we are being attacked! We are so glad we aren't staying in the shelter tonight. We run up to our tent and try to work quickly at getting the tent open, jumping in, and zipping it up before any follow us in. We aren't quick, but it doesn't seem as though we let too many in. As we're lying there looking up, the outside of our tent has now come under attack. Gnats galore! I guess we're in for the night.

Day 52 (Friday, May 28)—Culture Shock Number Two

Good Hiking! Long Sleeves
Happy Trails! Beans

Well, there you go! We slept on the flat ground, and FROG says he had a horrible night's sleep. Another plug for the slant! No, I imagine it had a lot to do with the night being hot, and we were sticking to our sleeping bags all night. Being dirty, sweaty, and hot doesn't make for a good night's sleep. I still prefer this circumstance to freezing all night though!

It was supposed to rain during the night, but it didn't. It waits until we are on the trail, and then the skies let loose! It is a seven-mile walk, all downhill and very rocky. It is a slow but not steady walk for me. My turn to fall this time; those wet rocks trip me up. As I'm lying on the ground, FROG asks if he should get a picture so y'all can see. "Um, *no*!" I'm sure it would be a good picture and all, but is that the first thing you think of when I fall? To snap a picture? It's worth saying again: we just might be taking separate vacations after this!

The Mountain Laurels are out in full bloom! Even on a rainy day, we stop to enjoy their tiny pale pink and white cup-shaped flower. We don't really think they have much of a smell, but we did find out they are poisonous. How can something that is so pretty be so harmful?

We've come to yet another memorial along the trail, a plaque that reads: "On December 7, 1968, 783 feet southwest from this point, WADE A SUTTON, North Carolina Forest Service Ranger, gave his life suppressing a forest fire, that you might more fully enjoy your hike along this trail." We are so very thankful for all those either volunteering or paid to keep us safe along the trail. Thank you for your time and service.

As we approach Wright Gap, the name "Wright" conjures up some not-so-great memories of our hike up Wright Peak in the

Adirondacks in New York. We can't help but reminisce about it as we continue our hike.

Our bucket list once included climbing all forty-six peaks in the Adirondacks. So, in April 2016, we drove to the Adirondack Loj and parked at Heart Lake. We had plans to hike to the peak of Wright. The trail starts at the Marcy Dam Trail and then splits off to the Algonquin Peak, and then splits off from there to Wright Peak Spur Trail. (Stay away from all trails that are spurs! Why will we never learn this?)

I am not sure what we were thinking (obviously, we weren't thinking, which was the problem!). April is not a good time to be climbing up any mountain peak with ice and snow. We did come prepared with crampons on our boots, so at least we had that going for us. It was a ten to twelve-foot vertical climb up huge boulders to reach the peak summit. It was an extremely slow climb up, many times on all fours and hanging on for dear life. As we're struggling to get to the top, a young couple just seems to bound up the boulders like it's nothing, and they don't have any crampons on! Talk about humbling!

We enjoyed a 360-degree view once we finally crawled our way to the top. It was really windy at an elevation of 4,580 feet, so we didn't stay long. Now ... to have to get back down this ice slope without falling off it. Talk about being fearful! Much was done on our backside, sliding down the boulders until we could stand upright and walk down the rest of the way.

It took us 9.5 hours to go 7.6 (strenuous!) round-trip miles. It was the most difficult hike we've ever done. I have never been so sore and exhausted in my life. I did not think I would be able to finish it, but by GOD's amazing grace, I completed it and told Brad I *never* wanted to hike again! I meant it at the time, but obviously I didn't carry through with it. Compared to this hike, the AT is a cakewalk!

What makes us laugh is what happens after the hike. We shuffle our way into our hotel room, totally hurting and exhausted but so hungry. We don't usually eat at McDonald's, but it was the closest place to grab some food, so Brad decides to walk over and grab us some Big Macs and fries. It is right across the street, mind you. By the time Brad returns with the food, it is *cold*. He was walking so slowly on his return; it was more like a shuffle. I'm going to date myself again. If you've seen the *Carol Burnett Show* with Tim Conway playing the old man, he shuffled exactly like he did on his return. Didn't matter. We ate our cold food and passed out! FYI: the forty-six peaks are no longer on our bucket list.

> If you can find a path with no obstacles it probably doesn't lead anywhere.
> —Frank A. Clark

We have been walking in solitude for days, and then *boom*! Culture shock number two is Nantahala Outdoor Center (NOC) in Bryson City, North Carolina. People everywhere! It is Memorial Day weekend, so that for sure added to the amount of people who may normally have been here. NOC is an outdoor wonderland for the outdoor enthusiast. The Nantahala River runs through here, so they offer whitewater rafting, canoeing, ziplining, paddling instruction classes for adults and kids, restaurants, a general store, an outfitter store, lodging accommodations, and a train that comes through daily that brings people in. It's a little city of its own. After we get over the shock, it is fun to sit and watch so many families enjoying outdoor activities together.

Day 53 (Saturday, May 29)—Flip-Flops

We are so thankful that we were not in our tent last night; we slept with the window open, and it poured all night long! We are scheduled to be out on the trail today, and it's going to be so wet and muddy. We will be NOBOs as we slackpack from Tellico Gap back to NOC, 7.9 miles.

It took us a while last night to find a shuttle driver, due to it being a holiday weekend. Every driver was busy and couldn't squeeze us into their schedule, but thanks to driver Fred, who took pity on us and asked his friend Jim if he could help us out. Jim came to our rescue but with a high price tag. We bit the bullet and agreed on the price.

We arrive at Tellico Gap about 9:00 a.m. to a lot of fog. Our stop at Wesser Bald, a massive observation tower with open deck, would have been spectacular I am sure, if we had only been able to see the view. Our Guthook app says, "The views from the tower are outstanding in all directions." Enjoy our outstanding view.

Wesser Bald

By the time we walk another 2.5 miles, the fog starts to lift and burn off, so that when we take our snack break, we start to see those outstanding views that were promised to us.

This section of the trail is easy sailing—oh, wrong sport, hiking. We had been told by a mother/son duo that this was their favorite section, and now we see why. The terrain has been easy, and the views of the rolling mountains are just spectacular! Blue sky, low humidity, little wind—a grand day, indeed!

We've been asked a lot lately if we are going to *flip-flop* our hike. For us, this would mean to walk one way (SOBO to Springer) and then connect back up to where we started (Groseclose, Virginia) and walk NOBO to a certain section of the AT. I say we'll do the flip part, but the only flop I am going to be doing at the end is in a lounge chair with my flip-flops on! No flip-flopping here!

Right before our hike ends today, we see tree roots that look like the AT symbol and the last Flame Azalea that we're going to see on the trail. At the time, we didn't know it would be our last, but it was. Maybe someday when we are done hoboing it, we will have a Flame Azalea in our front yard with a white blaze on it as a reminder of our time spent on the AT. And maybe we'll put a lounge chair next to it with flop-flops on it for good measure.

AT Tree Roots

After our hike, we stop by the office to reserve one more night and to pick up our bounce box so that we can do our laundry.

No birthday suits today! Only one birthday a year, and FROG's already gone over his limit—three since we started our hike in April: his actual birthday, Hot Springs mineral bath, and recently at Fontana Dam.

Our boots are soaked and muddy, just as we thought they would end up being after today. We put things out to dry, take a shower, and are going to get food at the restaurant by the river and watch the kayakers practicing their twists and turns.

It's an early night; sleeping was a little rough last night. There is a bunk bed in our dorm room, but it is of two sizes. The bottom bunk is a twin, where the top bunk is a double. I've seen it the other way around but never like this. FROG and I tried to sleep on the bottom one together, and it was just too scrunchy. I felt like a sardine in a can all night. He will be retreating to the top bunk tonight so that I can break free from my sardine can and spread out. Good night, sleep tight or rather … mighty fine!

Day 54 (Sunday, May 30)—Surprise!

Ahh, sleep was much better last night for both of us. It took a while for FROG to climb the ladder up to the top bunk, but once he got there, I think his boyish excitement took over since he's never slept in a top bunk before and really liked it. Coming back down, well, that's another story.

We had decided yesterday that we would stay another night. We want to take a day to totally relax, attend the church service, eat, shower, watch the kayakers and river rafters, write in our journals, eat, shower, shop in the store, eat, shower, mail our boxes, and eat and shower some more!

It is a cold morning. The River of Life Church service is scheduled to start at 8:30 a.m. by the river. We arrive early and are greeted by Terry, who welcomes us to service. She is very friendly, and we instantly feel welcome. It looks as though this is a core group that meets every Sunday and welcomes those who are visiting NOC to join them. There is music, a message by Rev. Dickert, and a time of reflection by the river. We are chilled to the bone but glad that we attended.

To warm up, we stop by the little blue bus, Slow Joe's Coffee and Donuts, to see about getting some hot chocolates. When it is our turn at the window, we find out they don't serve hot chocolate. What? There are kids all over the place here, and no one ever requests a hot chocolate? We, of course, don't say this out loud but leave shocked. FROG and I have never developed a taste for coffee, but usually we are able to get something else, either a hot tea or chocolate. I guess around here when they say, "Coffee and donuts," they mean just what they say.

Right now, until the sun comes out, it's still too cold to just hang outside, so we head back up to our room to get our packs ready for the trail tomorrow. Our room is a good quarter mile away (and uphill) from the main center, so making trips back and forth does get tiring. When we finally arrive and use our key, it does not work. We try again—nothing. We try key number two—nothing. We are definitely locked out of our room. I am pretty sure because we added another night to our reservation, something got mixed up, and because we were supposed to check out today, it automatically locks us out at checkout time. Neither one of us wants to walk back down to the office to straighten it out, so we get the brilliant idea to call the front desk from our cell. It's only brilliant if you have access to the number, which is inside the room.

Then FROG remembers that the number is in his recent calls when he called to make reservations a couple days ago. High five, FROG! You *are* brilliant! He calls, hoping that they can just reactivate the key from their office without having to go get new keys. Of course, they can't; you need to go to the office to get new keys. Ugh! It's back down to the office we go, chilled bones and all.

We saved eating at River's End restaurant for this afternoon. We have a table overlooking the Nantahala River. It is a beautiful spot, and it has finally warmed up outside, so there is a slight breeze coming through the window. There are whitewater rafts coming through with so many excited faces as they paddle through the rough waters. It's been a fun few days here watching all the goings-on. So many people, but we've gotten used to them and the busyness and think, *What a great place to bring our grandkids.* We love the idea of having adventures with them more than just buying them things. I really think they are seeking the attention (memories) instead of the things they will someday forget.

> Fill your life with adventures, not things.
> Have stories to tell, not stuff to show.
> **—Unknown**

Do you remember what items I have been missing? It seems superfluous after just writing the quote above. FROG has decided to surprise me with new hiking clothes! For FROG, this is a big deal, and I certainly don't want to disappoint his generosity, so I can't possibly tell him no. We finally have warm weather, and I am in need of shorts and another sleeveless top, so we head into the outfitter store to see what they have. I can't get much (he knows that!), but I have fun looking at all my choices. I grab a few things and head to the dressing room to try them on.

It's not long before I hear FROG having an in-depth conversation with some ladies while I'm in the dressing room. I can hear his voice, but I can't quite make out the conversation he is having. It amazes me how he can just strike up a conversation with anyone, anywhere. When I come out, he has informed me that while having a conversation with these two women, they told him they had snacks and drinks in their vehicle and wanted to give us some for our resupply. Trail angels! We never would have known if he hadn't started talking to them. If it hadn't been for their dog and FROG asking if he could pet him, they would not have found out we were hikers. We don't look like your average hiker, so they wouldn't have known. Not only do I leave with new shorts, a skort, and a sleeveless shirt, we also get a whole lot of snacks to take with us tomorrow. What a blessing!

Our last errand for the day is to get our bounce box sent on to our next big stop, Around the Bend Hostel in Hiawassee, Georgia, sixty miles away. I have gone through my clothes to send my old clothes forward to make room for my new clothes.

The hardest part was to surrender my fleece-lined sweatpants that Sandi gave me when we were in Erwin, Tennessee. I love those fleece pants, and they gave me such warmth for so many nights. I hesitantly put them in the hiker box in the common room. I really am not in need of them anymore; they don't fit in the bounce box, and they are just extra weight right now. It's a sad moment. (Sidenote: I did go back to the box, and if they had been in there, I was going to reclaim them. They were gone. Made me doubly sad. But I do wish the new recipient many nights of warmth as I had.)

With our bounce box in tow, we head back to the outfitter store to get it sent forward. Every day, the Great Smoky Mountain Railroad comes through and makes an hour stop at the center, allowing passengers time to eat, shop, or just hang out and watch all the water fun activities going on. We hit it just as they have reboarded, so we aren't able to cross over the tracks until it continues on its way. We aren't in any hurry, so to wait and wave as they head out is an added treat.

I almost caused a big upset! I can't even blame it on FROG. Well, I could, but we both know it was totally my doing. When we went in to get our package sent, I thought the form asked where we lived (the return address), but instead it asked where we wanted the package sent. Duh! The paperwork was all filled out, unbeknownst to us, with the wrong forwarding address on it until another worker looked at it and confirmed the address. It was headed to New York instead of Hiawassee, Georgia! Thank goodness another employee looked it over so we could see our error. We consider that a GOD-corrected moment. We can't be without our bounce box, as stated before. No more birthday suits; we need our clean clothes.

Day 55 (Monday, May 31)—False Advertising

Jim is early and waiting for us as we arrive at our designated place at 8:00 a.m. to be shuttled back to Tellico Gap and continue our hike SOBO today. Jim is an interesting guy who, like everyone, has a story, and we enjoy listening to him tell it. He not only "knows the Lord"; he is "saved"—his words. We pray GOD's very best for him.

> **May God bless you on your journey and in life. See you again, I am sure of it. Jim**

Only because it's early yet and we haven't walked much, we decide to take a 0.1 side trip to see the view at Rocky Bald. Our memories of Rocky Top in the Smokies were worth it, so we're banking on this Rocky to be just as nice! And it is!

We are greeted by a group of four and their dog—their *friendly* dog, I might add! They camped up here last night and were just breaking camp to head NOBO to NOC today. Two of them were speaking French, so it was interesting listening to them speak. Times like this, I wish I secretly knew the language so that I could respond in their language and watch their reaction. Okay, so I think strange things sometimes.

The day is warm and sunny. The clouds are sitting just above the mountaintops, but the view is still spectacular! What a morning!

An early morning walk is a blessing for the whole day.
—**Henry David Thoreau**

HOBOS GOING SOBO IN THEIR OBOZ and we never looked back ...

Rocky Bald

We don't do a lot of looking ahead at what is coming up—we want the element of surprise—but we couldn't help ourselves. We had to peek. We expect to cross a couple more balds, and all boast of having magnificent views. No PUDs in our immediate future! Copper Ridge Lookout is where we decide to take our lunch break and enjoy the views of the countryside. Pictures just don't do it justice. We've tried, but the blue haze and the greens are just unbelievably beautiful!

Cold Spring Shelter is literally on the AT—well, a hand slap close as you walk by it. We are in need of water, and the pipe to draw from is right in front of the shelter. Not having to go any distance down a hill to get it—this is turning out to be the best day! We meet up with a solo female hiker drawing her water and find out she just graduated from college and, before starting work, wants to thru-hike the whole AT. *That's the plan*, as everyone out here says as a disclaimer, in case it falls through. We encourage everyone we meet that they can do it. I think about how far we have come, 420 miles as of this point; if we can do it, anyone can!

Licklog Gap: I'm not sure who comes up with these names or the reason for them, but this is one worth mentioning. There seem to be plenty of logs here you could lick, if you so choose.

Another place we would recommend you add to your bucket list is Wayah Bald Lookout Fire Tower. You can drive to the trailhead parking lot and take the short, paved path (easy, 0.3) that leads all the way to the lookout tower. If you want to see jaw-dropping gorgeous views of the surrounding mountains in Georgia, Tennessee, North and South Carolinas, you need to go. You will not be disappointed. I guarantee it!

Wayah Bald

While at Wayah Bald, we meet another couple going NOBO, and they give us a great tip. "See over there?" He is pointing south over in the mountains. "That is Siler Bald. It is off-trail, but it is so worth the hike up. You will see this from over there and will have the satisfaction that you've been here." It's almost seven miles away, so it definitely will be something we will get to see tomorrow. We will make sure we do it. We are always so thankful for our tips. *Well ...* let me rephrase that. We are always so thankful for *most* of our tips. This one, yes. The ones where they say, "You're almost there," or "Just around the corner," or "Just another mile," we have learned to take that with a grain of salt. I know people mean well, but it all is so dependent on how fast one walks. We are slow, so if they say we're close and then we're not, how disappointing! It's just best not to know how much farther.

HOBOS GOING SOBO IN THEIR OBOZ and we never looked back ...

> **Hike your own hike; don't worry about Mike. Go your own pace; it's not a race.**

Our final stop for the night, Wine Spring Campsite. There is room for a few tent sites here, and we are the first to arrive. After setting up camp, we head to the spring with our glass and *no wine*! How can they advertise a wine spring if all that comes out is water? This is when you wish Jesus was here to turn water into wine for us. After walking eleven miles, it sure would have been nice to have had a glass of wine. No one else showed up to camp here; they must have gotten the email.

Day 56 (Tuesday, June 1)–They're Back!

Not much sleep last night—the owls are at it again! I'm not sure if there's a different mating season for different regions, but it was quiet for a while, and now it has started back up again! They are so loud! I need a *birdologist* to enlighten me on this subject. What is taking them so long to get this mating thing figured out?

FROG let me sleep in due to lack of sleep last night, but I'm thinking it might be more because he is afraid I will be cranky all day if I don't get more sleep. There might be some truth to that. I hear him out and about, whistling as he gathers our water for the day. He is happy and loving every minute of being out here, despite the ups and downs we've encountered. FROG's man cave has always been the woods. At home, he could spend hours just gathering wood and walking our property, enjoying the quiet and peacefulness of nature. He is in his element out here. I let him have this time by himself as I slowly get myself ready for the day.

Our plans today are to hike 8.1 miles to Winding Stair Gap trailhead, where we will be picked up by Sherpa Al. Then we will figure out where we'll stay in Franklin, North Carolina, for a couple nights. We seem to be taking a lot of nero/zero days this section of the AT; I am not complaining at all! This is one thing we discussed before starting our backpacking venture; we both agreed that we wanted to take our time and see all there is to see along the trail. If a town was coming up, and we wanted to stop, we would do it. I think as we near the end of our hike on the AT, we are delaying it as much as we can.

Terrain is easy this morning as we head down into Wayah Gap, crossing FS69 three times before getting here to sit at their picnic tables and enjoy our breakfast/snack before our climb up Siler Bald. It is here that we meet "Vulture," who is having an easy day slackpacking. She proceeds to tell us that she loves vultures and used to work with them—hence, her trail name. She is so friendly and wants to talk, so we are in no hurry and listen. She warns us of a homeless guy (hmmm ... we avoid telling her we're homeless) who has really weirded her out and to watch out for him. I know I've said this before, but it amazes me how many solo female hikers we've come across out here. We pray that GOD keeps them all safe from all those weirdo homeless people!

We have decided, in 1.5 miles, we will take the couple's advice from yesterday and hike the 0.2 side trip up to the summit of the bald to see the views. It's off the trail, so, as you know, it is not something we would normally do. FROG says we can just leave our packs at the bottom, hike up, look around, and head back. I just wish it had been that easy.

We're at the intersection: if we go right, we head up to the summit; if we go straight, we stay on the AT that will start the descent into Winding Stair Gap, our destination. As we look to the right, we both let out a loud groan. It is all open meadow, so you can see that it goes straight up, but it doesn't look like it's too far up to the top. (Hah! Beware of false summits!)

After our initial groan, we discuss whether we really want to take the side trip or not. "Well ... it is supposed to be the most spectacular summit on the southern part of the AT. We're here. We planned to, so let's do it."

Neither one of us decide to leave our packs at the bottom. I am feeling uneasy about doing that, so I am taking mine, and FROG decides to take his as well. FROG starts out in the lead, but we have discovered that when hiking uphill, he needs to stop more often than

I do, only because I lose my momentum if I stop too often, and it's hard to for me to get going again. So, he will move over and let me pass when we are going uphill. Today is no exception. I pass him and keep going. It is a hard climb, and with our packs, that much harder. I reach what we thought was the summit, and I wait for FROG to catch up so we can share in the misery together. Once he reaches me, we groan again, and I turn to keep going. He kids with me, "You doing 'the Rick' on me?" I laugh and say, "Yeah, I guess I am," and stop and wait with him as he catches his breath.

"The Rick" goes back to when Brad went backpacking with his friend Rick in the Tetons for two weeks in 1982. Rick was probably two hundred pounds and very much in shape. Brad was about 150 pounds and, compared to Rick, definitely not in as good of shape. Rick would take the lead, and once he got farther ahead, he would stop to wait for Brad to catch up, which would allow him time to rest, but once Brad caught up with him, he was on his way again. Brad never got to rest.

I would also do this when taking the lead, so we labeled it "the Rick," but it's all in fun. Brad would tell you those two weeks backpacking with his buddy were right up there as one of his top five memorable things he's done in his life.

When I reach the true summit, I can't help but yell down to FROG, "Wait until you see this! It is definitely worth every hard step we took!" I am looking all around and have become enamored by all I'm seeing around me. We have started running out of words to express the beauty we have been seeing. Spectacular, majestic, magnificent, wow, awesome, stunning, breathtaking ... you name it, it is! This was made for us to see at such a time as this! Glory be to GOD!

We decide not to make it a quick stop as previously said but sit and enjoy and eat another snack. As we're eating and staring out at our view, we notice the top of the mountain directly in front of us. "That must be Wayah Bald, where we were yesterday," FROG says. We can see the fire tower where we were yesterday.

After sitting here for some time, another couple arrives to enjoy the view with us. We learn that she is a principal and he is a physical education teacher, both looking very fit and trim and not breathing hard at all. Hmmm. So not like us at all. We make an immediate connection as we read his shirt, "Redemption," and know that we share in the love of our Creator and remark on this fact.

They have been doing sections of the AT and warn us that hiking through Georgia is pretty difficult. FROG remarks that nothing could be harder than what we've already experienced in the Smokies, the Roans, and the Grayson Highlands. (They were right. FROG was wrong.) The next big climb we have coming up is Albert Mountain; we keep hearing from everyone that it is so hard, so we ask them about it. They agree it is challenging, but she pipes up and says, "But it's fun. You'll enjoy it." Well, that's an interesting way to explain that climb. She is the only one who said it was fun. After looking at them and how incredibly fit they both are, I'm sure they did think it was fun. Hah! We'll see tomorrow just how fun it really is.

Another four miles, and we make it to Winding Stair Gap, where the AT crosses US Route 64. We will wait in the parking lot for Sherpa Al. We called him from the trail an hour ago to agree on a time he would meet us. When we arrive, there is no sign of him yet. No problem as I plop down on the pavement and lean against my backpack to wait. FROG can't plop, so he just meanders around the parking lot. He comes across a piece of paper that has a name and address on it, but what surprises us about the note is that the address is Endicott, New York. For our New York family and friends, you know that is very close to home.

We have no idea what Sherpa Al looks like or what he is driving, so when a man shows up in a truck, we think this might be him. As he jumps out of his truck, I ask him if he is the infamous Sherpa Al, and he nods in the affirmative. We gather up our gear as he runs over to the piped spring with some empty water bottles and fills them with water. We stand there waiting for him as he runs back, jumps in his truck, and leaves. Well, I'll be! We stand there dumbfounded. "I guess that wasn't Sherpa Al," we say as we watch him drive away. Thank goodness we hadn't thrown our backpacks in the back of the truck, thinking that was our ride.

HOBOS GOING SOBO IN THEIR OBOZ and we never looked back ...

When another man arrives, we are hesitant to approach him and stand back until we see that he is definitely Sherpa Al and is here to pick us up. He apologizes for being late, but he had to pick up another hiker who was slackpacking and take her to get a burger before he could come and get us. He mentions her trail name as Vulture. We are both shocked and excited to say, "We know her!" He laughs at the odds of that as he drives us into Franklin, North Carolina, where we will stay at the Microtel for three nights

> In every walk of nature, one receives more than he seeks.
> —John Muir

Our Support Team:

This is amazing!! Thank you so much for posting! (Not hot on separate vacations, but thankful you are still married!!) Denise L.

You are "earning the view," as they say! Bethie T.

You inspire me!! May God continue to walk with you and bless you with His presence. Cheryl K.

Wow! What an amazing journey! Y'all are certainly made of sterner stuff. Pat T.

WOW! Majestic views! Those are the times when you take a deep breath and congratulate yourself for the courage to walk there! Bev G.

Just amazing! And I LOVE your commentary!!! Denise A.

Again—thank you for all your posts & such smart advice in living life to the fullest! God Bless you guys always! Nancy K.

I am so enjoying your blog ... you definitely have a knack for informative and hilarious descriptives!! I look forward to more of the same. Stay as warm as you can, when you need to be. Thinking of you as you trek onward!! Linda H.

So happy to hear you are enjoying your adventure! Shelby S.

Beautiful pictures and stories. Love you guys, Glad you are having a great adventure!! Tracy M.

We Will Never Look Back

> You will tread upon the lion and the cobra; you
> will trample the great lion and the serpent.
> **—Psalm 91:13**

We distinctly got the message "We will never look back" when we were seeking direction in our lives. It happened twelve years ago in 2010. Brad was having an awful year at school. Actually, this was his second year in a row that he had been given some students with discipline problems, and he was thinking maybe retirement would be sooner than we had anticipated.

I had been doing research on the computer about where we would live once retirement did happen for us. The thought of a tiny home was very appealing to us, so I was looking at places in Texas that had established tiny home villages that we could go and look at. One caught my eye in eastern Texas, located in Canton. We decided to take an impromptu trip (so unlike us!) to check it out. I had made contact with Rachel at the resort, and we were going to be able to stay for free for two nights in one of the tiny homes to see if we liked it.

We would fly to Dallas, rent a car at the airport, and drive an hour to Canton. It just happened to be a weekend of First Monday (the world's largest flea market, with more than five thousand vendors), so we were going to be able to see what that was all about as well. We were apprehensively excited (if that's such a thing).

Living in Texas appealed to us for a few reasons. Our kids/grandkids were out west, the weather was favorable in the winter, and there was no state income tax. We weren't sure this was where we would end up, but we thought we'd at least give it a try to see if we liked it. Recently, some friends of ours from church had moved to the area, so we were going to plan a visit to see them as well. It was all falling into place. That had to mean something.

Our flight to Dallas went smoothly, but I knew once we landed, Brad was starting to feel tension about renting a car due to the traffic around the airport. Not knowing where we needed to go brings on a lot of fear. They were wonderful at Alamo Car Rental and gave us detailed instructions on how to get out of the airport and connect up with the interstate. We knew GOD's hand was in it all because it went so smoothly, and the traffic wasn't bad at all.

Our drive to Canton was a pleasant surprise. We had only ever been to southern Texas, so that was our impression of Texas. Eastern Texas is nothing like that; it's country. It looks a lot like where we're from, Upstate New York.

When we arrived in Canton, we had no problem finding the resort and where we needed to go to check in. Our tiny home cabin met all our expectations, and we were in love with the resort. It seemed perfect and too good to be true. It was.

Our hope was that we could purchase a tiny home, place it on one of the lots, and then be able to live in it full-time. That was not how it worked there. You purchased the tiny home, used it when you wanted, but you had to rent it out when you weren't staying in it, and you would never live in it full-time. Which is fine now, but what happens when we can't travel anymore and need something for twelve months. Then what? We've paid for this tiny home but aren't able to use it on a full-time basis? And it seemed as though it was more the property of the resort than it was ours. The tiny home would stay, and we would have to sell it if we needed to find something full-time. We didn't let it discourage us. We started planning and designing our tiny home with Rachel, picked out our lot, and put money down to proceed forward.

We were given a golf cart to use during our stay, so for all the traveling we did throughout the property, we used our cart. Funny thing happened with that. It was Brad's first time really driving a golf cart. We were driving it around, and the horn kept blaring. We couldn't get it to stop going off. It was loud and drawing so much attention. It was embarrassing! Something was really wrong with the cart. *There must be a short; it's defective.* Hah! The only thing short and defective was the operator! He kept pushing on the horn, which is located on the floor of the golf cart! *That* was really embarrassing when maintenance had to let us in on that bit of information! I'm pretty sure we were laughed at by the locals, but they couldn't have been laughing any harder than we were at ourselves!

The resort offered shuttle service over to First Monday, so this was where we heard it first. The bus driver was talking to us about her decision to move to the area and said, "We made the move here and never looked back." *Okay, that is good—confirmation that this is a good area and she is happy here.* Didn't faze us at all until bus driver number two picked us up, and we told him what we were doing there, and he replied, "I made the move to this area and never looked back." What? The exact same statement, the same day, two different people. Coincidence? I don't tend to believe in coincidences at all.

Our time at the resort is over. It's time to head back to Dallas to stay with our friends Deb and Bill. We haven't seen them for a few months, so it is going to be a fun time to get together and catch up on what's been happening. I am telling Deb all about our experience at the resort and how we're not sure if it really is something we want to do or not, but we will pray about it. Her comment was "We made the move to Texas and never looked back." Boom! The exact phrase again! She had no idea that we had heard that exact phrase twice already. By now, it's gotten our attention, and we knew it meant something for us. We had to travel two thousand miles to hear the message that when we're ready to make the move, we will never look back.

When we returned to New York, we visited with friends, and they shared their experience of retirement, and I kid you not, Mary turned to me and said, "We made the move and never looked back." Our jaws dropped in amazement. *There it is again!*

And if four times is not enough, we hear it one more time. Brad's friend Rick moved out of the country, and in one of his letters back to Brad, he said, "I made the move and never looked back." Okay, GOD, we have definitely heard You and believe that when it's time to move, we will never look back! No coincidences at all. That is a personal GOD who really speaks to His children when they seek and ask.

Our plans at the resort and with Rachel fell through. It just wasn't the right time to be making a move. Brad continued to work four more years at school—happily, I might add—and retired in 2014 after putting in twenty years. As I mentioned before, he was meant to teach. He had some rough years, but it was the most rewarding job he ever had!

In retirement, Brad continued to sub at school, which really meant he went in four times a month and did his own science program at the two elementary schools where he previously taught and did this for five years. He had plans that I would continue working after he retired, but after two months, I also retired from working office management in the real estate business so that we could pursue other activities together.

Those activities included working at schools in Jamaica, first on our own, and then we got involved with the humanitarian group Great Shape! Inc. (See appendix A for more information on Great Shape! Inc.) and taught in classrooms in Negril and Ocho Rios, doing hands-on science experiments.

During this time, we also took four different mission teams from the Owego Nazarene Church to work with Nazarene churches in the West District of Jamaica under the leadership and direction of Reverends Lionel and Jennifer Brown. Many tasks were completed, including but not limited to: construction teams building offices at the Gamertsfelder Medical Centre; medical teams who worked at the infirmary, Gamertsfelder Medical Centre and did diabetes testing at churches; sewing teams who made uniforms and pillowcases; and the education team who held children's programs at the churches, and handed out much-needed school supplies to the children.

We also did individual mission trips to Antigua under the leadership and direction of Pastor Christopher Weekes at Bolan's Church of the Nazarene and worked at many schools in the area, arranged by his wife, Andrea. We have felt so blessed to be able to provide them with much-needed school and science supplies.

All glory goes to GOD in what was provided and accomplished by these mission trips. We could not have done what we did without Him and the help of every team member who went with us.

In 2018, we made the decision to become winter Texans and chose the Hill Country area. The reason for this area is that we were hoping to get both of our families together during spring break. Our grandchildren didn't really know one another, and we really wanted to get them together. We chose the area based on the activities that were available for them to do. The grandchildren instantly bonded, and so every year after that, we have come back.

It was here where we met Bev and Claude, our morning pool buddies. We would get up early every morning, meet in the pool, and try to solve the world's problems. Never quite solved anything, but we had a lot of fun, and many topics were discussed, one of which was our idea of hiking the AT. Right from day one, they were enthusiastic and encouraged us to do it.

They told us of their adventures hiking the Chilkoot Trail, a thirty-three-mile trail from Alaska to British Columbia, Canada, in 1988. I remember Bev sharing how she was so paralyzed with fear climbing up the pass, up and over the huge boulders; she just wasn't sure she wanted to do it, but by putting one foot in front of the other, taking that step of faith, she ended up having an amazing adventure that she would have missed out on had she not done it. Now they have so many wonderful memories of the people they met and experiences they had together. In her words, "Climbing the pass itself was difficult in early August, and I was as frightened as I've ever been in my life. When we got to the top above 4,500 feet, the water was pure and clean, so we didn't have to sanitize it. Amazing experience walking through a living museum of artifacts and history."

> The way you become brave is one terrifying step at a time.
> —Bryant McGill

I needed to hear this; it confirmed my decision. I was feeling that same fear she felt and not quite sure if I could do it, but if she ended up having such an amazing adventure, I was pretty sure there was one waiting for me as well. (And there was!)

I knew that if we were going to walk the AT, one of the factors in doing so would be selling our house first. Since we spent winters in Texas and then were going to be on the trail for three months in the spring, we couldn't be away from the house for six months; we would have worried about it the whole time we were away.

It sounds like it was a rash decision to just up and sell our home, but it really was a three-year process and didn't come lightly or easily. Brad built this house forty-three years ago, and he had put so much into it for so many years. It had become his dream house. I had remodeled and decorated and made it my dream house as well. I loved it, but it was just a house. Our *home* was anywhere we were together. I could leave it; it took him just a bit longer to realize he could too.

The winter of 2020, we were back in Texas with our friends in the pool. I had just prayed that morning on what we should do with the house. Should we go back to New York and put our house on the market or not? I specifically asked GOD to make it so clear if we should sell or not. There was no clear direction when we were in the pool, but we had made plans with Bev and Claude and Ann and

Hugh, our other close friends we met in Texas (who actually live five hours from us in Upstate New York), to go to the Gristmill River Restaurant in Gruene for lunch that day.

As we're seated at the table, we start talking about our plans of backpacking the trail and how we're thinking about selling our home. There is discussion back and forth about it, and then Bev says, "When we sold our home, we never looked back." My mouth dropped as I turned to Brad. I asked GOD if He could specifically say those words to me; then I would know it was Him and the direction we needed to go. Bev had no idea about those words until I told her the next day in the pool that the Lord used her to speak to me. If you seek Him, you will find Him. There was no doubt what we were supposed to do.

Upon returning to New York, when it was safe to do so (we were going through the COVID pandemic), we put our house on the market on a Wednesday morning, and by four o'clock that afternoon, we got our first offer, and it was for more than we asked for. The next day, we got two more offers. We ended up going with our first offer and asking them if they could match one of the other offers that was slightly more. They did so, so we ended up getting $12,000 more than we asked for. If that wasn't enough, we got two more contingent offers just in case the original offer fell through. Five offers, the same number of times twelve years ago that we were told we would never look back. Coincidence, I think not. Personal GOD, I think so.

Right now, we are happy being wandering nomads and moving from one place to another with no permanent place that we call home. There will be that day that we are ready to settle somewhere, and when that time comes, we have no doubt that the Lord will lead us and let us know where it will be, and when it happens, *we will never look back*!

> Not all who wander are lost.
> —J. R. R. Tolkien

Franklin, North Carolina, to Helen, Georgia

"Because he loves me," says the LORD, "I will rescue him;
I will protect him, for he acknowledges my name."
—Psalm 91:14

Day 57 (Wednesday, June 2)–Albert Mountain

Checking into the Microtel Inn & Suites in Franklin, North Carolina, yesterday afternoon was a breath of fresh air from the moment we stepped up to check in with Nettie to when we went to our room. She is originally from South Africa and told us a lot about her life—how she became a US citizen, how COVID has affected workers at the hotel, and most of all, she shared of her love of the Lord. What we have found in the South is that so many feel free and excited to share their faith and are very bold in doing so.

To be able to have a bed and bathroom … ahh. I truly hope I never take those two for granted ever again. They are truly two of the most luxurious things in life, and when you don't have them, you really do miss them. I am learning to be content in both situations, but in all honesty, I sure prefer having those luxuries.

Today we will get shuttled by Sherpa Al to Mooney Gap and will walk back to Winding Stair Gap, the NOBO side, which will be an 11.3-mile slackpack day. We will be climbing up and over Albert Mountain, the dreaded (but fun?) mountain so many have been talking about. Our advantage: no full backpacks.

We are out front waiting for Sherpa Al to arrive when another hiker limps outside and sits on the bench in front of us. He has twisted his ankle and has been here for almost a week, resting it so that he can continue. We have heard so many stories of ankles being twisted since we've been out here. It is so easy to have that happen, even if you are going slowly. So far, so good for us. We have 109 miles to go, and we pray we make it without any casualties.

Sherpa Al is late but has called to say he would be late (hmmm … I wonder if this has anything to do with Vulture and taking her someplace again). No problem. We're not sure we're ready to tackle this mountain yet anyway.

**Today is the tomorrow that you
worried about yesterday.**

Another guy comes out, not a hiker, and we can tell he is definitely in distress and needs to talk. We find out he is in the area due to his son's death; the funeral is today. His young son was driving a motorcycle on one of the winding side roads in the hills, took a corner too fast, and died instantly. The father mentions he is not from the area and recently made plans to meet up with his son here later in the month. They never had that chance. It really pulled at our heartstrings, and in a situation like that, there are just no words. All we could say is, "We are so sorry." Letting him talk and share was the only solace we could give. We did pray later for him and his family, that the Lord would give them His peace and comfort as they went through this tremendous loss. The mountain we have to cross today doesn't even compare to the mountain his family is crossing today and the days to come.

Sherpa Al has arrived, and with a downcast spirit, we get in his car. I have never lost a son, but I have felt loss due to death. You feel as though the world should just stop, but it keeps going. People around you are still living and doing, as they should, but our world has come to a standstill. (We pray that this family has felt the love and comfort only the Lord can provide.)

It's hard to bounce right back after such news, but we know we need to lift it up to the Lord to carry their burden; it isn't ours to carry. I am reminded of a story about a person pulling a wagon up a mountain, but since we are backpacking, we will change it to carrying a backpack up a mountain ...

We start out carrying a backpack with just the right amount of items (weight) that we need to successfully carry it up to the top of the mountain. But the first person we meet on the trail talks about his divorce, and so we add that burden to our backpack. The next person we meet talks about a death in her family—more weight added to our backpack. The last person we meet has lost his job and is not sure what to do; we add that to our backpack. Soon we are crying out to the Lord that He gave us too much to carry and that our pack weight is way too heavy. The Lord then replies, "I never gave you all those extra burdens to carry. You decided to add them to your backpack and carry them." We are never meant to carry this additional weight. He wants us to lift it up to Him in prayer and release it into His hands. Our backpacks will then become manageable again, and we can successfully hike to the summit of the mountain.

Sherpa Al helps to redirect our thoughts to what we will be encountering today on the hike. "First thing is Albert Mountain. It's a really tough one." Yep, that's what we've been hearing. "But ... is it fun?" I ask. He is easy to talk with, so we tell him what the principal said yesterday about the mountain. He laughs. "Not sure I'd call it fun, but let me know what you think at the end. There's a fire tower at the top. You can only go so far up to the top, and then it's blocked off."

HOBOS GOING SOBO IN THEIR OBOZ and we never looked back ...

Slackpack day!

> These mountains that you're carrying, you
> were only supposed to climb.
> —**Najwa Zebian**

We are at the infamous Albert Mountain. As we stand at the bottom and look up, all we can see is huge boulders to climb up and around that will eventually take us to the top. As stated before, we are very thankful to not be carrying a full backpack. The fear of falling backward would have been on our minds throughout. With lighter packs, we are ready. We can do this!

Remember our story on climbing Wright Mountain in the Adirondacks? This mountain is like that but to a much smaller scale (and no ice!). Who would have known that our past experience climbing that traumatizing mountain would have conditioned us for this one? We had heard so much about this mountain from the

NOBOs and how difficult it was. Our thoughts on it: we think it is not bad at all, and we have to add … it was *fun*!

The steps up the fire tower to the top are an open grate, so you can see the ground as you keep going up. I'm glad no one else is here right now as we *slowly* make our way as far up as we're able to go before it is blocked off. The floor is at least not open, but it's still scary being up so high, so I am starting to feel queasy and uneasy. Of course, FROG is all about taking a picture of me standing at the railing, hanging on for dear life, as I try to smile and squeak out a "Hurry!"

Albert Mountain Fire Tower

"It's supposed to be right around here," says FROG as he looks at the Guthook app. We are standing at the area where the hundred-mile marker should be and are just not finding it. Same thing happened with the two-hundred-mile marker, and we had to get creative, so I pick up a bunch of sticks nearby and make a one hundred out of them. We officially have one hundred more miles until we hit Springer Mountain. We can't believe how close we are to the end!

HOBOS GOING SOBO IN THEIR OBOZ and we never looked back ...

Hundred-mile Mark

Lunch break at Long Branch Shelter. Really nice shelter, double decker, built in 2013. Ah, man, I so wish we could stay here tonight. If I ever say something like that and mean it, you better believe someone's taken over my body!

This walk is right up there as one of our favorites. It's been fun, views have been remarkable, terrain has been easy, we had a big milestone marker, and to top it off, another rhododendron tunnel at Glassmine Gap. (Will be our last one, but at the time, we didn't know it.)

Now ... great way to end our day is at Shoney's to pig out at their all-you-can-eat-buffet trough! Oink! Oink!

Day 58 (Thursday, June 3)—Zero Day

Reality has set in. We are in need of some more green stuff. And I'm not talking about a spinach smoothie or a salad full of greens, although that would benefit us greatly if we had more of those. No, we are in need of more moola. When we first started this venture, we had no idea how much money we would need for three months. It turns out our estimation wasn't even close. It isn't a cheap endeavor, at least not the way we have done it. We could have saved money if we hadn't stayed in hotels or private rooms in hostels, or didn't slackpack and have to get shuttled, or if we hadn't eaten out as much as we did. But as I stated before, it needed to be a journey we both enjoyed, and those things make me happy, and therefore, he is happy. Happy wife, happy life. Happy spouse, happy house. I'm sure if he was doing this alone or with his buddies, it would have been a lot less costly but definitely not as much fun as it was with me. Hahaha.

We contact Macon County Transit and ask for a pickup at Microtel and are told to be out front by 10:00 a.m. As we're sitting out front, our limping hiker friend comes out and sits across from us again this morning. He's still not doing well and wonders if he should throw in the towel and go home. The wise thing to do is to protect that ankle and not damage it further. Just like FROG, he had dreams of being out here, or he wouldn't be here, so it's a decision that is not easy for him to make. (We are not sure what he ended up doing, but we hope he has healed and is living his dreams again.)

We are on our way to Mountain Credit Union on the bus transit. This bus system seems so much easier to understand than the one in Gatlinburg. No color or direction to figure out. You just get on the bus and tell them where you want to go. Easy Peasy! It took us quite a while to get where we needed to go with all the stops we had to make, but what is our hurry anyway? We have learned to slow way down, so this delay is nothing out of the ordinary for us.

Errands complete, reservations made for the next hostel twenty-nine miles away (Around the Bend), backpacks repacked, multiple showers taken, shuttle service set up for tomorrow with Sherpa Al's son, and we are free to go spend some of that moola. *Let's eat!*

Day 59 (Friday, June 4)–Bears?

We are bummed that we miss seeing Nettie this morning when we check out, so we don't get her to sign FROG's book. Of all days, how dare her take this one off! She was such a delight and would have had a great message for y'all. She's one of those people who has the southern hospitality down to a tee. This is the right job for her, and I imagine she brightens many people's lives by being where she is. She brightened ours, and we hold special memories of her that we carry with us (and what we carry doesn't even add weight to our backpack).

We are picked up by Sherpa Al Junior bright and early to take us back to Mooney Gap to continue hiking SOBO. We are only twenty miles from the Georgia border, so, if all goes well, we should hit that tomorrow. Excitement builds as we realize just how close we are to the finish.

We haven't seen any bears yet on the AT, but we have just heard reports from NOBOs that at the next shelter coming up, Carter Gap, there was an invasion by bears last night, and a Boy Scout troop and leader were there at the time. Although it was an exciting time (I'm sure mixed in with some fear) for the boys and their leader, all they could do was let the bears have the run of the place. They had hung their food as you're supposed to do, and these professional thieves knew just what to do. Up the tree they climbed and reached far enough out on the limb to keep smacking the bags until they fell. Free-for-all! Fifty meals devoured that the leader had brought for the boys to eat for this weekend's journey. They had eaten all their *bear* necessities!

You can, I'm sure, sense our hesitation upon entering this shelter. We slowly walk in and are scanning the place left and right to make sure there is no activity still going on. It is quiet. Thank You, Lord. We look at the tree where we were told it happened, and yep, there are scratch marks on the tree and clawing on the ground all around the base. It must have happened, and I am not sorry I missed the show.

It's lunchtime, and of course I am afraid to pull out our lunch, thinking this could bring them back to this area with the yummy smell of our chicken. I am banking on the fact that they have eaten so much last night that they are sleeping it off. But I can tell you we did not stay long. We quickly ate and were ready to boogie on out of there as soon as we were done. (Days later, we heard they closed this shelter due to excessive bear activity. Um … you think!)

It is a nice day, a little cool. It was supposed to have rained the last couple days, but it didn't. We are finding it very difficult to find water and are getting very close to needing some. Small creeks are dried up, and pipes have only a drizzle of water coming out. We could be in trouble soon if we can't find water.

While we were in Franklin, I heard from my friend Bethie that a young guy she knew from church was out hiking the AT and to keep an eye out for him. He recently started his thru-hike and was headed NOBO, so our paths should cross soon. I really don't know what he looks like, just that his name is Noah. We see a young solo hiker headed our way and wonder if this is him. FROG casually starts talking to him, as he does to almost everyone who will stop and talk to him. (There are those who don't even look at him and just keep walking. Those are the smart ones. Of course, I'm kidding!) I assume FROG will ask him his name, but he doesn't. So, I blurt out, "Are you Noah?" He looks at me with a blank stare and says no. I explain why I asked, and he says he hasn't run into anyone with that name. Strike one.

We are making great progress. The trail is favorable and flat so far, and the views ... Oh! My! Goodness! Did I tell you yet how beautiful the rolling hills of North Carolina are? I know, but it's worth mentioning again. We can never get tired of looking out into the vastness before us.

HOBOS GOING SOBO IN THEIR OBOZ and we never looked back ...

We have walked 13.1 miles today and are just so tired. We know we are soon going to hit a busy parking lot and are secretly hoping for trail magic. No one has mentioned it to us, but we really aren't seeing a lot of people hiking NOBO anymore either. It's become quiet, and sporadically, we see a few hikers here and there. I'm not sure why we are talking trail magic, but I think it has a lot to do with just being so tired we don't want to cook our meal tonight. How nice it would be to have it prepared for us. If we do this again, we need to see if we can find someone to hike with us who will cook our meals, and since we're dreaming, they will carry our packs for us as well. Dream big, they say!

> We have a BIG GOD, dream BIG!
> —Rev. Lionel Brown

Nope. We need to cook our own meal tonight. Deep Gap is full of cars but no people anywhere. We see on our app that there are campsites just across the road, down in the woods, so we head in that direction to Kimsey Creek Trailhead campsites. There is already a tent set up, but there are plenty more available. We choose one close to the water source and are hoping we can get enough water for our meal tonight. The creek is close, but only a trickle is coming out of the pipe. It will take a *long* time to fill our bottles, but we are in desperate need of water. What else can we do? Our dinner is late but simply wonderful as we eat our big, juicy steak, baked potato with sour cream, and chocolate cake with a dollop of ice cream for dessert. Dream big!

Before we settled down for the night, we made contact with our phone support team of family to let them know how close we were to the Georgia border. We have been in contact with them almost daily since we started to let them know where we are and how we're doing. Their support has been very much needed but also very entertaining. We had quite a chuckle as we announced to the group, "We hit

Georgia tomorrow. Woohoo!" My brother, David, who is very quick-witted and is quite the wordsmith (and lawyer), responds, "Sounds like premeditated assault. Don't let Tennessee."

I, who am not as witty, sent a message after we crossed into Georgia: "We went through with the assault. We both hit Georgia, and we're pretty excited we did it. She had no idea what hit her! No one saw it, so not worried about Tennessee."

My brother continues his play on words: "But the question remains—what did Delaware? Was it her New Jersey? I think you were spotted—Arkansas. Keep having fun; that is the Maine thing!"

Thanks for your support but especially the laughs!

Day 60 (Saturday, June 5)—Welcome to Georgia

We woke up in the middle of the night *again* with loud noises all around us! This time I can't blame the owls! Seems we set up our tent where the local teenagers hang out to party hardy! It went on for a good hour at least as we lay there listening to them cackle and hoot and holler as young kids do. It is the weekend, so we really can't fault them for being out and having fun and doing what teenagers do. Regardless, we didn't get a full night's sleep, got up late, and were not on the trail until 9:15 a.m. That is really late for us.

Our plans are for Plum Orchard Gap Shelter, 11.3 miles away, and passing by the North Carolina/Georgia border in seven miles! A day we didn't dare dream about sixty days ago. One thing I can say for sure is we never looked ahead or looked back; we took it one day at a time, one step at a time.

Until now. We are so close you can almost feel the end, so it's become harder to not focus on the finish line and start counting down the miles until we reach the end. It's not even that we want it to end; it's just knowing it's the end that's messing with our heads.

We tried to get water this morning before we left, but it was so slow going (just like we were in getting around) that we only had a couple full bottles this morning instead of our normal four bottles.

Water is still scarce out here on the trail. We are hoping that the shelter has a good water source tonight when we get there.

On our way out, we meet another young solo hiker, and I immediately ask if he might be Noah. Nope, not him. Strike two.

Who comes up with the names of these side trails? We have just arrived at the junction of the AT and Chunky Gal Trail #77. I can guarantee you a woman did *not* come up with that trail name! And it makes you wonder, if this is number seventy-seven, are there seventy-six other trails with that same name? Just not right. I can bet the man who named this trail is not in a successful relationship with a woman!

Lunch is at Muskrat Creek Shelter, where we meet two guys just finishing up their lunch. They tell us of encountering a bear last night at the Standing Indian Shelter. What is with all the bears lately? They told us the bear wasn't at all frightened by their presence and kept coming closer to get some of their food. They weren't comfortable staying, so one of them distracted the bear while the other packed up their food and left. Of course, every time I hear of these stories, I start to get antsy and think every noise and tree might be a dreaded bear.

Views, views, views! Between yesterday and today, we have been so blessed with amazing landscapes to look at. As we're standing there agape in wonder, two hikers approach and stand there with us. Conversation, as noted before, always centers on where people are from. Seems one of their wives is from a town outside where FROG grew up. It's been remarkable how many people we've run into who live close by where we lived for most of our lives. New York state isn't our home right now, but we both know we'll always call it home.

We are within 0.1 mile to the border when we meet a guy taking a break off to the side of the trail. He just passed the border going NOBO. We talk to him some about our trek, where we started and that we are headed to Springer Mountain. He is completely amazed that we've done this and says to us, "You have every right to scream and yell once you hit the border line."

Scream and yell we did! Three states, 467 miles, sixty days, with seventy-eight miles yet to go! I agree with our friend; it is completely amazing, and I'm really proud of both of us!

North Carolina / Georgia State Line

If we weren't in dire need of water, we would have camped up along the trail instead of walking 0.2 mile to Plum Orchard Gap Shelter. That's a long way off-trail, but we've heard there's water below. And water we need!

And water there is! It's flowing abundantly, and it's so easy to fill our bottles quickly compared to last night. It's going to be a good night. I can tell!

It's a nice shelter (as far as shelters go)—double decker, plenty of room for many. Currently there is no one set up to sleep in there, and all have chosen to tent. With ours, there will be eight tents scattered throughout. But where is the plum orchard?

We find a nice flat spot to put our tent up. I tell FROG it's not supposed to rain tonight, so we aren't as careful as we usually are with making sure the footprint is completely under the tent. (Why don't we learn from our past mistakes?)

It didn't rain; it poured! The weather in the mountains is so unpredictable. I paid the price, as my side only got wet. Thankfully I have a pretty good air mattress that separated me from the wet bottom, so I was protected from getting a wet bottom!

But wait! See! We were on a flat surface, so it collected and had nowhere to go. What would have happened if we had been on a slant? Would it have gone down the hill instead of gathering up under the tent? I'm starting a new slogan: "Camp on the slant! For dryness, privacy and a good night's sleep!"

Day 61 (Sunday, June 6)—And Then There Were Three

What a night! This wasn't as bad as the rainstorm we had on day 24, but it was worse as far as how wet my side got. But we faired so much better than two of our fellow tent mates who were out behind the shelter. Their tent was completely submerged, and they had to abandon their site for the shelter, where we found them this morning. Every single item they own is drenched. We feel horrible for them. I am surprised when she mentions she is a meteorologist. Shouldn't she have predicted this storm was coming? Well, we all know, they aren't right most of the time anyway!

Everyone else seems to fare better than they did, but all got wet in some way or another. We (or rather FROG) have to carry a wet tent, but it's a short day, 4.5 miles to Dick's Creek Gap and then to Around the Bend Hostel, where we'll stay a couple nights.

> **Nice to meet you both at Plum Orchard Shelter. No plums but lots of rain. Keep hiking. All the best. Nina**

> **I am Saiyay and met you at Plum Orchard Shelter. Good to see you, today is 6/6, Sunday.**

About a mile into our walk, we are greeted by a dog followed by a family of four. We are assuming this is their dog, but once they catch up to us, they say they don't know whose dog it is; it just started following them. There are no tags to show ownership, and it sure looks like he's eating just fine, which is good. We offer to take him with us, and when we get to the parking lot, maybe there will be someone there looking for him.

Our Traveling Companion

Everyone after that assumes it is our dog when he goes up to them, and we have to say what the other family said. It's not ours; we're looking for the owner. One young couple that is thru-hiking is so close to adopting him as their own but ends up saying they better not take it, so we continue our journey as three.

After three miles, we meet up with an older guy (yes, older than us), and the dog immediately bonds to him. We ask him if it's his dog, and he says no. It ends up we can't get the dog to follow us any farther; he has adopted this man. Someday when we're not homeless, we may get another dog. We so much enjoyed the two we had, Sammy and Shadow, and have great memories with both. But for right now … and then there were two again.

The journey today is short. It takes us three hours to walk to Dick's Creek Gap. When we get to the parking lot, we are not sure which way we are to go. Seems to be a pattern for us. We like to kid each other that if we ever were on *The Amazing Race* together, we would probably be eliminated in the beginning because we don't do well with figuring out where we need to go.

We notice there is a young man sitting at a picnic table, resting from the hike, so I volunteer FROG to go and ask him if he knows where we are to go. And while you're at it, ask him if he's Noah. Strike three. We're out! We never did run into Noah, but we hear that he made it all the way to Maine. Yay, Noah!

Our not-Noah hiker friend did know where the hostel was and pointed us in the right direction. "It's just around the bend." Well, they certainly came up with an appropriate name for their hostel. It is a half-mile walk beside a busy road with traffic, which I find pretty nerve-wracking. But once we break out and see it, all the stress I am feeling dissolves. We are home. Well, home for the next two nights anyway.

We instantly love Lisa and Gordon, our great hostel hosts, owners of Around the Bend. They are new owners and have fixed the place up to be so inviting and accommodating to the hiker. This place has everything! The common area has a full kitchen, table and chairs, couches, massage guns, foot massagers, and the best hiker box I've seen so far. There are two modern bathrooms and lots of hot water for showers, resupply available, treats/drinks to buy on the honor system, private rooms, a bunkhouse, and mini cabins. Slackpacking options and shuttle into town available daily. We just might not leave here and permanently call this home!

We choose a small mini cabin that has two twin beds in it with great Wi-Fi, and right next door is a port-a-john, so we don't have to go far at night if we need. What more can we ask for? I guess room service would be a welcome option.

They have our bounce box and our resupply box full of goodies. Ah, clean clothes and more food! An afternoon of doing our chores—laundry, drying out the tent and shoes, restocking our food bag with resupply—followed by showers! It's not all fun and games until we get the chores done.

We talk to Gordon about slackpacking tomorrow from Unicoi Gap back to the hostel. It's a seventeen-mile hike, and we are pretty sure that even with a light pack, we wouldn't be able to do that much. Our trail legs did not arrive with our boxes, so we have to decline his offer to take us there. We will just take a zero day; it's supposed to be a rainy day tomorrow anyway.

An easy night of frozen pizza, ice cream, and sodas and a wonderful foot massage in the living room / common area. We won't even think about how many other gross feet were also in the massager. No, let's not go there.

Day 62 (Monday, June 7)—Trip to Town

It's pouring out! What a great day to be taking off and just hunkering down in our cabin. It gives us time to get last-minute things done and get a shuttle lined up to pick us up in two days at Unicoi Gap to drive us into Helen, Georgia. It was on day 34 when we were told to include this in our plans. I can't believe it is finally upon us. It seemed so far away twenty-eight days ago.

Mission accomplished! Our venture as Hobos and not showering has embarrassed my little sister! As anyone who has a younger sibling knows, when growing up, they can be a pain and embarrass you in front of your friends. When calling my sister today, she pleads, "Please take a shower; you are embarrassing me." Yes! Payback is great! If that isn't bad enough, FROG and I break out in our most beautiful singing voices (gag!) and sing a lovely (horrendous) duet of "Happy Birthday" to her. It's a tradition; we do it every year. She should be so thankful that it worked out that we were off-trail and had good reception so we could continue that tradition. You're welcome, Suzanne!

You can only play cards so long, and then cabin fever sets in. We decide to go up to the common area and hang out and see who is there, if anyone. This is where we meet a universalist and a spiritualist. Well, we sure have a diverse bunch here at one time, which sure leads to interesting conversation. When it comes down to it, everyone is searching for the truth. They didn't convince us or sway us from what we believe—there is no other way to GOD than through Jesus Christ. We enjoyed our conversations and listened respectfully as each shared their stories and beliefs. Who says you can't talk religion amicably?

We've been waiting all day for our trip into town. Lisa is driving us, and when we're in the Ingles grocery store getting our dinner, she will go to the post office to send our bounce box back to Sheila. We have sixty-nine miles left and don't feel we will need the bounce box again before that. We could have been a lot more creative in picking out our dinner since we have access to a kitchen, but our choice? Subs! We haven't had one of those in such a long time, and it sounds so good. And of course, to finish it off, we have picked up a slice of carrot cake for dessert.

Our favorite conversation happens after we return from our downtown outing. Terrance (Texas T) has arrived at the hostel, and there is an immediate connection between him and FROG. We share the same faith and enjoy listening to his story, the journey GOD has him on now, and his plans for hiking the AT. We wish him all GOD's best as he continues his journey in life. See you on the other side.

Met FROG and Faith today. Talked about our Father in heaven. Great to meet people with like mindedness. Be safe! Be bold! Be strong! Texas T.

Day 63 (Tuesday, June 8)—Dinosaur Spotting

Lisa drives us back to Dick's Creek Gap so we don't have to walk the road again. Very thankful for that. Our plan is to walk eleven miles to Tray Mountain Shelter. The trail is very wet and muddy, but at least it has stopped raining.

We have hit our first four-thousand-foot mountain in Georgia, Kelly Knob. It is mostly covered in trees—slight views but nothing picture worthy. On the PUD side, I'd say.

Kind of like how we feel our day is going today. It has been a rough day mentally. The closer we are getting to the finish, the harder it is to enjoy and to not just concentrate on the miles and start clicking them off as we do them. Much of the day is just hiking with little talking. We are both deep in our own thoughts. We've been on a high for so long, and soon it will end. We are filled with mixed emotions and experiencing something new that we haven't felt this whole journey. We will be fine; we just need a day to process our thoughts is all.

> Don't count the days, make the days count.
> **—Muhammad Ali**

Wait! What's that? Hidden in the trees? Looks like some kind of dinosaur. FROG thinks it looks like a prehistoric flying bird. What do you think? And an egg? This is interesting. I thought dinosaurs were *eggs-tinct*! I am thankful for this diversion. It is good to laugh. I *crack* myself up!

The Dinosaur

The Dinosaur Egg

When we arrive at Tray Mountain Shelter, there are already tents set up for the night around the shelter, with a large group hanging out at the shelter. FROG has hopes to set our tent up inside the shelter after hearing the forecast for tonight. As it turns out, the ones hanging out at the shelter are the owners of the tents set up and will not be using the shelter tonight. FROG is thrilled, and I am fine with it as well. I will be protected from all the pesky critters running around at night tonight.

Inside the shelter

It takes a while for us to fall asleep due to the lightning and thunder storm happening all around us. We are so thankful we aren't out there in it and are thinking of those other three tents that are set up and enduring this storm. We hope they are faring okay. We do end up having a young guy as a shelter mate. We don't ask, but I'm sure it isn't Noah.

Day 64 (Wednesday, June 9)–Reubens and Bratwursts

We wake to wetness all around, but guess what? We are not wet, and nothing we own is wet! I have to admit the shelter was perfect for last night. FROG says, "What? Can you repeat that please?"

"Yes, staying in the shelter was a perfect idea." Having our tent set up, minus the fly, was comforting to me, knowing I was well protected from the critters and the light and sound show that lasted well into the night. It was pretty to see the sky light up and the sounds. I almost could imagine watching fireworks, minus the color.

FROG is relieved that he doesn't have to carry a wet tent as we head to Unicoi Gap, a short day of only 5.6 miles. There will be many ups and downs today, our first being only 0.4 mile away, Tray Mountain. It will be our second over four-thousand-foot mountain in Georgia. FROG thought this journey through Georgia was going to be easy. Hah! The joke's on him!

We heard that Tray Mountain has a beautiful view of the Chattahoochee National Forest. We cannot attest to that. When we arrive there, it is so foggy we can't see very far in front of us, let alone any view. Even though we can't see it, we still believe it is there.

> Faith is like radar that sees through the fog—to the reality of things at a distance that the human eye cannot see.
> —**Corrie ten Boom**

A mile down from Tray, we are able to look back up to the summit to see where we have just been. There is fog all around, but we can still see the tip of the mountain. We were there; now we are *the view* that we would have seen up there. Whoa … mind-boggling!

Climbing up Rocky Mountain has its challenges, but once we hit the peak, we are not only rewarded with a stunning view, we hear laughter coming from the other side of the summit, and someone sees us and is calling out to us. At first, we are not sure who it is and think he must have us confused with someone else he knows. You would have thought we were king and queen of the mountain or something the way he yells to us. Hey, maybe I have earned my queen status back again. He yells out, "What a blessing to see you two again." We turn around to make sure he isn't talking to someone behind us. Nope, no one there. We respond excitedly back so as not to be rude and try to hurry over to where he is so to get a better look.

"Oh, it's you! Terrance!" We met him two days ago at Around the Bend. We had no idea we would see him again; it really is a blessing to run into him again! He had been dropped off this morning at Unicoi Gap to walk the seventeen miles back to the hostel and has a hiking partner with him. We instantly like her as well. This is another time we wish we were walking their direction; we would have enjoyed forming a tramily with them.

> The best portion of your life will be the small, nameless moments you spend smiling with those who matter to you.
> —Unknown

Darrell and his grandson are right there at the gap to pick us up at 12:30 p.m. when we arrive. He offers us ice-cold water as we throw our packs in the back of his truck. Refreshing! It is an enjoyable ride as we learn a lot about Darrell and his family and the ministry he is involved in, with his wife. They offer Christ-centered biblical counseling. After this venture together, we may need to look him up!

Alpine Helen, Georgia, takes us completely by surprise! It is a German town with a lot of shops, restaurants, and tourists. As we are driving through, we can't help but look this way and that at all the goings-on around us. This really looks like a fun place to visit.

Thank you to our hiker friends who told us to definitely put this on our schedule.

Darrell takes us to SureStay, where we hear they have hiker rates available. We reserve two nights at fifty-five dollars each night, but we're thinking of adding one more night just to have a day to relax and hang out here in town. The desk clerk responds, "Well, for Friday night, the rate goes up to two hundred and eighty-nine dollars."

"No, we're good. Two nights is fine," FROG and I both respond.

After arranging a slackpack day tomorrow with Darrell and checking into our room, we don't even bother with showering yet. We'll just dine outside. It's time for Reubens and bratwursts!

> When I look at GOD's beautiful creation, I am reminded that, since He is powerful enough to do that, I can trust Him with my life as well.
> —Unknown

Our Support Team:

Bears! No way! I wouldn't be hiking anywhere near that area!! No way! No how! My biggest fear! Tracy M.

Love traveling in my mind with you on your adventure! Stay safe and healthy! Way to go you guys!!!! Shelby S.

Delightful pictures! Thanks for doing this and sharing it. Penny C.

Wow! Just Wow! Each week I look forward to hearing all about your adventures and seeing all your pics. I just love it! Keep on trekking! (and laughing). Maryann V.

Thank you for the updates. Amazing, beautiful & pretty! Darlene M.

HOBOS GOING SOBO IN THEIR OBOZ and we never looked back ...

Amazing! Thanks for sharing!!! You should write a book. Michelle E.

I love your journal. Kudos my friends! Georgene C.

Just Amazing! Sandy T.

Awesome! Louise S.

Awesome, as always! Thank you for taking us along! Linda H.

Here's to a continued safe journey! This really is such an amazing accomplishment!!! Denise A.

> The journey of a thousand miles begins with a single step.
> **—Lao Tzu**

15

The Finish: Helen, Georgia, to Springer Mountain / Amicalola Falls State Park, Georgia

> He will call upon me, and I will answer him; I will be with
> him in trouble, I will deliver him and honor him.
> —Psalm 91:15

Day 65 (Thursday, June 10)—Longest Slackpack Day

We feel sorry for those who had to endure last night. We had all intentions of sitting outside to eat, but when we arrived at the restaurant last night, the weather did not cooperate. It started to rain just as we got there, so we had to eat inside. We really should have showered first.

We are up early today since it will be a long day, 14.3 miles from Hogpen Gap back to Unicoi Gap. We are definitely cranking out the miles, so after today, we will have only thirty-eight miles left to go. We can feel the end. We're not doing very well with not counting miles and just enjoying them now. We try. It's just not working. We are doomed—we are focused on the end.

To take our minds off each step closer to the end, we reminisce about our trip thus far. I ask FROG what some of his favorite things in each state are that we've seen or done so far:

Virginia: wild ponies in the Grayson Highlands, Damascus Diner, and the Virginia Creeper Trail.

Tennessee / North Carolina (since we never knew which state we were really in): views of Watauga Lake, Jones Falls, and Laurel Fork Falls; our thirteen-dollar breakfast at Mountain Harbour; hiker feed in Erwin put on by the local churches; Hot Springs mineral bath; 360-degree views at Max Patch; Fontana Dam views; Wayah Bald views; Siler Bald views; and Nantahala Outdoor Center.

Georgia: we haven't seen much yet, so Helen so far. (Since our finish, we would add Neels Gap / Mountain Crossings, Long Creek Falls, Springer Mountain, Amicalola Falls State Park.)

I agree with his answers, but I'd add Overmountain Shelter (in North Carolina) where my kingdom resides and my open throne sits. Hahaha. We both agree that the list isn't conclusive by any means. We've seen so much, and it's hard to narrow it down. The overall journey has been phenomenal, and we hold so many wonderful memories.

The first ten miles are flat and of gradual grade, so it is a good pace we keep. Peaks at Poor Mountain, Sheep Rock Top, and our tallest mountain today, 4,010 feet, Blue Mountain are PUDs! All PUDs! Tree-covered peaks—what a disappointment! Then we hit rain and rocks galore! Walking is slow and easy so as not to slip and fall as we descend into Unicoi. By the end of our hike, our feet hurt, and we are completely whipped! We definitely outdid ourselves today.

We can see the parking lot on our descent and see that Darrell is waiting for our return. I'm not sure how long he has been waiting, but it's so nice to know we don't have to wait for his arrival. I am ready to unwind, take a bath, and hopefully have energy to walk into town to get something to eat later.

It's our last night in Helen, and we need to get out there and have one last meal here. Walking into town is slow and calculated as we take each slow step. We are tired and sore, but we are determined. We choose a restaurant by the river to watch the tubers coming down the river as they go through the rapids. We belly-laugh as we watch people flip up and off their tubes, which seems to be happening a lot with this group. I'm sorry—I'm sure that sounds so mean, but we do wait to make sure everyone is okay and that they are laughing too before we let loose with our laughter. What a great night of cheap entertainment. They paid for it; we get to enjoy it for free.

It was a good stay. Helen, Georgia, will definitely be on our list as a town to return to in the future. Add it your bucket list, and we'll meet you there.

Day 66 (Friday, June 11)—Mountain Crossings / Neels Gap

Darrell is prompt and waiting for us as we check out of the hotel. What a nice morning as we throw our gear in the back of this truck—and we're off to Hogben Gap to hike SOBO. Our goal is the infamous Neels Gap! We've heard so much about it and can't wait to see it. I'll explain more once we get there. Just know we have great anticipation to arrive there. It will be a seven-mile day, so shouldn't be too bad. Hah!

Saying goodbye to Darrell was bittersweet. We know we will see him again someday, but until then, we pray many blessings for him, his family, and his ministry. It is always good to have those moments where you take the time to pray for one another. Great way to start the day!

> A day without prayer is a day without blessing, and a life without prayer is a life without power.
> —**Edwin Harvey**

HOBOS GOING SOBO IN THEIR OBOZ and we never looked back ...

At the start of our hike, we run into a solo hiker who has spent the night just inside the woods at the trailhead. He was planning to thru-hike to Maine, but just after thirty-eight miles, he is ready to end it. He is not a happy camper by any means. We realize that this is not for everyone, and unless you try it, you will never know. We give him many kudos for giving it a try.

> You'll never know until you go!
> **—Unknown**

The junction to our first shelter that we come to, Whitley Gap, is 1.2 miles off-trail. Does anyone actually walk to that shelter with it being so far off-trail? We didn't even consider it! They say there are great views as you walk there, and when you get there, a picnic table and privy, but that is just craziness! We wave and head the other way.

Wow, the views today on the summits of Cowrock Mountain, Green Cliff Top, and Wolf Laurel Top. You can look out and see valley views and the Wildcat Mountain ridge. A slight view from Levelland Mountain if you look just right through the trees, you can see just a wee bit of it. But who said Georgia was going to be easy, FROG? It is an extremely hard climb up and over boulders and rocks. It takes us five hours to just go seven miles! It is *not* as easy as we thought it would be today. Georgia is not for wimps!

What a welcome relief as we arrive at the infamous Neels Gap. Walking through the stone walkway and seeing the shoes hanging from the trees seems so surreal! Tears are in both of our eyes to know we have made it to this iconic place.

The Stone Walkway at Neels Gap

Neels Gap is about thirty miles from the start of the AT (for NOBOs); it is the first outfitter store, Mountain Crossings, you come to; it is located after the dreaded "Blood Mountain" descent (we have yet to do this); and it's the only place on the AT where the trail goes through a building structure. But the coolest thing about it is, when you arrive here, you will see tons of shoes hanging from the trees outside. This is the place where one of two things may occur, both ending with their boots thrown up in the trees. (1) They decide to quit hiking after realizing this really is a tough trail, or (2) they realize the boots they had started with are not good and go in the store and purchase new ones.

HOBOS GOING SOBO IN THEIR OBOZ and we never looked back ...

Iconic picture of boots in trees, Neels Gap / Mountain Crossings

Mountain Crossings is a huge outfitter store filled with anything a backpacker may need in food or gear. They also help with advice, do shakedowns for free (look through your pack and help eliminate what you don't need), and will mail things back home for you. There are a lot of extras in the store as well. FROG says that before we leave in two days, we will buy a couple AT shirts. All right! New clothes!

We had made reservations with Craig at Misty Mountain here in Blairsville, Georgia, and he is expected to pick us up soon. It sounds like a really nice place, so we are looking forward to another night of luxury. Have you noticed how this part of our journey has been one luxury after another? I am *so* happy and have asked FROG if we can backpack this way from now on. We need to find a trail that you hike all day and end up with all the comforts at night—hut-to-hut system, I think they're called. *That* would be my next choice if we did something like this again.

Craig has arrived and tells us to put our backpacks in a huge bin in back of his truck while he runs in the store; he will be back in a few minutes. Shortly after he leaves, we see him talking to a woman on the deck of the store, pointing to his truck. She is soon standing next to us, asking if this is the right truck going to Misty Mountain. We assure her she has the right truck, and she puts her backpack in the huge bin as well. She tells us this was a blessing from GOD, the timing of this; she was feeling as though she needed to take a break and had just walked into the store to see if there was some place they could recommend she stay, and then Craig showed up. That is definitely a GOD moment.

We learn our house mate goes by the trail name of "Patches" and is hiking the AT to raise money for Children and Youth Programs through the American Legion. Her son is going to meet up with her soon, and then they will hike the trail together. She is a beautiful soul who shines with the love of Jesus and isn't afraid to let you know of her love for GOD and what He has done for her. Her boldness is awe-inspiring! May we be as bold as she is in sharing our faith.

Misty Mountain Inn & Cottages is a huge Victorian home that has several rooms inside and cottages out back. We have a room in the house in one of the upstairs rooms that has a *tub*! We had a choice, and you know us, we want to be able to soak our weary bones! The room is five-star for sure! We have made plans to stay two nights, and tomorrow we will do a slackpack day. Craig is very accommodating and even does our laundry for us! I am liking this place *a lot*! (We were some of their last guests under this ownership, so we feel blessed.)

We are thankful that Patches has a Chik-Fil-A app and has ordered all of us food for tonight, to be delivered to us soon. We can hardly wait! It is just the three of us tonight, so we sit out on the front porch and talk about what brought us out here and learn more about each other's lives as our food arrives and is devoured in a matter of minutes.

> **Met FROG and Faith today. What a blessing. The Lord and I have to continue to grow closer and the trail continues to show God's wonderous works. Who would have thought our paths would have crossed. All I know is God is so good and**

simply amazing. I have only been on the trail for 7 days, have accomplished so much and have *so* many people praying for me. He continues to bring believers in Him to me. Great to share the stories with one another on God's love. Such a joy to meet Faith & FROG. Isaiah 40:31—Won by One. Patches

Day 67 (Saturday, June 12)—Blood Mountain

Patches told us all about Blood Mountain last night and that it wasn't going to be easy, but our advantage is a day pack; her disadvantage was a forty-five-pound backpack. We have tried to process and prepare the best that we can from all the comments we've been hearing about it. We are hoping we are mentally ready—physically, who knows. Maybe it will be a lot like Albert Mountain was and end up being fun. We will soon find out.

We woke in the middle of the night to another thunder and lightning storm. Relief as we look around, as it hasn't seeped in and we're nice and dry. Realization hits as we remember we are inside and so we don't need to worry. Ahh ... we are safe.

We slept in until 7:30 a.m. and slowly get ourselves around for the day. We will be leaving here about 9:00 a.m. and hopefully will be on the trail by 10:00 a.m. Patches will be dropped back off at Neels Gap to walk NOBO, and then we will get dropped off at Woody Gap to hike back to Neels Gap (10.8 miles), so we will be NOBOs today as well but will be hiking the section she hiked yesterday. We stop by the convenience store to pick up breakfast sandwiches first so that we have something tasty on the trail to eat; this will be a nice change from protein bars or oatmeal, which we normally have for breakfast.

It is another sad goodbye. We have thoroughly enjoyed visiting and sharing with Patches and have made a really nice connection. We know that if we were hiking with her, she would be part of our tramily, but instead, we are content knowing that she is a part of our heavenly family. GOD bless you, Patches, as you continue your journey on the AT and in life!

Our New Sister, Patches!

Craig has hiked the AT before so is quite familiar with the section we will be hiking today. On our way to Woody Gap, he fills us in on what to expect and warns us about taking a wrong turn after descending from Blood Mountain. If you take the wrong path, two hundred feet down there will be a sign that says, "You are no longer on the AT, go back up." Well, my goodness, why doesn't it warn you at the top of the path that it is not part of the trail instead of that far down? Maybe they secretly have a camera down there monitoring how many people they can easily lead astray. Such a conspiracy theorist! We will definitely be looking out for that and will hopefully not take the wrong turn.

Our first stop is at Preacher's Rock / Big Cedar Ledges. What a great place to sit and enjoy our breakfast sandwiches. We aren't the only ones to think to stop. The view is remarkable! There are several groups of people hanging out, each looking straight ahead, all lost in their own thoughts. It doesn't seem to be a place that requires conversation, just quiet contemplation.

HOBOS GOING SOBO IN THEIR OBOZ and we never looked back ...

I know we are both thinking about what we have accomplished in what really is a short time but seems like a long time. Being out here makes it seem as though time has slowed way down. I think not being busy with everyday busyness really has its advantages. How can we wrap this all up and take it back into reality with us? If only.

The trailhead was packed with cars, so we knew it was going to be a busy trail, and it is, but nothing like it is on the summit of Blood Mountain. Getting to the mountain isn't too bad at all; we are not sure what all the fuss is about. Hah! Bask in the easiness now ... we had no idea.

Just before we approach the summit, we see a privy off to the left side. I am not aware that just ahead is the shelter on Blood Mountain, so I find this odd that there is a privy out in the middle of nowhere. Just seeing it, my system seems to signal a need. FROG is probably right in giving me the trail name "Miss Privy" if I didn't already have one. I don't like them, but I sure prefer them, and my bladder seems to respond when I see them. I know, I know, we've had this conversation before.

The shelter is a large stone hut at the top of the mountain. It is somewhat dank inside but would be a good place to stay if the elements were bad up here. Last night during the rainstorm would have been perfect. Although we hear that if you sleep near the chimney or walls, you will get really wet, as the roof leaks. Now I wonder, how perfect would it really be then if the potential to get wet is pretty probable?

We take time to climb the huge boulder next to the shelter to see the view along with *many* other hikers. It is definitely worth the climb up, but we aren't able to sit and enjoy it—too crowded. If we had only known you can get the same view if you walk behind the shelter, and no one is there! We did stay and enjoy the view, but if we had known what was ahead, we'd still be sitting on top of that mountain today.

Blood Mountain is the highest mountain in Georgia on the AT (4,458 feet). It is said that this is the sight of the battle between Cherokee and Creek tribes for control of the territory. The Cherokees won the battle that was fought at Slaughter Mountain and Blood Mountain.

There is no way we could have processed or prepared for what we endured on our descent. It was brutal! *Fun* is not a word I would give it. Thank GOD for our trekking poles to help us maneuver over the large boulders and down through crevices. And you know that path we were warned to watch out for? We were headed straight for it, and had it not been for a couple that just came back up and told us not to go that way, we would have most definitely taken the wrong path. The problem was the trail kind of led you in that direction, which was very confusing. See! It must be a conspiracy of some sort!

We have finished our hike today and have returned to Neels Gap. I feel we have definitely earned a soda, ice cream, and a new shirt! We left the store with all three and are sitting outside looking at the view off the side deck of the Blue Ridge Mountains. It's so beautiful and peaceful here. Reflecting back on today …

We are happy to report that no blood was shed on this mountain on our descent, but we did have a lot of sweat and tears! It was *tough*, and we only did it with a day pack on. Our new friend, Patches, did it with a forty-five-pound backpack on! That is one ahh-mazing woman!

Craig is picking us up after 5:00 p.m. and taking us to Jim's Smokin' Que BBQ, to pick up some food to bring back to the house. He told us that he's worked it out with our next hostel, Above the Clouds, and will be dropping us off there tomorrow morning. This will be our last hostel on the AT. We have twenty miles left of the AT And then 8.8 miles down the Approach Trail.

> A great accomplishment shouldn't be the end of the road, just the starting point for the next leap forward.
> **—Harvey MacKay**

HOBOS GOING SOBO IN THEIR OBOZ and we never looked back ...

Day 68 and Day 69 (Sunday, June 13 and Monday, June 14)–Our Final Hostel

What a beautiful, sunny Sunday morning. FROG is up early and has discovered that there are scales on the front porch. He knows he has lost a lot of weight. Curiosity has gotten the best of him; he needs to find out. He has lost as much as his backpack weighs—twenty-six pounds. I avoid the scales like the plague. I am not curious; I don't want to know.

Craig has taken us to Above the Clouds, where we meet Nimrod, who is Lucky's (the owner) sidekick and runs the place. What a character he is! He is such an interesting person who has so many stories to share; he is one of those people you meet in life that you feel so blessed and richer because you met him.

It has been arranged that Nimrod will take us to Hightower Gap today, and we will slackpack from there back to Woody Gap, 11.9 miles. We are still just checking off the miles and know that after today we will only have 8.6 miles left of the AT. Unbelievable!

The hike today is easy as we think more about our journey to where we are today. We laugh as we again reminisce about the trail and how we were clueless that it would be so difficult. We do believe the Adirondacks in New York prepared us for much of it, but it is definitely something that, unless you are determined and motivated, it can get the best of you. So many things learned about one's self while out here—that's for sure. FROG has made a comment that he thinks it should be a requirement for all young adults just starting out in life to do something like this to learn that you don't have to have a lot in life to survive and be happy. They are capable of doing more than they think they can, and let's face it: they're young, and they have more energy and stamina than us old folks!

It's been a fun experience, but I still think we should find a hut-to-hut system that includes only *flat* trails. Last night, I did some research on the internet as we were in the comfort of our luxurious room at Misty Mountain and found that there is the Great American Rail Trail that goes through twelve states. It is just over 3,700 miles of trail from

Washington, DC, to Washington state, a former railroad, so it is *flat*. Flat, y'all! It might just be calling my name! Could you imagine how fun that would be, even if you only did a small section? All the towns you'd go through and the people you'd meet—what great experiences and fun it would be. I am not sure about the hut-to-hut part. I guess it would depend on how close the towns are that you walk through and what they offer. I think I will add that to my bucket list. It's not quite complete yet, but when they're done, you might just hear that we're going to be walking (or biking?) that trail. Any takers out there?

As we approach Justus Creek, there is a group of four guys hiking together, just lying in the water, whooping it up and having the best time. It is a hot day, so we understand the impulse they have to just get in, clothes and all. We do catch one of the fellas as he is taking his shirt off, and FROG yells over to make sure he isn't going any further than his shirt. He says it will cost us if he goes further. We're broke; don't bother. A great group, having a blast and enjoying their last day together out hiking.

The view at the end is the icing on the cake for the end of our day. Nimrod picks us up at Woody Gap to return us to a full house at the hostel. If going NOBO, this is the first hostel hikers come to; for us, it is our last. I think with this hostel, it may give the hikers the wrong impression of hostels. This one serves both breakfast and supper, included in its rates. This is the first and only hostel that did that for us. We come back to a delicious dinner of burritos, rice, and beans. It is way more than I could finish, but it is so good. Nimrod is not only a great guy, he's a great cook!

We were supposed to have the private cabin in the woods, but once they showed us the private room in the house, we took that one instead. It is cozy and right next to the bathroom, which is a huge plus for me! I will take inside plumbing any day!

Breakfast is just as good and filling as we enjoy eggs, toast, bacon, and potatoes. We kid Nimrod that we may just decide to stay here permanently! What great service! Lucky is *lucky* to have Nimrod helping him with running the hostel.

Today is a zero day of getting the rest of our things ready for the final trek. Nimrod is doing our laundry (see why we may never leave?), and we are going through the rest of our things to see what we can ship back to our cousins—whatever we aren't going to need for the next 8.6 miles of the AT and then the remaining 8.8 miles down the Approach Trail.

We have gathered up two boxes of things to ship back. The only things we need are some clothes, one night of food, two days of snacks, water/filter, and toilet paper. Our backpack is like carrying a day pack by the time we get done. We are so excited for the end.

> **To Brad & Lori—you both truly embody that which John Muir taught us ... sauntering through our holy land along the AT. It has been a pleasure to share your company. Happy Trails! Nimrod**

Day 70 (Tuesday, June 15)—The End of the Appalachian Trail

We started the AT with so many questions, and today we end it with so many questions. *What does the end look like? How will we feel when we get there? How does the Approach Trail connect to the AT? Will we feel satisfied or empty?* We know it's going to be a whole bag of mixed emotions, just like when we started.

Our morning is filled with excitement as we get ready to get shuttled back to Hightower Gap by Lucky. It has been a wonderful and enjoyable stay, but it's time to finish this bad boy!

As we're saying our goodbyes to everyone (there is a big group heading out NOBO), we talk to one of the hikers who is roughly four hundred pounds (give or take) and carrying an eighty-pound backpack that he swings up over his head and then down onto his back. That in itself is impressive. He is out to lose weight and get in shape and then will join the military. He has plans to hike the whole thing. We wish him the best and wonder if he reached his goals.

A hug and a reminder from Nimrod to make sure we stop at Long Creek Falls on our way to Springer. Most people are so focused on the start—or, in our case, the end—that they pass by and don't stop, but it's so worth the stop, he says. We promise to stop and look.

We pass many streams and bridges, go right on past Hawk Mountain Shelter and Hawk Campsites and Hickory Flats dirt road, then take the side trail to see Long Creek Falls. It is as Nimrod said, so worth the trek in. It is beautiful. We are fortunate that a father and his son are also enjoying the view and are able to take a picture of us in front of it.

Long Creek Falls

We are just so focused on the finish that we keep going, bypassing any stops along the way. More streams and bridges, Stover Creek Shelter ... all in our past, no stops today.

We have reached USFS 42, the parking lot that is one mile to the summit of Springer Mountain. This is the parking lot that is used to shuttle people up to the start if they wish to skip the Approach Trail that connects to the beginning of the AT. The Approach Trail is not something that is required to be a purist; you just have to start at the very beginning of the AT. If you take the parking lot route, you have to hike in a mile and then turn around and walk the mile back to continue on. If you start at the Approach Trail, you hike *up* for 8.8 miles to connect to the beginning and then hike on. Listening to a lot of NOBOs, it seems more started at the Approach Trail for the full experience.

Our last mile is *hard*! It is uphill and rocky! We travel slowly and easily and are passed by many. It is a busy area, as there are many day hikers wanting to reach the summit and the start of the AT.

When we hit the summit, truth be told, we don't realize we are at the top. The only reason we figure it out is because there are a lot of people sitting up here, scattered all around. Our ending is nothing like I had envisioned. I act more stunned and confused than I do happy and ecstatic like I should have been. We find the plaques to signify the AT and the secret drawer in the rock where you sign the register that you are here.

FROG is finally coming out of his stupor. He does before I do and announces our huge accomplishment to anyone who will listen. There are shouts of congratulations all over by everyone who is sitting here. A gentleman jumps up and says, "Sit right here by the plaque, and I'll get your picture." We sit. I am still dazed and just sit there until he says, "You two need to show more excitement about what you have just accomplished!" That is when I finally wake up! We both let loose and hoot and holler—just like the owls!

We did it! We reached the summit and, for us, the end of the Appalachian Trail!

The Finish on the AT!

We Weren't Defeeted (defeated)!

We stay here for about a half an hour and then start our descent into Amicalola Falls State Park, on the Approach Trail. We are on the home stretch now. FROG was worried about how this trail connected to the AT, but it is easy to find where to connect. We are not following white blazes anymore but blue blazes. Where in the *blue blazes* are we? I'll tell you: 8.8 miles away from the finish line. That's where!

We were originally thinking we would stop at the first shelter, Black Gap Shelter, and end our hike for the day, which would give us a 7.3-mile hike in tomorrow. But when we reach the shelter, we are still full of enough energy and decide to keep going. Every additional step we take, that much less tomorrow. I'm so smart! Although ... as we're sitting at the shelter taking a break, it takes a young kid to show us how to download information we need for this particular trail into our Guthook app so we can follow it. We had no idea. Not so smart—humbled once again.

We hike another 1.7 miles and decide to stop at a designated tent site and set up our tent for the very last time. The very last time, y'all. It is a really buggy night, so we don't get to stay outside long while eating our dinner; we have become the dinner for these pesky gnats, so it's time to recline from our dine. Tomorrow is another big day! See y'all at the final finish line!

Day 71 (Wednesday, June 16)—Wave That Checkered Flag!

Our last day on the trail. It is so hard to sink in. We try to comprehend what we have accomplished, but we just can't.

Our last morning of routine: pack up our sleeping bags, mattress pads, pillows, and tent, all placed in their stuff bags and in our backpacks so we can finish our hike. A little nutrition and hydration, and we are on our way.

We are 5.6 miles from Amicalola Falls. The anticipation is building as we get closer to the stone arch (our finish line!). We hike in silence, both deep in our own thoughts about how it will end.

We reach the lodge at Amicalola Falls State Park first, before we make that final descent. We plan to stay here for the night to rest up, shower, and eat a big dinner before we get picked up tomorrow by Sheila and Randy. Our room is not ready, but the staff is kind enough to let us leave our packs there in their office as we continue our hike.

Culture shock number three! There are people everywhere as we hike down the 604 steps to the bottom of the 729-foot waterfalls. The falls are incredibly beautiful! (A must-see! Add to your bucket list!) We figure it must be easier climbing down the steps than climbing back up.

Amicalola Falls

We finally come out at a picnic area and a large parking lot. But where is the visitor center and the stone arch? We stand there in a daze, full of confusion. We ask a gentleman where it is, and he directs us one way (we found out later we should have gone the other way – Hah! So like us!) which leads us on a slightly longer journey to the end and certainly not how we anticipated the finish.

We arrive out front of the visitor center. Okay, well, where is the stone arch? More confusion. We walk through the center and notice out back ... the arch! *There it is!* It is a bittersweet moment. We are so proud of ourselves, but at the same time it's what we've been doing for two and a half months; we are sad because we will miss being on the trail and the experiences we had there.

HOBOS GOING SOBO IN THEIR OBOZ and we never looked back ...

The Finish Line at Amicalola Falls State Park

We turn around, walk back through the stone arch, and head back up to the lodge. Thank You, Lord for an *amazing* adventure! We met so many wonderful people, saw so much beauty, and realize our health really is our wealth!

As we're lying in bed that night, we look out the window, and there before us is a beautiful sunset. The Lord gave us one the first night on the trail and has given us another one on our last night. We are so blessed!

As we continue to admire the sunset, I am reminded of the dream I had on the road to Damascus. If you're familiar with the Bible, you know that Saul (who later became Paul) had a Jesus encounter on the road to Damascus that changed the course of his life. Since I knew we would be walking to Damascus (of course a different Damascus), I kiddingly asked the Lord if I would have an encounter on our way to Damascus too. I feel truly blessed that He answered my prayer and gave me a special encounter with Him. I am ready to share my dream ...

My Jesus Encounter on the Road to Damascus (Virginia)

It was the night before we were to arrive in Damascus (April 13) that I had a dream that was so real it felt like I was in GOD's presence. I remember climbing a mountain, and to the right of me was a man standing off to the side. Then I climbed just a little bit higher up the mountain, and Jesus was standing at the right. As I looked higher up the mountain, there was another man off to the right. I had no doubt the man I was standing beside was Jesus, and the moment I turned and came face-to-face with Him, it was like I was no longer dreaming. It was so real; I was actually in His presence. I started jumping up and down, laughing, and saying, "You're here! You're really here!"

He got a big smile on his face and said to me, "Grab your paper and pen." I was so excited and thought He was going to give me some wisdom to bring back to share with everyone. So I went and got my paper and pen. Upon returning, He was gone. I remember being sad that I didn't know what I was supposed to do with the paper and pen, and then I woke up.

The next day on the road into Damascus, I shared my dream with Brad. He was flabbergasted. He then shared with me that he had been praying about writing a book to share our adventures on the Appalachian Trail (I had no idea he was praying about it), and he felt this was confirmation that we are to write a book.

I was still not 100 percent sure that was what it meant even after I had someone on our support team say (the day after the dream) that they couldn't wait for the book, which caused my mouth to drop and wonder. It finally hit me after several more people from our support team said we should really write a book. I finally got the message (I'm a little slow) that what you do with a paper and pen is *write*. From that day on, I carried my paper and pen so I wouldn't miss out on anything. This encounter has changed the course of our lives. Here we are, a book later.

> To truly live is to thirst for adventure. It's watching a bird take flight and wishing for wings. It's climbing a mountain simply to discover what lies beyond. It's traveling forever, not to reach your destination, but in the relentless pursuit of a distant horizon.
> **—Wash**

Our Support Team:

Congratulations! We are so very proud of you two and will miss living vicariously thru your amazing stories about this life changing adventure. What a challenge physically, mentally, spiritually! Life is indeed meant to be lived and you are doing just that. So, what's next? We have loved the pictures and stories and look forward to attending the book launch when you're ready. Lori this is a book meant to be! Love you both and can hardly contain my joy and gratitude to know you've had this incredible experience living your dream. Bev G.

Amazing journey! Congratulations!!!!!! Michelle E.

So AMAZING, God Bless you guys! It picks up my day when we get you're "latest" set of pics & your note! Safe Travel always. God Bless you. Darlene M.

You did it! Awesome! That's a lot of miles in 71 days!!!!! Love your blog and pictures! Glad you are safe and back to civilization! Shelby S.

Terrific adventure! Congrats on your accomplishment. Thanks for the pics & stories. Ahhh, the feeling of getting off the trail, hot showers & a soft bed. Patti T.

Such a wonderful accomplishment and such beauty along the journey! Denise L.

Such BIG BIG UP's!!! Congrats to you both! One Love my friends! Georgene C.

What an adventure—you are brave and hearty souls!! Tammy S.

Congratulations to both of you! Amazing! Ann P.

HOBOS GOING SOBO IN THEIR OBOZ and we never looked back ...

Woot WOOOOOOOOOT!!! How AWESOME!!!! Such an accomplishment!!! Loved the armchair adventure!! Three cheers for hot showers!!!!! Denise A.

Congratulations!!! So glad you made it safely and were able to fulfill this dream together! What an accomplishment!!! Sending lots of love and big hugs from all of us in Ohio!! Christine K.

Wow! Can't believe you did it! Congratulations! Can't wait to see you guys now. Louise S.

Congratulations to a persevering, adventuresome twosome!! You are my hero and heroine, a job very well done!!! Peg P.

Happy Dance! Bethie T.

Congratulations!!! What an amazing adventure you had! Thank you for sharing it with us! Sue L.

Congrats! Awesome job! Thanks for sharing the journey with us. Cathy L.

You are amazing!! Congratulations! Sam L.

Yay!!! Good for you two!!! Can't wait to hear all about it!!! Tracy M.

Soooo excited for you! Yay!!!! Cheryl K.

I am so happy for you guys! What an accomplishment! Diana T.

You are totally amazing! So glad that you did this together! What an adventure! Casey M.

Congratulations!! You two are amazing!! And thank you for sharing your adventure with us all. Linda M.

Amazing! Thank you for sharing your adventures! Patti R.

What an adventure to do together. What an excellent example of strength, trust and faith. The world is a brighter place with both of you in it. Absolutely amazing trip with a bittersweet happy ending. Mary K.

Amen, thanks for taking me (us) along on your adventure! But, I gotta know what and when is next? Allen S.

U guys rock! Not many people could do that! Congrats! Chrissi W.

You guys are awesome! Way to go! Meg F.

Bravo!!!! High 5's!!! Marion P.

Congrats!! Coleen B.

Yeah, way to go! Cathy L.

Congratulations to the both of you! You are amazing and inspiring! I just went back to the beginning of your journey (even before you left) and am rereading each entry! It may take me longer to read it than you took to hike it, but it's worth it!! Linda H.

Amazing!! Great job you two! Renee M.

You two are amazing! Good for you. Donna M.

Amazing and Exciting. Definitely want to read about this journey. Congratulations on an amazing accomplishment! Valerie T.

God did bless the journey and both you Lori and Brad in many special ways along this long journey that will be a treasured memory for life. Make more!!!! God Bless. Joyce P.

HOBOS GOING SOBO IN THEIR OBOZ and we never looked back ...

You Wandering Nomads are amazing! Congratulations!! Linda M.

Congrats on the journey! Rob M.

Congratulations to you both! Tammy S.

Amazing!! BethAnn K.

Congratulations on your adventure!! Will have to go back and read from start to finish!! Lila H.

I am sitting here in Sandra's Cantina enjoying a margarita and waiting for my lunch to be served while reading this latest story! Picture me laughing out loud time after time, giggling like a little girl—and everyone in this restaurant turning to stare at me! Don't care! I was so into loving your story that nothing else mattered ... well, except this delicious margarita! Pat T.

> There were so many unknowns going into this adventure. There were fears and dangers, but we overcame all of them to have an experience of a lifetime!
> **—FROG and Faith**

16

What We Have Learned

> With long life will I satisfy him and show him my salvation.
> —Psalm 91:16

FROG:

- The very first thing we learned was that we could do it. We started planning and buying equipment over a year ago. Then we hiked the Northville-Placid Trail in the Adirondack Mountains in New York State for sixteen days and 132 miles. We did 545 miles and four states in seventy-one days. That is a huge accomplishment in our lives.
- The bus ride from Monroe, Georgia, to Wytheville, Virginia, was a terrible start. We left our car at my cousins' near Atlanta, Georgia. The bus was crowded with people yelling at each other. It was the worst of humanity on full display. We couldn't wait to get off the bus and out into GOD's creation.
- We never had a morning that we woke up on the trail and dreaded the hike. We usually had about twelve hours of

horizontal time or sleep at night. When we woke up, we would go through our daily chores of breaking down camp, packing up, getting ready for the day's hike, and having some morning nutrition and hydration. It was a routine that just got us back on the trail hiking.
- We did not expect to run into so many great people. We knew going into this that being out backpacking meant we had something in common with other hikers. But the conversations we had and the journal entries that were written were just such treasures. Our lives have been enriched and blessed by each person we met on the trail.
- There is more uphill than downhill. Yes, we know, this is physically impossible. But when you hike the Grayson Highlands, Roan Mountains, and Smoky Mountains, you will begin to agree that there is more uphill than downhill!
- Pack weight is everything. We should have learned our lesson hiking the Northville-Placid Trail in the Adirondack Mountains. We thought we learned our lesson when we eliminated items on that hike. Then we did the same thing on the AT and eliminated items on day 2 of that hike. If you aren't sure you are going to use it, don't take it. Only carry what water you need and just plan ahead for water sources. Put many different items in one stuff bag. Four to five pounds makes a huge difference.
- Staying dry is a necessity! Yes, you will get wet, but some things have to stay dry. A full rain poncho seemed to us the best approach. The backpack has to stay dry, especially the sleeping bag. You can dry out wet shoes and socks. You have to stay dry in your tent because it will rain. Learn how to set up your tent and where to set it up. If you keep the necessary items dry, you will have an enjoyable adventure.
- The scenery and the wildlife were more than we expected. The snorting of the wild pigs at night in the Smoky Mountains and the screeching of the owls during mating season. The beauty of Jones Falls, Siler Bald, and the beautiful Flame

Azalea, and the Mountain Laurels. It was GOD's creation on full display.
- We stopped at Greasy Creek Friendly hostel to pick up a mail drop, and above the doorway was HYOH—hike your own hike. The first few days, we hiked about seven to eight miles per day. Later on, we built up to about ten to twelve miles per day. We had one day of fifteen miles, and we were exhausted! Most every hiker we met was much younger than we were, and they were hiking fifteen to twenty miles per day. Hike what you can and enjoy the journey.
- Baths, running water, beds, and chairs—oh how you forget! We still remember our first bath in Damascus, Virginia, after seventy-five miles of hiking. It felt so good! Our air mattresses under our sleeping bags were okay, but the feel of a soft bed was a treat. I am not very flexible, and just getting in and out of the tent was an adventure. Faith can sit Indian style on the ground, but I cannot. So, a chair, picnic table, or any elevated flat surface makes life much more comfortable.
- Don't get rid of your cold-weather clothing too soon. The months of April and May can be unpredictable. Also, elevations up over 6,000 feet can offer different weather. I got rid of my gloves, winter hat, and long johns too soon. You want to reduce weight, but *weigh* all of your options.
- It's okay to go with plan B or C if plan A does not work out. We had all intentions of hiking through the Smokies, but due to excessive bear activity, we had to bypass thirty miles to get to the next available entry, which was near Gatlinburg. We missed those thirty miles but felt we more than made up for them by extra miles we put in with going to water sources off-trail, shelters off-trail, side trails, walking through towns, and our finish at Amicalola Falls State Park.

Faith:

- I know you're all wondering ... I never did quite master the farmer blow. It started out that I got more on me than on the ground, but at least now I get less on myself than I used to.
- We are not good selfie takers or even good photographers.
- It's a good idea to make sure all your bills are set up on autopay before you leave for an extended trip, especially if it is your cell phone, your only link to the outside world.
- I may need to go into therapy over this ... it's this whole losing weight thing! We've walked 545 miles, y'all. Wouldn't you expect that you would lose a significant amount of weight walking that many miles? Well, one of us did, and one of us did not! I wonder if you can guess who's who! FROG lost twenty-six pounds, and I ... drum roll ... lost five pounds! Okay, so at least I lost some weight after gaining, but c'mon! (Please don't misunderstand. It's not that I thought I needed to lose weight or that I only walked to lose it. I'm just standing up for the women out there who work just as hard to lose it, but it's much easier for the men. Just. Not. Fair!)
- I am happy to report we never saw a bear or rattlesnake on the trail. Thank You, Lord! But nonpoisonous snakes we did see, which are very alarming when you come upon them.
- Although still an introvert, I opened up a lot more than I did in the beginning. There was a definite change from day 1 to day 71 as I got more comfortable with my surroundings and knew we were all experiencing the same type of experiences together.
- Still missing: we never received our trail legs. It was promised by the younger crowd that we would eventually find our trail legs and be able to walk fifteen to twenty miles a day. Hah! Never happened. Those faster ones are still missing, but we did find a slower, knock-off version that allowed us to walk twelve to fourteen miles a day.

- The bill on my baseball cap is still intact, surprisingly! FROG takes the lead when we hike to set the pace (I may have gotten a younger, faster version of trail legs than his older pair, which frustrates him, so I let him lead.) For whatever reason, he will stop quickly without any warning, and wham! I run into his backside! I guess I've just as many times gotten him back (not intentionally) with hitting his boots with my trekking poles by following too close.
- Although we loved all the opportunities we had to eat, we never did develop hiker hunger. We never were ravenous or required large amounts of food like we saw with so many hikers.
- Except for the *long* trek to get to Greasy Creek Friendly, FROG did an excellent job of setting up our mail resupply boxes and getting them shipped to various stops. I take back what I said, and he is once again allowed to be in charge of mail drops.
- Carry extra coins in your bounce box for laundry. You never know when you might encounter a coin shortage.
- I did break up with my trekking poles; we have parted company. I have a feeling that someday soon we will be back together again. I hope we can work through some of our past issues.
- I had planned to burn my hiking clothes when I got off the trail. I couldn't do it; they were a part of me for so long. Instead, I donated them to other hikers, and maybe my clothes will make it all the way to Maine, just like the shirt FROG forgot on a tree limb and the neck gaiter he lost.
- I have Morton's neuroma (inflammation of the nerve endings in my left foot), so I don't wear socks when the weather is warm to prevent my foot from overheating, which enhances the pain in my toes. Not wearing socks leaves me very susceptible to blisters and hot spots breaking out on my feet. My reason for telling you this is to share with you a product that works if you're also susceptible to

blisters—Hike Goo. Even when I bought new hiking boots on the trail, I never had any problems. This goo really works! I sound like a commercial. I'm thinking they need to give me promotional fees for promoting their product! Instead, I will just say thank you to "Willow" (NPT and AT thru-hiker) for introducing me to the product.

- Purists we are not. Those who are considered purists are very strict in their walk on the AT. They make sure they pass every white blaze on the trail, never take a slackpack day, never take a bypass route, never cut miles out to avoid bear activity, and never take any shortcuts to get to the end faster. We have broken every one of those rules. Yep, we are nonpurist rule breakers and have no shame!
- If you lean back too far with your backpack on, you can and most likely will fall backward and won't be able to get back up.
- Shortcuts (or spur trails) aren't always easy or the best choices to make. Quote by Beverly Sills: "There are no shortcuts to any place worth going."
- Enjoy the journey and not just the destination. Make the journey the destination.
- Try not to have such high expectations. Our finish line experience didn't meet what we thought would happen and caused some anxiety when we should have been full of excitement.
- Don't always get upset with how things turn out; there may be a divine reason why it happens the way it happens. Trust GOD to lead.
- This hike has been more than we could have dreamed or imagined. We have met so many wonderful people, seen so much of GOD's magnificent creation, and have been blessed to experience it together! I kid about us taking separate vacations after this, but I'm truly only kidding. We went through seventy-one days, twenty-four seven, and I can still happily report we are still each other's best friend.

FROG and Faith:
If there is one important thing that we learned on the trail, it is that people are searching. People are hiking the trail but also looking for answers to what this life is all about and wondering about this beautiful creation they're walking in. The answer is simple, and the process is even simpler. You can never try hard enough or be good enough. The answer is the reality of Jesus Christ. By humbly asking for forgiveness and asking Jesus to be in your life, you will begin to see changes. Because Jesus loves you so much, He has given you a free will. He has left that decision up to you.

> Earth and sky, woods and fields, lakes and rivers, the mountain and the sea, are excellent schoolmasters, and teach some of us more than what we could learn from books.
> **—John Lubbock**

Epilogue
What's Next

Now to him who is able to do immeasurably more than all we ask or imagine, according to his power that is at work within us.
—Ephesians 3:20

Monday, June 21—HOBOS GOING NOBO IN THEIR RAV-O!

As we head north in our Toyota RAV-4, we decide to make a stop in Groseclose, Virginia—our starting point. We would love to be trail angels to those still out on the trail, to pay it forward for all the generosity that was extended to us while on the trail. We have a lot of food, toilet paper and wipes, hand sanitizer, clothes, and waterproof bags that we can hand out.

The trailhead where we started in Groseclose, Virginia, Route 11, is quiet and deserted. It is an area that isn't a spot with a lot of traffic going through, and today is no exception. No one is around. We are feeling disappointed that we're not able to bless anyone when we finally spot two hikers walking down the road. Oh yeah! Here we go.

I designate FROG to yell over and tell them we have goodies if they want them. He does. They yell back, "Thank you, but we don't need anything." We wanted so badly to bless someone, and, well, that didn't happen! It's almost as though you want to go over there and pull them to the car and say, "Please take something—anything! We want to bless you!"

That does not go as hoped or planned. We are happy they are doing well and happily on their journey, but we are filled with disappointment. We remember being so excited to run into trail magic and to see trail angels. Now what to do?

As we head north, I get another idea. "Hey, how about we stop in Harper's Ferry (the headquarters for the Appalachian Trail) and see if we can leave our goodies there for those walking through?" That proves to be a successful idea. Headquarters is very open to our leaving four boxes of things to have hikers go through to see if they need anything. We are fortunate to see one hiker go through and take what he needs, which brings much joy to us.

Appalachian Trail Conservatory / Harper's Ferry, West Virginia

We put a lot of things on that table that day, thinking it would be our last AT adventure …

We miss the woods, the quiet solitude, and the simplicity of life we felt while hiking on the AT. Adjusting back into society was a lot harder than we thought it was going to be.

Our world while hiking had become smaller but in so many ways much larger and richer. Time slowed way down, as we took one day at a time, one step at a time, it allowed us to really enjoy each other, GOD's creation around us, and those we met on the trail. Life was less busy and complicated and more relaxed and simple.

There were no distractions from knowing what was happening in the world, and we didn't miss it at all. We learned to live with just what we had on our backs, and we discovered you can survive with little. We were reminded of how we tend to take for granted the luxuries of indoor plumbing, a nice, comfy bed, chairs, and (for me) a few more choices for clothes and shoes.

But overall, we realized what truly brings happiness is not having *things*; it is enjoying time with GOD, His creation, the adventures that He gives us, each other, and the people He puts in our path.

I think about all we learned and experienced on the trail, and I wonder ... maybe we're not meant to fit into the puzzle anymore; maybe, just maybe, we are meant to stand out.

> Returning home is the most difficult part of long-distance hiking. You have grown outside the puzzle and your piece no longer fits.
> —Cindy Ross

Our Support Team:

Such wonderful insights! Hugs! You will always "fit" in our hearts!! Denise L.

Well you best fit somewhere into our puzzle! Miss and love ya. Tracy M.

A lesson to contemplate! Your adventures have changed your world, bravo!! Peg P.

It sounds like you better start planning the next third of the trail!!! Yes, to a simpler more present life. Linda M.

WOW! Thank you for sharing the "lesson." Agree—love the woods & water = all that they give to your heart, brain & ability to calm your life. God bless you two! Darlene M.

Very nicely put. After our last camping trip (though we are not roughing it in anyway) I realized that one of the reasons I'm really enjoying it is there is no "I should be doing" this or that. It eliminates any pressure to accomplish a task. Spent time with family, friends and on the water—not more complicated than that. Tammy T.

Beautiful, more truthful words could not be spoken. Minimizing is really maximizing on what truly matters—Love, of each other, our creator and our beautiful world. So happy to have shared in your postings!! BethAnn K.

Thank you for sharing your adventures with us! A joy to follow you! Ariel S.

Wow, girl! Your message is thought-provoking! Pat T.

> Somewhere between the start of the trail and the end is the mystery of why we choose to walk.
> **—Unknown**

Months Later

We hear the calling once again; we can't seem to stay away. GOD willing, we will put on our hiking boots yet again (April 2022) and conquer another quarter of the Appalachian Trail. I never thought I'd be saying we were going to journey farther, but there's just something magnetic and mysterious about being on this trail. We can't wait to get back!

FROG's (and now Faith's) dream continues ...

> A dream you dream alone is only a dream. A dream you dream together is reality.
> —John Lennon

UPDATE: The journey did continue ... on April 24, 2022 we put on our Oboz once again and hiked SOBO from Duncannon, Pennsylvania to Groseclose, Virginia – a 600-mile trek filled with a lot of adventure and drama! We can proudly say we have hiked half of the Appalachian Trail, 1100 miles!!

Our Support Team:

I can't tell you how much I enjoyed reading your journaling of "Our Trip, Part One"! You are a consummate storyteller and made me feel like I was walking that path right along with you ... except that I didn't get tired! Can't wait for Part Two! Pat. T.

Yeah! Can't wait to hear of your adventures! Nancy K.

So excited to travel with you both again from our recliners in our living room. Mary K.

I'm so excited for you! Both the continuation and the book! Cathy L.

May God continue to both bless and keep you! Denise L.

Wonderful! You are great writers! Can't wait! Bonnie B.

That's so awesome! Yay! Diana T.

Oh wow!!! I would never have guessed that!!! Suzanne M.

That's wonderful! Sue L.

Good for you! Shelby S.

This is great!!!!!! Denise M.

> In all things of nature there is something of the marvelous.
> —Aristotle

"For I know the plans I have for you," declares the Lord, "plans to prosper you and not to harm you, plans to give you hope and a future." (Jeremiah 29:11)

Appendix A
Glossary of Words and Terms
(Brought to you by FROG)

AT: Appalachian Trail (from Springer Mountain, Georgia, to Mt. Katahdin, Maine, for 2,190 miles.)

base weight: The weight of your backpack plus all the gear that's inside it, not including food, water, and fuel in that weight. Your base weight is mostly determined by your sleeping bag, backpack, and tent (Big 3). Most backpackers will try to have a base weight of fifteen to twenty pounds.

bounce box: A box of extra supplies that you will need to replace while on the trail, all kept in a box that you keep sending yourself from post office to post office, such as clean clothes, change for laundry, detergent, socks, toothpaste, snacks, toilet paper, first aid, shower wipes, and so on.

bubble: A large group of hikers who hike through an area at the same time.

cameling up: When you reach a water source, you refill your water bottle, attach a filter to the top, and drink all the water in the bottle. This allows you to stay hydrated without carrying heavy water bottles. A lot of ultralight hikers do this.

CDT: Continental Divide Trail (from the Mexican border to the Canadian border, following the Continental Divide for 3,028 miles.)

double blaze: Two white painted markers to indicate a direction change in the trail.

duck cover: A waterproof cover for the backpack only.

false summit: When you think you see the top of a mountain, but as you keep climbing, you realize what you see is not the top or summit.

flip-flop: Start at one part of a trail and hike for any distance one direction and then go back to where you started and hike the opposite direction. Example: Start hiking in Harpers Ferry, WV and hike north to Mt. Katahdin (the northern terminus of the AT), return to Harpers Ferry (by air, train or car) and hike south to Springer Mountain (the southern terminus of the AT)

Frogg Toggs: A full waterproof poncho that covers the backpack and the hiker.

footprint: Ground cover that goes down first before the tent.

Garmin InReach: A two-way satellite communicator that works where cell phones do not.

giardia: A tiny parasite (germ) that causes diarrheal disease giardiasis. It is found in water that has been contaminated with feces from infected people or animals. So filtering is a must.

Great Shape! Inc.: Great Shape! Inc. (greatshapeinc.org) empowers children and families of Jamaica and the Caribbean by providing access to education and health care. They need volunteers for their programs: iCARE, Teach the Teachers, SuperKids, and Thousand Smiles. Contact Georgene Crowe at georgene@greatshapeinc.org for more details.

Guthook app (recently renamed Far Out): An app you can purchase and download on your phone that includes locations for shelters, campsites, water sources, towns, and other needed information for a particular trail. We purchased the sections we needed for the AT; access is not dependent on the internet and runs like a GPS.

hiker box: A box located at a hostel, motel, or other hiker destination that contains extra items left by hikers. This could include food, clothes, shoes, and so on.

hiker feed: When a church or other organization puts on a meal for a number of hikers.

Hiker Goo: Lubricant applied to feet to reduce friction from foot to shoe.

hiker hunger: An abnormal, excessive hunger developed after hiking a length of time.

hiker midnight: Because of exhaustion from the hike, hikers will go to bed by 9:00 p.m.

Hobos, SOBOs, Oboz: Hobos refers to homeless wanderers, SOBO stands for southbound, and Oboz are hiking boots.

hostels: Places of lodging along the trail other than a tent or motel, consisting of either private cabins and/or bunkhouses.

HYOH: Hike your own hike.

LASH(ers): Long-awesome (our version) section hiker. We were called this.

loaner clothes box: A box of clothes, usually at a hostel, that you can use while you wash all of your dirty clothes.

mail drop / resupply boxes: Boxes of food and/or supplies that you send to yourself ahead of time to a certain post office or hostel. The difference between this and a bounce box is the bounce box will follow us, and the resupply is food/supplies just for the week.

nero day: A day you do low mileage on the trail with a full pack.

NOBO: Hikers walking from south to north (Georgia to Maine), northbound.

NPT: Northville-Placid Trail (132-mile trail located in the Adirondacks in New York state.)

official versus unofficial campsite: An official campsite is marked at the site or designated in a publication or app, and an unofficial campsite is not.

PCT: Pacific Crest Trail (from the Mexican border to the Canadian border, going through California, Oregon, and Washington for 2,653 miles.)

PUD: Pointless ups and downs—when reaching a mountaintop and there is no view.

purist: A hiker who will hike only from white blaze to white blaze; they will never take a shortcut or alternate route.

ridge runners: A park ranger within the Great Smoky Mountain National Park who monitors overnight campers at the shelters, keeps trails clean, answers questions, and so on.

section hikers: A hiker who hikes only a part (section) of the trail at a time.

slackpack: Being transported from a hostel or hotel to a portion of the trail that hasn't been hiked. The full packs would be left behind, and a day pack would be used, with just what is needed for that day's hike. If you are hiking south, you would be transported to a portion of the trail south that has not been hiked and then hike north back to the hostel/hotel. This is a way to get in miles on the trail without carrying a full pack.

SOBO: Hikers walking from north to south (Maine to Georgia), southbound.

stealth camping: Has a double meaning; could mean when you come into a campsite later at night and leave before other people get up, or it could mean just setting camp up in an unofficial campsite.

switchbacks: A zigzag trail that increases the distance but reduces the steepness of the trail.

thru-hiker: A hiker who hikes the entire 2,190 miles from Springer Mountain, Georgia, to Mt. Katahdin, Maine (or vice versa) within a year's time.

trail angels: People who provide food, drink, and transportation along the trail. They are usually former hikers but not necessarily.

trail legs: After hiking for a time, you build up endurance and are capable of hiking more miles per day.

trail magic: Food and drink provided for free.

trail names: Names you use on the trail instead of your real names; we were FROG and Faith.

tramily: Trail family—other people on the trail you might hike and camp with over a period of time; they become your trail family.

triple crown – When you complete a thru-hike of the three main hiking trails: AT, CDT and the PCT.

ultralight: Carrying a base weight of ten to twelve pounds.

VCT: Virginia Creeper Trail is a thirty-five-mile trail located in southern Virginia.

white blazes: A white painted marker approximately four inches tall and two inches wide that indicates the trail on the AT.

work-for-stay: Some hostels allow you to do work at the facilities to pay for your stay.

yo-yo: To hike the entire length of a trail and then turn around and hike back to the beginning.

zeek: Week off.

zero day: A day you take off and don't do any miles on the trail.

Appendix B
(Brought to you by FROG)

Setting Up Camp

Toward the end of the day as you get tired, you need to find a place to set up camp. Unless there is a lot of elevation, an average day for us was ten miles.

There are shelters about every seven to ten miles. A standard shelter is a three-sided building with an open front, with sleeping room for six to eight people. Another name to describe it would be a lean-to. If it's raining and there is room, this is definitely a positive option for the night. Otherwise, the downside is the floor being so hard (no give like the ground offers), it can be noisy, there's no privacy, and the mice and snakes!

Our usual preference was setting up near a shelter. This offered three advantages: they are usually near a water source; they have a privy (unless you are Tennessee); and there is a bear hang or a bear box. We only stayed in a shelter three times, and twice it was because of the weather. We normally preferred the privacy of our tent.

The next consideration is finding a flat spot without rocks or roots. If the spot is sloped, you will roll into each other during the night. If it is raining out, you don't want to roll against the outside of the tent. And there is nothing more uncomfortable than sleeping on a rock or root all night long. You want a good night's sleep so your body can recover.

Probably the best part of setting up camp is taking off the backpack and shoes. You have been carrying a backpack all day long with a weight of about twenty-five pounds, and it feels good to take it off and set it down. When the hiking shoes/boots and socks come off and the Crocs come on your feet, it is a feeling you can't explain unless you go through it.

Time to set up the tent. Lay out the footprint in the flat spot that you found without any rocks or roots. The footprint will add more protection from the ground moisture, but make sure it doesn't stick out beyond the tent (tuck it under). This is in case it rains; it won't collect on the footprint and run under the tent. The tent has two parts. Once the poles are extended from the bungy cords that hold all the poles together, the inside of the tent can be set up. Since this is freestanding, this part of the tent can be placed on top of the footprint. If it is at all windy, the tent can be staked to the ground (past experience says you probably should stake it down every time, just in case). Second is the waterproof fly part of the tent, which is attached over the tent. You now have a waterproof shelter.

Faith is much more flexible than I am, so she will now crawl into the tent, and I will stand outside and inflate the air mattresses, then pass them into the tent along with the sleeping bags and deflated pillows so Faith can blow those up and set up our beds. There is enough room for both of our backpacks, but we usually only kept Faith's bag inside and put my backpack outside under the vestibule of the fly part of the tent. Our four hiking poles are used as additional stakes to hold the fly away from the tent (with an added touch of our dirty socks on top of the poles to air out, and my theory is it kept the bears away too). Our shelter is now complete.

We kept all cooking supplies, food, wrappers, and toiletries outside of the tent. Our supper usually consisted of a freeze-dried meal that needed boiling water added to it. Our dessert was a Snickers bar as a reward for the day's hike. And we always drank a lot of water, with Nuun's added to it to replace electrolytes so we wouldn't get leg cramps from walking and sweating so much. We always took a water bottle with a Nuun inside the tent with us to drink at night. If there was a bear hang, anything that had any odor went into that. If there was no bear box or bear hang, I would try to find a limb on a tree to hang these items, but I will be honest: it was sometimes almost impossible to find a low enough limb on a tree to be able to reach to use as a bear hang. If there was no other option, the items were in our odor-proof plastic bag and placed in my backpack under the vestibule part of the tent.

Water was always a need. There was usually a water source within a tenth of a mile from the shelters. We would filter enough water to fix our supper, to drink during the night, and have enough to get started in the morning.

We would need at least an hour to set up camp, fix meals, and be sure we are ready for the next day. Now it is time to climb into the tent—usually about 7:00 p.m., some nights sooner than that. Lying down on our air mattress and sleeping bags—a great feeling! Time to let our bodies recover from a long day's trek, but first a card game of 3-13, then to sleep.

Filtering Water

The most essential aspect of backpacking for an extended amount of time is drinking a sufficient amount of water. You do not want to dehydrate!

Before you filter water, you need to know where the water sources are located. This is one of the advantages of having the Guthook app, which is now called Far Out. The main sources of water are springs, streams, and, at lower elevations, creeks.

We used the Sawyer Filtration system. We would gather water in bags and then filter that water through the Sawyer into clean Smartwater bottles. For the majority of the hike, we would fill all four one-liter bottles when we filtered water, but because water has so much weight (2.2 pounds for each liter), later in the hike we got a little smarter because of the added weight. We would plan ahead for what water we would need and where the upcoming water sources were located.

There appeared to be a very creative way of placing a spout on the smaller water sources. To be honest, I don't know what plant the leaf came from. The oblong green leaf was placed where there was a small trickle of water so hikers could put their water bottles underneath it to collect water.

We carried one dirty bottle to collect the water and then filtered that water into our clean drinking bottles. The common problem with drinking unfiltered water is called giardia. That can get you sick and off the trail for a week or longer.

The best advice is to drink a lot of water and filter everything that you drink or cook with.

Our Meals

I planned out eight resupply mail drops of food that we sent to ourselves and picked up at post offices or hostels. I strategically planned them out, which averaged about every fifty to sixty miles apart.

Breakfasts: protein bars, protein drink, cold-soak oatmeal (add filtered water to oatmeal and let set overnight, add fruit in morning), hot tea/cider.

Lunches: peanut butter and jelly, or pouched seasoned chicken, or salami/pepperoni with cheese on tortilla shells, beef jerky.

Snacks: beef jerky, fig bars, protein bars, nuts/raisins, fruit bars, granola bars, fruit roll-ups, gummis, applesauce, Snickers and Payday bars (our reward at end of day).

Dinners: Ramen noodles with beef jerky, instant mashed potatoes with bacon, dehydrated meals (lasagna, spaghetti, chili mac, chicken and dumplings, beef stroganoff, potato or bean/cheese soups). We added a packet of oil to add a healthy fat to meals.

Equipment We Wish to Promote

There are many books out there that will give you pointers on equipment to buy and use, but we have included the items that we know we could not have lived without:

Tent. Our tent was a great choice. It was the three-season, three-person Big Agnes Copper Spur HV UL3 (2019) we bought at Recreational Equipment Inc. (REI) (weight: 3 lbs. 14 oz). The reason for the bigger size was we could bring our backpacks inside in rainy weather, with enough room leftover for our air mattresses and sleeping bags. We went through several rainstorms and never got wet.

Sleeping bags. REI Magma 15 Men's Long (comfort level 28 degrees, 1 lb. 14.6 oz) and REI Magma 15 Women's Regular (comfort level 17 degrees, 2 lbs. 14 oz). It was amazing how cold it could still get in April and May; some nights got into the thirties. We stayed warm, but some nights we also wore our down vests to bed for added warmth.

Air mattress. Sea to Summit Ultralight Insulated Air (Long, 1 lb. 4.9 oz, R-value 3.3) and (Regular, 1 lb. 1 oz, R-value 3.8). It was the Airstream Pump Sack based on Bernoulli's principle, so, of course, I had to make sure we both had one of these! It took very little effort to inflate and made for a good night's sleep.

Duck's Pack Rain Cover by REI (5 ounces)—waterproof cover for your backpack (only needed if your backpack does not have a cover included).

Hiking shoes/boots. No matter what you wear, after eight to ten hours of hiking, your feet will be tired! We both started out with the Xero's minimalist shoe, but they didn't hold up with the terrain that we had to hike on. We both switched to Oboz and were very pleased with them.

Superfeet Trailblazers—shock-absorbing foot inserts for your shoes/boots.

Hike Goo. Every day, Faith doused her feet with this to prevent blisters and hot spots, and it worked. She never had any blisters on her feet.

Adventure Wipes—large shower wipes for cleaning up after a long day's hike. If you can't take a shower, just being able to wipe off the grime is the next best thing.

Trekking poles are highly encouraged! Any brand or style you choose will be good. We can't imagine trying to hike this trail without the use of poles to help us when ascending and descending steep, rocky places. I threw mine a few times, and Faith fought with hers a lot, but we are so glad we had them!

Guthook app (will also invest in Garmin InReach for next trip).

Acknowledgments

Thank you doesn't seem enough for those who prayed, supported, and encouraged us along our journey to get us to where we are today. We will forever be indebted to all of you.

- Cousin Sheila and her husband, Randy, for letting us leave our car and belongings at their house; giving up their comfortable bed so we could have it (knowing we wouldn't have that luxury soon); taking us to the bus stop in Monroe, Georgia; sending out our mail resupply boxes of food and supplies (and receiving boxes back from us); meeting us in Gatlinburg, Tennessee, and bringing us money when we ran out and shuttling us around town; our day trip to Cades Cove and Pigeon Forge; picking us up at the end of our adventure in Amicalola Falls State Park, Georgia; and your hospitality before and after our journey.
- Our trail angels from afar: our son, Ryan, and family, Laura, Ryan Jr., and Lauryn (box sent to Damascus, Virginia); our daughter, Miranda, and family, Ken, Bryce, and McKenze (box sent to Hot Springs, North Carolina); and Tracy and Walt (two boxes sent to Fontana Dam, North Carolina) for sending us mail resupply boxes. The variety and amount of food sent was so appreciated and very much enjoyed.
- Sister Suzanne for being our personal assistant, collecting our mail, and figuring out what was important and needed immediate attention and what was junk. We may just keep you as our personal assistant forever since you do such an amazing job!
- Our daily phone support system of brother David, sister Suzanne, our kids, Miranda and Ryan, cousin Sheila, and

stepmom, Ann. Your comments and encouragement were truly needed as we endured all those days of cold and rain. It was comforting to know our support was just a text away.

- Brother David and sister-in-love, Margie, stepmom Ann, and friends Bethie and Paul for opening up your homes to us Hobos so we had a place to stay after the hike. Your willingness to adjust your busy schedules last minute to accommodate us was truly a gift. We thank you all for your generosity and hospitality. You took such great care of us; we might just decide to move in with one of you! Watch out!
- Bev and Claude, our morning pool buddies in Texas who encouraged our plan from day one. Without your love and support, I'm not so sure we'd be sharing our story. We thank you both for reading and editing our first draft. You two are the best! Claude, you have an incredible gift of drawing. The images you made for our book are top-notch and perfect!
- Ann and Hugh for being there for us (opening your home, keeping our vehicle, storing our bins, sending supplies back to you from the trail) when we hiked the Northville Placid Trail (NPT), which ultimately prepared us to do the Appalachian Trail. You are our special Texas / New York friends!
- Dan and Dorothy, who called us throughout to make sure we hadn't been eaten by bears. Thanks again for our sign: *Campers in sleeping bags are like soft tacos.*
- Fred and Pat / Miranda and Ken for allowing us to store our possessions in your storage unit and basement, respectively. Your generosity in offering your space to lighten our load so that we could hike the trail as Hobos means so much. We didn't need Allstate, we knew our things were in good hands.
- Our online support team of family and friends who followed us and encouraged us along the way. There are so many of you whose names can be found throughout our book. Having the love, prayers, and support that all y'all gave us

was our driving force and the inspiration we needed to write our story.

- Our shuttle drivers: Rambunny, Nimrod, Lucky, Darrell B., Sherpa Al, Jim L., Mike K., Minnie, Sandi A., Craig, and Travis. Each and every one of you were a true blessing to meet.
- Sandi A. for praying for us and being a wonderful friend and support. Your generosity in giving Faith those fleece pants was such a welcome and *warm* gift. We truly hope our paths meet again this side; if not, we know beyond a doubt we will see you again.
- Mickey and Minnie, you were at the right place at the right time for us. We thank GOD for both of you and your generosity in rescuing us from further injury from a blown-out shoe by taking us into Hot Springs. You are true trail angels.
- WestBow Press for all your help in getting our story in print for family and friends to enjoy.
- ★ Most of all, our Lord and Savior, Jesus Christ, for allowing us this amazing adventure together and for keeping us safe throughout. We couldn't have done it without You!

About the Authors

Lori (Faith) and Brad (FROG) Lewis have been married for thirty-seven years. They have two adult children and have been blessed with four grandchildren. They are both retired, Brad as a schoolteacher and Lori as an administrative assistant / bookkeeper. After retirement, Brad continued his love of teaching in schools in Jamaica and Antigua, with Lori right by his side as his assistant. They have led four mission teams from their church to work at churches in Jamaica. They have always loved the outdoors and have hiked the Adirondack Mountains in Upstate New York, as well as several national parks within the US, especially their favorite place in the Grand Teton National Park. Hiking the AT was a dream come true and an experience of a lifetime!